In Solidarity

In Solidarity: Friendship, Family, and Activism Beyond Gay and Straight shows what being an ally (in this case to LGBTQ+ persons and communities) requires, means, and does. Through prose, poetry, performance text, and film, the work takes readers inside relationships across sexual orientation and serves as an exemplar of activist scholarship. *In Solidarity* makes a unique and compelling contribution to courses on LGBTQ+ studies, sexualities, gender, identity, relationships, or the family.

Lisa M. Tillmann, Ph.D., is an activist researcher, social justice documentary filmmaker, and professor of Critical Media and Cultural Studies, a program she founded at Rollins College. She has participated in numerous activist initiatives, many centering on LGBT civil rights. She authored the book, *Between Gay and Straight: Understanding Friendship across Sexual Orientation*, produced the film *Weight Problem: Cultural Narratives of Fat and "Obesity,"* and co-produced the films *Off the Menu: Challenging the Politics and Economics of Body and Food* and *Remembering a Cool September.*

Innovative Ethnographies

Series Editor: Phillip Vannini, Royal Roads University

The purpose of this series is to use the new digital technology to capture a richer, more multidimensional view of social life than was otherwise done in the classic, print tradition of ethnography, while maintaining the traditional strengths of classic, ethnographic analysis.

In Solidarity

Friendship, Family, and Activism Beyond Gay and Straight

Lisa M. Tillmann

Routledge
Taylor & Francis Group

NEW YORK AND LONDON

First published 2015
by Routledge
711 Third Avenue, New York, NY 10017

and by Routledge
2 Park Square, Milton Park, Abingdon, Oxon, OX14 4RN

Routledge is an imprint of the Taylor & Francis Group, an informa business

Library of Congress Cataloging in Publication Data
Tillmann, Lisa.
  In solidarity: friendship, family, and activism beyond gay and straight/
  by Lisa Tillmann.
  pages cm. — (Innovative ethnographies)
  Includes bibliographical references and index.
  1. Gays—Computer network resources. 2. Sexual orientation. 3. Social
  acceptance. 4. Social networks. I. Title.
  HQ76.25.T55 2014
  302.3—dc23
  2014024679

ISBN: 978-1-138-77791-0 (hbk)
ISBN: 978-1-138-77792-7 (pbk)
ISBN: 978-1-315-77233-2 (ebk)

Typeset in Adobe Caslon and Copperplate Gothic
by Florence Production Ltd, Stoodleigh, Devon, UK

MIX
Paper from
responsible sources
FSC
FSC® C013056
www.fsc.org

Printed and bound in Great Britain by
TJ International Ltd, Padstow, Cornwall

CONTENTS

Preface

Purposes, Audiences, and Classroom Applications

Deep, committed, and loving relationships across lines such as class, nation, sex, race, religion, ideology, ability, age, gender, and sexual orientation can help light the way toward a more equitable and just society. *In Solidarity: Friendship, Family, and Activism Beyond Gay and Straight* shows what being an ally requires, means, and does.

My first book, *Between Gay and Straight: Understanding Friendship across Sexual Orientation*, stemmed from my Ph.D. dissertation (1994–8). The work chronicled my journey from small-town girl—heterosexually-identified and raised Catholic in the 1970s and 1980s—to emotional, relational, and political ally to an urban network of gay male friends. The essays and website materials (see http://www.insolidaritybook.com) collected for *In Solidarity* demonstrate how I have mobilized the raised consciousness acquired along and since that journey in my continued research, campus and community advocacy and activism, teaching, and everyday life. The *Beyond Gay and Straight* in the subtitle hails my first book and suggests movement: from working with and for a community of gay men to befriending and engaging in civil rights activism with and for persons in the bigger tent of LGBTQ+;[1] from employing but insufficiently troubling categories such as "gay" and "straight" to foregrounding them as social constructions, useful for some purposes but also limited and limiting; and from a wish to explore what lies between "gay" and "straight" to envisioning a place beyond, where everyone will be treated with humanity, dignity, and equity.

I hope professors and students will be drawn to the work's utilization of autoethnography, interviewing, and participant observation and to its contextualization in relevant literatures. *In Solidarity* reflects and contributes to fields of study such as Communication, Sociology, Cultural Studies, LGBTQ+ Studies, Women's Studies, Gender Studies, and Psychology. The work will feel at home on syllabi for courses on qualitative methods, feminist methodologies, gender and communication, sexualities, queer methodologies, documentary film,[2] creative nonfiction, identity, emotions, interpersonal communication, close relationships, friendship, the family, activism, and social justice.

Through prose, poetry, performance text, film, and photographs, *In Solidarity* and its website[3] take readers/viewers inside relationships across identity groups and serve as exemplars of collaborative[4] and activist scholarship.[5] Through aesthetic variety and accessible, evocative composition, *In Solidarity* will resonate with academic audiences as well as with lay members of and allies to marginalized communities.

To readers who identify as LGBTQ+, I offer this work as testament to my personal and political commitments to securing full legal and social equality. To fellow allies, may *In Solidarity* provide companionship and strengthen your resolve and tenacity. To prospective allies (i.e., everyone else), consider this an invitation to solidarity.

Notes

1   I use LGBTQ+ to be inclusive of lesbian, gay, bisexual, transgender, and queer, plus identities such as intersex, pansexual, and asexual. See the Introduction for further discussion.

2   See the film *Remembering a Cool September* on the book's website.

3   Please visit insolidaritybook.com.

4   See especially Chapters 1–4, Chapter 10 (co-authored with my friend and colleague, Kathryn Norsworthy), and the film *Remembering a Cool September* (co-produced with my friend David Dietz).

5   See especially Chapter 10.

References

Tillmann, Lisa M., and David Dietz. *Remembering a Cool September* [motion picture]. United States: Cinema Serves Justice, 2014. http://cinemaservesjustice.com/Remembering.html.

Tillmann-Healy, Lisa M. *Life Projects: A Narrative Ethnography of Gay-Straight Friendship*. Ph.D. diss., University of South Florida, 1998.

——. *Between Gay and Straight: Understanding Friendship across Sexual Orientation*. Walnut Creek, CA: AltaMira Press, 2001.

INTRODUCTION[1]

June 26, 2013, 9:55 a.m. I sink into a magenta leather rocker recliner in the back bedroom of my home away from home—that of my friend Deena Flamm[2] and of her wife Kathryn Norsworthy, my friend and colleague. I am flanked by Deena on my left and Margaret McLaren, another friend and colleague, on my right. Kathryn sits in a cream leather swivel chair to Margaret's right. Deena's beige recliner borders a bank of windows. The typical Florida summer skies promise both heat and rain, perfect to nourish the already-thriving plumbago and lantana in the backyard.

It is the U.S. Supreme Court's final day of rulings this session. Beginning at 10:00 a.m. the Court will announce its decisions on Proposition 8, which bans same-sex marriage in California, and on the constitutionality of the Defense of Marriage Act (DOMA). Signed in 1996 by President Clinton, DOMA defines marriage as a relationship between one man and one woman and bars same-sex couples, even if legally married, from receiving federal rights and benefits.

This day already is historic: the 10th anniversary of the U.S. Supreme Court decision in *Lawrence v. Texas*, a six-to-three ruling that struck down sodomy laws in 14 states, including ours. Prior to this ruling, same-sex partners (and, in some states, different-sex partners as well) could be arrested, prosecuted, and convicted as sex offenders for engaging in consensual relations, inclusive of oral sex—even in the privacy of their own homes. Two of the three *Lawrence* dissenters—those who argued that states had a right to police the bedrooms of consenting adults— still sit on the court today: Clarence Thomas and Antonin Scalia. No one expects them or George W. Bush nominee Samuel Alito to have evolved on lesbian and gay rights.

Sporting a red t-shirt from last year's Come Out with Pride festival, Margaret adjusts her gold-rimmed glasses. "Surely we can count on Obama's people: Sotomayor and Kagan."

"Ginsburg's a given," I add, "and who's the other Clinton nominee?"

Deena consults Jimi Hendrix, whose face covers the front of her grey t-shirt. When he doesn't answer, she begins typing on her laptop. "Wikipedia says . . . Breyer, Stephen Breyer."

Feline interloper Buddy leaps from Kathryn's lap, shedding hair across her purple t-shirt emblazoned with a raised fist. Kathryn predicts, "I bet George W.'s chief, John Roberts, goes the way of Thomas, Scalia, and Alito—the White male Catholic contingent."

"Roberts did save the Affordable Care Act," observes Margaret.

"The other wild card is Anthony Kennedy," I say. "He's in the White male Catholic contingent, but he also wrote the majority opinion in *Lawrence*."

"While Reagan rolled over in his grave," quips Deena.

"Was he dead in 2003?" I ask.

"Wikipedia says . . . no," Deena replies.

"Rolled over from his nap," amends Margaret.

We anxiously sip the strong Italian roast coffee Kathryn made, mine creamed and sweetened to perfection. I grip the hand-thrown pottery mug tightly.

Deena flips from one cable news station to the next. We watch film from yesterday's 11-hour filibuster by Texas State Senator Wendy Davis. Her protest temporarily fended off a restrictive abortion bill that will be signed by Governor Rick Perry next month.

Flip. Earlier today, police staged a "perp walk" starring a handcuffed Aaron Hernandez, tight end for the New England Patriots. A little less than two months from now, a grand jury will indict him for murder.

Flip. A former employee has accused celebrity chef Paula Deen of racial and sex discrimination. On this morning's *Today Show*, Deen tearlessly "cried" through Tammy Faye makeup, "I is what I is, and I'm not changing."

Flip. CNN takes us live to Sanford, Florida (17 miles away) to the trial of George Zimmerman. Jayne Surdyka testifies about the fatal altercation, which occurred outside her home, between gun-zealot Zimmerman and unarmed teenager Trayvon Martin. Don West, Zimmerman's attorney, says, "I have shown you state's exhibit 41, and you're talking about a window . . . Is that correct?"

Ms. Surdyka replies, "Yes."

West follows up: "So your vantage point in terms of looking down would have been towards the . . . courtyard. Is that correct?"

"Yes."

Cut to the CNN studio in D.C. "This is it!" says Margaret.

"I'm Wolf Blitzer in Washington with our breaking news coverage."

"Ooh . . . shit!" exclaims Deena, a bit like Clarence Carter in "Strokin," one of our group's dance favorites.

Wolf continues, "We're expecting rulings literally at any moment now . . ."

Kathryn, raised in small-town Georgia but a practicing Buddhist, calls out, "Good God almighty!" Nerves raw, we barely can take in the content or meaning of the coverage.

"Let's go to Brian Todd," directs Wolf, ". . . outside the United States Supreme Court. Brian, a lot of folks are anxiously awaiting the decisions . . ."

Brian replies, "That's right, Wolf. Very anxiously awaiting . . . The moment is at hand, the decision coming down in just minutes. I have one same-sex couple with me here." The camera brings into frame two young women, both smiling and wearing sunglasses. "Molly Wagner and Sharon Burke," Brian introduces, ". . . students at American University. They have braved the swamp-like heat of Washington, D.C. to be here. Molly, why?"

As she speaks, Molly glances fondly toward Sharon. ". . . This is something really important to us . . . We're here. We're not going away, and the decision impacts us directly." CNN goes split screen, the couple on the left and the Supreme Court building on the right.

"What about you, Sharon?" asks Brian.

"I'm just hoping the court is on the right side of history this time . . ."

"All right, guys," says Brian, "thank you. Anyway, we've got—"

"Brian, hold on for a moment," interrupts Wolf, ". . . I want to alert our viewers. The justices have now announced that a critically important case, the Defense of Marriage Act, whether it is constitutional or not constitutional, has been reached." My chest tightens. "This is *United States versus Windsor.*"

Wolf calls upon correspondent John King at the CNN "magic wall" (a large LCD touchscreen) to provide background. "The respondent in this case is Edith Windsor, who had a same-sex spouse who passed away. She wanted to get the benefit of the estate tax you would get if you are married. The federal government said we can't do that because the federal government does not recognize same-sex marriage . . ."

"We know all this already," says Deena.

Kathryn surmises, "They're buying time while the analysts examine the decision."

Deena's and Kathryn's future, like that of millions of same-sex couples, will be shaped by today's rulings. They married on June 12, 2011, the anniversary of the Supreme Court decision in *Loving v. Virginia*, which struck down anti-miscegenation laws in 16 states and granted legal status in every U.S. state to Richard Loving, a White man, and his wife Mildred Loving, a woman of Native- and African-American descent. The demise of DOMA would not have the reach of *Loving v. Virginia*, but it would lay important groundwork for challenging bans against same-sex marriage in 35 states, including ours. Kathryn's and Deena's marriage, though recognized by the state of Massachusetts, has no legal status federally or in Florida.

The wait—and weight—feel excruciating. Chief Political Analyst Gloria Borger discusses the shift in public opinion on same-sex marriage. Correspondent Tom Foreman reviews the justices' statements and questions from three months ago as attorneys argued *U.S. v. Windsor.*

Deena checks the SCOTUS[3] blog every minute. Kathryn searches her phone for updates. I cross and uncross my legs, observing, "This is like watching election results come in."

The camera cuts from Wolf to a split screen: on the right, a raucous crowd; on the left, a dark-suited, bespeckled Jeff Toobin, Senior Legal Analyst, who says the words: "DOMA is gone."

In unison, we raise our hands above our heads and let out a whoop they likely can hear down the block.

About the Project[4]

Personally, and then academically, this project began in 1994. That May, the man I had been dating long distance, Doug Healy, graduated from pharmacy school and relocated to Tampa, where I had just completed my first year of graduate school at the University of South Florida. Doug's employer assigned him to a pharmacy managed by David Holland. As colleagues and friends, Doug and David clicked immediately. David came out to Doug and me by inviting us to meet him at Tracks, which I knew to be a gay nightclub in nearby Ybor City. Neither Doug nor I, both 23 at that time, had ever had an openly gay friend before. Both of us had grown up in the rural Midwestern United States with conventional ideas about sexuality and sexual orientation. Nonetheless, we agreed to meet David at Tracks, and as it turned out, this was only the beginning.

Later that year, David mentioned to Doug that he played softball. A former three-sport athlete still new to Tampa and longing for male friends, Doug asked excitedly if David's team, sponsored by a bar called the Cove, needed players. "Uh . . . yeah," David hedged, "but I should tell you that my team is gay, and in fact, the whole Suncoast league is gay. However, we do have a provision that allows each team to have two straight players, so if it doesn't bother you, it doesn't bother us." At the start of the next softball season, Doug became the Cove's right centerfielder, a position he played for the remaining four years we lived in Tampa.

This was the mid-1990s: after *Bowers v. Hardwick*,[5] before the first U.S. state legalized civil unions, before even *Will and Grace*.[6] At that time, neither mainstream media nor academic research offered in-depth explorations of close friendships between men with divergent sexual orientations.

Working toward my Ph.D. in Communication, I came to recognize the unique opportunity presented by the Cove team: I could investigate

Figure I.1 David Holland, Lisa Tillmann, and Doug Healy.

an understudied relationship ethnographically. Because men's friendships tend to be constructed and maintained through shared activities
like sports, this approach seemed organic. In the fall of 1995, I began
a three-year interview and participant observation study for my
dissertation.[7]

Over the course of this study, friendship emerged not only as a subject
of my research but also as its primary *method*.[8] In my dissertation, I
coined the term "friendship as method," positing friendship as a kind
of fieldwork and establishing its methodological foundations in interpretivism,[9] feminist research,[10] participatory action research (PAR),[11]
and interactive interviewing.[12] This mode of qualitative inquiry involves
researching with the practices, at the pace, in the natural contexts, and
with an ethic of friendship.[13]

On Saturday, October 10, 1998, I took a break from preparing an
opening statement for the oral defense of my dissertation and learned
of the brutal beating of Matthew Shepard, a 21-year-old student at the

University of Wyoming. The headline in that morning's *St. Petersburg Times*: "Gay Man Clings to Life after Attack." In the printed photograph of Matthew, I saw the faces of my research participants, who also had become my closest friends. Matthew Shepard died of his injuries on Monday, October 12. His memorial service, picketed by members of the Westboro Baptist Church with their now-infamous signs blaring "God Hates Fags" and "Matt in Hell," took place Friday, October 16, the same day and time as my defense.

I spent the next two years converting the dissertation to a book, *Between Gay and Straight: Understanding Friendship across Sexual Orientation*.[14] To me, the most powerful section is its epilogue, which portrays the oral defense. About a dozen of the men I had befriended and studied attended, having read the dissertation. After my Ph.D. committee asked their questions about the project's methods and implications, we opened the discussion to the group. Many friends/participants spoke about how the project had affected their lives: helping them move toward self-acceptance, assisting them in coming out to their families, and inspiring them to get more involved in political and grassroots efforts.

Though most members of the Cove team eventually relocated (including Doug, when I accepted a position at Rollins College in 1999), the group kept in regular contact. By the time I published *Between Gay and Straight* in 2001, all the men featured had come out to their parents and siblings.

As time passed, I began to notice that in many of the men's families of origin, the conversation failed to move much beyond the initial disclosure. Some of my friends stayed away physically. Some continued concealing their relational lives and/or their HIV status. Few families of origin had integrated their partners. A dynamic of "don't ask/don't tell" seemed prevalent, with self-protection and self-censorship on all sides. I wondered why this pattern developed, even in families quite different from one another; what it might require to disrupt; and what the consequences, short and long term, could be.

I spoke to three friends, Matthew (Matt) Moretti, Raymond (Ray) Wise, and Gordon Bernstein, proposing that we take *Between Gay and Straight* "on the road": interviewing family members where they lived and doing fieldwork at key sites. All signed on.

Matt Moretti, my friend since 1996, took me to his hometown of Tremaine, Massachusetts.[15] We visited Matt's old neighborhood, church, and schools, and I interviewed three of his siblings (one lesbian- and two heterosexually identified). During that visit, it became clear that the "don't ask/don't tell" dynamic related far less to Matt's gay identity or his sister's lesbian identity than to the secrecy surrounding the family's long and widespread history of alcoholism.

Son of a military father (and later stepfather as well), Ray Wise had resided across the United States (Florida, Pennsylvania, and Colorado) and in Germany. He and I traveled to Buck Hill, California, to reconnect with his father Steven, a retired air force pilot and elder in the Mormon Church.[16] In a pre-trip interview, Ray described their relationship as "tense, distant," and said, "It's almost like visiting a stranger." Military tours, divorce, and custody arrangements had contributed to long periods of separation. In fact, though Steven had lived in Buck Hill for more than a decade, this trip was a first not only for me but also for Ray.

Gordon Bernstein and I visited Philadelphia and Atlantic City.[17] As with Matt, we toured key sites: his old neighborhood, schools, and synagogue. Interviews with Gordon's parents revealed the depths of his father's struggle to come out as the parent of a gay son. The ravages of ALS[18] on Gordon's mother and a family history of avoidant communication locked the Bernsteins in old patterns.

Amid the *Going Home* project, I received an unexpected email. The author introduced himself as Donovan Marshall, a man three years older than I, who also had grown up in the small, rural town of Lake City, Minnesota. He reported receiving *Between Gay and Straight* as a gift and feeling moved by it. Though I hadn't known him as Donovan, I clearly remembered *Don* Marshall, a star of track, theatre, and choir. Don had come out six weeks before his high school graduation in 1986, dropped out of school, and left town. In fact, I had written about him under the pseudonym Dev in my book as a guy from school whose sexual orientation peers questioned at the same time I had a huge teenage crush on him.

We began corresponding. I learned that Donovan's parents had purchased land for a vineyard on the edge of town and that he had moved back to Lake City with his partner Jackson Jones to help them run it. Fascinated by his return after all those years, I asked if he and his family would participate in the project. When they agreed, I made *my* going home trip.[19] Donovan provided a narrated tour of sites significant to his life and growing up, and I conducted video-recorded sessions with Donovan's parents, John and Barb Marshall, and an audio-recorded interview with Jackson.

Going Home enriches literatures on the family. Many family researchers quantitatively analyze retrospective survey data. Comparatively few studies investigate families ethnographically, yet this method of research and mode of writing offer "detailed information that can contribute to understanding how people experience their family lives in their environmental and cultural contexts and how it feels and what it means to be a family."[20] Further, existing family ethnographies tend to center on participants marginalized by class, race, nationality, and/or disability. *Going Home* examines the dynamics of four White, middle-class families—an extremely rare site of ethnographic investigation.[21]

My role as family ethnographer proved unconventional and instructive. Several (auto)ethnographers have written retrospective accounts of their own families.[22] Others have gained consent to interview and/or observe their kin.[23] Still others have involved family members as co-researchers.[24] In this project, my participants and I are friends, not family members. These men are insiders to their families of origin in multiple ways I am not. However, my identity as a heterosexual woman renders *me* an insider with most family members in one way my friends/participants are not. Unlike traditional anthropological studies, I do not leave home alone to study others/Others in their home environment. My friends/participants and I travel *together* as research collaborators to survey sites "not home" to me and simultaneously "home" and "no longer home" to them.

In LGBTQ+[25] studies, we find fewer ethnographers than literary critics or content analysts. At the same time, there is no shortage of relevant ethnographies; to prepare this Introduction, I reviewed 52 and identified over 150 more. Among the 52, the most common type of site investigated, by more than a factor of three, is bars and clubs, drag balls and shows, and circuit and house parties.[26] Another relatively common type of site, explored in six of the 52 ethnographies I reviewed, is sex-related: cruising areas, adult bookstores, bathhouses, and strip and sex clubs.[27] I do not critique or pathologize any queer space. I myself have socialized in raves and leather clubs and have documented my experiences there.[28] Indeed, bars and clubs have been central institutions for LGBTQ+ identity formation; community building, education, and outreach; and even political organizing.[29] Among relevant ethnographies, a type of site emerging in popularity is education.[30] Three of the 52 studies I reviewed focused on religious contexts,[31] only one on military experience.[32] None involved ethnographic fieldwork in participants' families of origin.

As the *Going Home* project drew to a close, my marriage unraveled. Since Doug had been my point of entry to the *Between Gay and Straight* network of friends, I spent the next several years working through who I was, on my own, vis-à-vis these particular men and LGBTQ+ communities more broadly. I already had been integrating into my teaching issues pertaining to LGBTQ+ identities, histories, and civil rights, and my campus and community activism centered on struggles for equality and justice. For example, I coordinated a successful movement to add gender identity and expression to my institution's Equal Opportunity policy and joined the Orlando Anti-Discrimination Ordinance Committee (OADO), a group of LGBT and ally activists instrumental in securing non-discrimination protections and domestic partner registries in Orlando and Orange County. I engaged in much of that activism alongside my closest colleague, Kathryn Norsworthy.[33] Over time, I became as close to Kathryn and her partner (now wife) Deena as to the network of gay male friends.[34]

My post-*Going Home* scholarship, in turn, began to reflect my more politically aware consciousness and engaged citizenship. I still wrote about emotional experiences within particular relationships, both with gay men and with Kathryn and Deena, but even more thoroughly and explicitly than before, I examined my relational experiences for what they had taught me—and perhaps could teach others—about human rights.

Historical and Cultural Context for the Project

Since the turn of the millennium, LGBT persons in the United States have achieved numerous legal victories. As mentioned, the Supreme

Court in 2003 struck down sodomy laws in 14 states. President Obama in 2009 signed the Matthew Shepard and James Byrd, Jr. Hate Crimes Prevention Act, enhancing penalties for crimes motivated by the victim's actual or perceived sexual orientation, gender, or gender identity. Two years later, President Obama repealed "don't ask/don't tell," enabling those with same-sex orientations to serve openly in the military. Since 2000, ten states have enacted non-discrimination protections on the basis of sexual orientation, bringing the total to 21 states,[35] and 17 have added protections on the basis of gender identity/expression, bringing the total to 18.[36] As indicated, the Supreme Court ruled DOMA unconstitutional in 2013, opening federal benefits to same-sex couples who marry in the District of Columbia and the 19 states in which it is currently legal.[37] Seventeen countries have established a federal right for same-sex marriage.[38] The day after its ruling on DOMA, the U.S. Supreme Court avoided consideration of a federal right by refusing to hear a case challenging a state ban on same-sex marriage. Given that bans have been ruled unconstitutional in several states, eventual SCOTUS consideration seems inevitable.

On the cultural front, today's U.S. media landscape is filled with more images of gay men and lesbians than ever before, and those images tend to be more diverse and complex than in the past. In 2012, voters elected Tammy Baldwin, the first openly lesbian or gay U.S. senator. In 2013, Jason Collins became the first active National Basketball Association player to come out as gay; for the first time in its more than 100-year history, the Boy Scouts of America voted to allow openly gay boys as members;[39] and leaders of Exodus International, the world's largest evangelical "ex-gay" organization, closed its doors and apologized for harm caused. In 2014, Michael Sam became the first openly gay player drafted by the National Football League.

With so much progress, we might assume that the fight for equality has been all but won, and LGBTQ+ persons no longer need—either personally or politically—heterosexual and cisgender[40] allies. But history offers no linear narrative of progress. Ground that has been gained also can be lost, and several fights remain. As of this writing, 31 U.S. states still bar same-sex couples from marriage. In 29 states, any of us still can be refused service in a shop or restaurant; denied a hotel room, house, or apartment; and even fired—for no other reason than identifying (or being perceived) as gay, lesbian, or bisexual. LGBTQ+ persons continue to be targeted for hate crimes; according to 2011 Federal Bureau of Investigation statistics, sexual orientation is the second most common motivator of hate crimes, behind only race.[41] Though a survey of over 8,500 youth conducted by the Gay, Lesbian, and Straight Education Network (GLSEN) found for the first time lower rates of victimization and better access to LGBT-affirmative resources and support,[42] the experience of many LGBT youth at home, in school, and in public life bears little resemblance to the television dreamscape of *Glee*. Parents, school administrators, and board members push back against efforts to institute inclusive curricula and anti-bullying policies and to form Gay–Straight Alliances.[43] Hostile climates contribute to LGBT youth's over-representation among runaways[44] and to sexual minorities' over-representation among youth who self-harm and who consider and attempt suicide.[45]

Approaches to Research and Modes of Writing

This work reflects interpretive and critical approaches to research.[46] Interpretive projects center on how individuals make sense of and meaning from their lives and experiences.[47] Critical research focuses on the distribution of power and circulation of ideology in society.[48] As an interpretive researcher, I work with participants to co-construct narratives meant to aid us and readers in navigating life's challenges and growing personally and relationally. As a critical researcher, I seek to expose and challenge injustice and to collaborate in movements to redress social inequality.

In the chapters that follow and on *In Solidarity*'s website, you will find poetry,[49] a play,[50] photographs,[51] video,[52] and prose (both nonfiction and fiction).[53] Also note the variety of standpoints: first person from my perspective, first person from participants' perspectives, second person, and third person. These composition decisions emerged from desires to experiment creatively and to offer aesthetic variety as well as from trial, flop, and trial again (and again, and again). More importantly, the modes of representation attempt to evoke the depth, significance, and evolution of my relationships with friends/co-researchers. In my earliest ethnographic work, I shared drafts with participants and revised the texts according to their feedback. My follow-up project, *Going Home*, involved many more check-ins with primary informants and, in two cases, collaborative workshop sessions with them and with one or more family members. Most recently, I co-authored and co-produced work with old friends/community members, Chapter 10 of *In Solidarity* with Kathryn Norsworthy, an academic who identifies as lesbian, and the film *Remembering a Cool September* (based on the story in Chapter 5) with David Dietz, a media production specialist who identifies as gay.

I thank you for taking this journey and invite you to mobilize emotions called forth and insights gained in service of the continued struggles for equity and justice, for LGBTQ+ persons and for everyone.

In solidarity,
Lisa M. Tillmann

Notes

1   Greg Willis took the photograph in this chapter, whose webpage may be found at: http://www.insolidaritybook.com/introduction.html. Saleem Yusuff oversaw the construction of the book's website, and Rajesh Kannan designed it.
2   In the use of names and other identifying details, I have followed the wishes of those featured. Some are real; others are fictional.
3   Supreme Court of the United States.
4   Some material from this section has been adapted from my Ph.D. dissertation, *Life Projects* (Tillmann-Healy 1998) and my book *Between Gay and Straight* (Tillmann-Healy 2001; used with permission, AltaMira Press).
5   *Bowers v. Hardwick*, a 1986 U.S. Supreme Court case, upheld the constitutionality of sodomy laws. In 2003, the ruling in *Lawrence v. Texas* overturned this decision.
6   *Will and Grace*, a U.S. sitcom (1998–2006), centered on the friendship between a gay man and a heterosexual woman.
7   See Tillmann-Healy (1998).
8   See the Appendix as well as Tillmann-Healy (1998, 2001, 2003).
9   See, e.g., Denzin (1997) and Jackson (1989).
10   See, e.g., Harding (1991), Reinharz (1992), and Roberts (1990).
11   See, e.g., Lather (1991) and Reason (1994).
12   See Ellis, Kiesinger, and Tillmann-Healy (1997).
13   See Tillmann-Healy (1998, 2001, 2003).
14   See Tillmann-Healy (2001).
15   See Chapter 1.
16   See Chapter 2.

17 See Chapter 3.

18 Amyotrophic Lateral Sclerosis, also known as Lou Gehrig's disease.

19 See Chapter 4.

20 See Descartes (2007, 35).

21 See Descartes (2007).

22 See, e.g., Adams (2011), Bochner (1997), Ellis (2009), Goodall (2006), Kiesinger (2002), and Poulos (2009).

23 See, e.g., Boylorn (2013), McGrath (2005), and Waterston and Rylko-Bauer (2006).

24 See, e.g., Davis and Salkin (2005) and Kiesinger and Kiesinger (1992).

25 I use LGBTQ to refer to lesbian, gay, bisexual, transgender, and queer. The plus sign expresses a desire to include other identities, such as intersex and asexual. There is no "catch-all" term that feels right to everyone. I have lesbian-identified friends who refer to themselves as "gay" and talk about "the gay community." I find "gay" insufficiently inclusive of women and gender minorities and thus use the term only to refer to self-identified gay men. Many of my academic associates use "queer" in the sense of queer theory to describe a person, group, space, act, or project that challenges heteronormativity (the idea that heterosexuality is "normal" and all other sexualities deviant); the binary construction of sex (male–female), gender (masculine–feminine), and sexual orientation (same sex–different sex); and their conflation (so that, e.g., male=masculine=heterosexual). But "queer" also carries its history as an epithet and has been criticized as overly male, White, and academic. Except when quoting others' words, I avoid the term "homosexual," loaded with its history as a psychiatric diagnosis.

26 I reviewed 20 ethnographies of this type. See, e.g., Berkowitz, Belgrave, and Halberstein (2007), Johnson (2008), and Westhaver (2006).

27 See, e.g., Brodsky (1993), Graham (1998), Hammers (2009), and Ridge, Minichiello, and Plummer (1997).

28 See Tillmann-Healy (1998, 2001).

29 See Correll (1995).

30 See, e.g., Crawley and Broad (2004), D'Augelli (2006), Pascoe (2007), Schacht (2002, 2004), and Smith (1998).

31 See Barrett-Fox (2011), Barton (2010), and Wolkomir (2001).

32 See Kaplan and Ben-Ari (2000).

33 See Chapter 10.

34 See Chapter 9.

35 U.S. states with non-discrimination protections based on sexual orientation are: California, Colorado, Connecticut, Delaware, Hawaii, Illinois, Iowa, Maine, Maryland, Massachusetts, Minnesota, Nevada, New Hampshire, New Jersey, New Mexico, New York, Oregon, Rhode Island, Vermont, Washington, and Wisconsin. See "State Nondiscrimination Laws in the U.S." (May 21, 2014).

36 U.S. states with non-discrimination protections based on gender identity/expression are: California, Colorado, Connecticut, Delaware, Hawaii, Illinois, Iowa, Maine, Maryland, Massachusetts, Minnesota, Nevada, New Jersey, New Mexico, Oregon,

Rhode Island, Vermont, and Washington. See "State Nondiscrimination Laws in the U.S." (May 21, 2014).

37 Marriage equality U.S. states are: California, Connecticut, Delaware, Hawaii, Illinois, Iowa, Maine, Maryland, Massachusetts, Minnesota, New Hampshire, New Jersey, New Mexico, New York, Oregon, Pennsylvania, Rhode Island, Vermont, and Washington. See "States" (May 21, 2014).

38 Marriage equality countries are: Argentina, Belgium, Brazil, Britain, Canada, Denmark, France, Iceland, Luxembourg, Netherlands, New Zealand, Norway, Portugal, South Africa, Spain, Sweden, and Uruguay. See "Freedom to Marry Internationally" (n.d.).

39 The Scouts' ban on gay adults remains.

40 Cisgender refers to a person whose gender identity and expression tend to conform to cultural expectations for a person of her/his biological sex (e.g., a biological female whose gender expression tends to be predominantly feminine).

41 See "FBI Releases 2011 Hate Crime Statistics" (December 10, 2012).

42 See Kosciw, Greytak, Bartkiewicz, Boesen, and Palmer (2012).

43 See, e.g., Sieczkowski (February 7, 2013).

44 See "LGBT Homeless" (June 2009).

45 See "Suicidality and Self-inflicted Injury" (April 18, 2007).

46 See Bochner (1985).

47 For examples of ethnographic and autoethnographic studies reflecting the interpretive approach, see Adelman and Frey (1997), Boylorn (2013), Drew (2001), and Poulos (2009).

48 I served as lead author of a curriculum in Critical Media and Cultural Studies, and I have taught in this department at Rollins College since its founding in 2007. Our program centralizes the analysis of power and inequality in the examination of the world's most pressing issues and challenges, including the environment and climate change (see, e.g., Pezzullo 2007), poverty and economic inequality (see, e.g., Royce 2009), war (see, e.g., Moeller 2009), mass incarceration (see, e.g., Alexander 2010), and the encroachment of corporate values on public life, including education (see, e.g., Giroux 2007).

49 For other examples of (auto)ethnographic poetry, see Austin (1996), Boylorn (2013), Hartnett (2003), Richardson (1992), and Tillmann (2009).

50 For other examples of (auto)ethnographic performance texts, see Foster (2002), Lockford (2004), Pelias (2002), and Poulos (2010).

51 For an ethnographic work in which photography plays a central role, see Neumann (1999).

52 See Tillmann and Dietz (2014) as well as Tillmann, Hall, and Dietz (2014) and Tillmann (2014).

53 For other examples of (auto)ethnographic prose, see Adams (2011), Alexander (2011), Bochner (2014), Ellis (2009), Jago (2002), Kiesinger (2002), Mingé and Zimmerman (2013), Morman and Non Grata (2011), Pelias (2004), Ronai (1995), and Tillmann (2011).

References

Adams, Tony E. *Narrating the Closet: An Autoethnography of Same-Sex Attraction.* Walnut Creek, CA: Left Coast Press, 2011.

Adelman, Mara B., and Lawrence R. Frey. *The Fragile Community: Living Together with AIDS.* Mahwah, NJ: Lawrence Erlbaum Associates, 1997.

Alexander, Bryant Keith. "Standing in the Wake: A Critical Auto/Ethnographic Exercise on Reflexivity in Three Movements." *Cultural Studies↔Critical Methodologies* 11, no. 2 (2011): 98–107.

Alexander, Michelle. *The New Jim Crow: Mass Incarceration in the Age of Colorblindness.* New York: The New Press, 2010.

Austin, Deborah A. "Kaleidoscope: The Same and Different." In *Composing Ethnography: Alternative Forms of Qualitative Writing,* edited by Carolyn Ellis and Arthur P. Bochner, 206–230. Walnut Creek, CA: AltaMira Press, 1996.

Barrett-Fox, Rebecca. "Anger and Compassion on the Picket Line: Ethnography and Emotion in the Study of Westboro Baptist Church." *Journal of Hate Studies* 9, no. 11 (2011): 11–32.

Barton, Bernadette. "'Abomination': Life as a Bible Belt Gay." *Journal of Homosexuality* 57, no. 4 (2010): 465–484.

Berkowitz, Dana, Linda Belgrave, and Robert A. Halberstein. "The Interaction of Drag Queens and Gay Men in Public and Private Spaces." *Journal of Homosexuality* 52, no. 3–4 (2007): 11–32.

Bochner, Arthur. "Perspectives on Inquiry: Representation, Conversation, and Reflection." In *Handbook of Interpersonal Communication,* edited by Mark L. Knapp and Gerald R. Miller, 27–58. Thousand Oaks, CA: Sage, 1985.

——. "It's about Time: Narrative and the Divided Self." *Qualitative Inquiry* 3, no. 4 (1997): 418–438.

——. *Coming to Narrative: A Personal History of Paradigm Change in the Human Sciences.* Walnut Creek, CA: Left Coast Press, 2014.

Boylorn, Robin. *Sweetwater: Black Women and Narratives of Resilience.* New York: Peter Lang, 2013.

Brodsky, Joel I. "The Mineshaft: A Retrospective Ethnography." *Journal of Homosexuality* 24, no. 3/4 (1993): 233–251.

Correll, Shelley. "The Ethnography of an Electronic Bar: The Lesbian Cafe." *Journal of Contemporary Ethnography* 24, no. 3 (1995): 270–298.

Crawley, Sara L., and K.L. Broad. "'Be Your(Real Lesbian)Self': Mobilizing Sexual Formula Stories through Personal (and Political) Storytelling." *Journal of Contemporary Ethnography* 33, no. 1 (2004): 39–71.

D'Augelli, Anthony R. "Coming Out, Visibility, and Creating Change: Empowering Lesbian, Gay, and Bisexual People in a Rural University Community." *American Journal of Community Psychology* 37 (2006): 203–210.

Davis, Christine S., and Kathleen A. Salkin. "Sisters and Friends: Dialogue and Multivocality in a Relational Model of Sibling Disability." *Journal of Contemporary Ethnography* 34, no. 2 (2005): 206–234.

Denzin, Norman K. *Interpretive Ethnography: Ethnographic Practices for the 21st Century.* Thousand Oaks, CA: Sage, 1997.

Descartes, Lara. "Rewards and Challenges of Using Ethnography in Family Research." *Family and Consumer Sciences Research Journal* 36, no. 1 (2007): 22–39.

Drew, Rob. *Karaoke Nights: An Ethnographic Rhapsody.* Walnut Creek, CA: AltaMira Press, 2001.

Ellis, Carolyn. *Revision: Autoethnographic Reflections on Life and Work.* Walnut Creek, CA: Left Coast Press, 2009.

Ellis, Carolyn, Christine E. Kiesinger, and Lisa M. Tillmann-Healy. "Interactive Interviewing: Talking about Emotional Experience." In *Reflexivity & Voice*, edited by Rosanna Hertz, 119–149. Thousand Oaks, CA: Sage, 1997.

"FBI Releases 2011 Hate Crime Statistics." *fbi.gov*, December 10, 2012. Accessed May 21, 2014. http://www.fbi.gov/news/pressrel/press-releases/fbi-releases-2011-hate-crime-statistics.

Foster, Elissa. "Storm Tracking: Scenes of Marital Disintegration." *Qualitative Inquiry* 8, no. 6 (2002): 804–819.

"Freedom to Marry Internationally." *freedomtomarry.org.* Accessed May 21, 2014. http://www.freedomtomarry.org/landscape/entry/c/international.

Giroux, Henry A. *The University in Chains: Confronting the Military-Industrial-Academic Complex.* Boulder, CO: Paradigm Publishers, 2007.

Goodall, Harold L. *A Need to Know: The Clandestine History of a CIA Family.* Walnut Creek, CA: Left Coast Press, 2006.

Graham, Mark. "Identity, Place, and Erotic Community within Gay Leather Culture in Stockholm." *Journal of Homosexuality* 35, no. 3/4 (1998): 163–183.

Hammers, Corie. "An Examination of Lesbian/Queer Bathhouse Culture and the Social Organization of (Im)personal Sex." *Journal of Contemporary Ethnography* 38, no. 3 (2009): 308–335.

Harding, Sandra. *Whose Science? Whose Knowledge? Thinking from Women's Lives.* Ithaca, NY: Cornell University Press, 1991.

Hartnett, Stephen John. *Incarceration Nation: Investigative Prison Poems of Hope and Terror.* Walnut Creek, CA: AltaMira Press, 2003.

Jackson, Michael. *Paths toward a Clearing: Radical Empiricism and Ethnographic Inquiry.* Bloomington, IN: Indiana University Press, 1989.

Jago, Barbara J. "Chronicling an Academic Depression." *Journal of Contemporary Ethnography* 31, no. 6 (2002): 729–757.

Johnson, Corey W. "'Don't Call Him a Cowboy': Masculinity, Cowboy Drag, and a Costume Change." *Journal of Leisure Research* 40, no. 3 (2008): 385–403.

Kaplan, Danny, and Eyal Ben-Ari. "Brothers and Others in Arms: Managing Gay Identity in Combat Units of the Israeli Army." *Journal of Contemporary Ethnography* 29, no. 4 (2000): 396–432.

Kiesinger, Christine. "My Father's Shoes: The Therapeutic Value of Narrative Reframing." In *Ethnographically Speaking: Autoethnography, Literature, and Aesthetics*, edited by Arthur P. Bochner and Carolyn Ellis, 95–114. Walnut Creek, CA: AltaMira Press, 2002.

Kiesinger, Christine, and Julie Kiesinger. "Writing it Down: Sisters, Food, Eating, and Our Bodies." Unpublished manuscript, University of South Florida, 1992.

Kosciw, Joseph G., Emily A. Greytak, Mark J. Bartkiewicz, Madelyn J. Boesen, and Neal A. Palmer. *The 2011 National School Climate Survey: The Experiences of Lesbian, Gay, Bisexual and Transgender Youth in Our Nation's Schools*. New York: GLSEN, 2012. Accessed May 21, 2014. http://files.eric.ed.gov/fulltext/ED53 5177.pdf.

Lather, Patti. *Getting Smart: Feminist Research and Pedagogy with/in the Postmodern*. New York: Routledge, 1991.

"LGBT Homeless." *nationalhomeless.org*, June 2009. Accessed May 21, 2014. http://www.nationalhomeless.org/factsheets/lgbtq.html.

Lockford, Lesa. *Performing Femininity: Rewriting Gender Identity*. Walnut Creek, CA: AltaMira Press, 2004.

McGrath, Jacqueline L. "Stories of Ruth: An Ethnography of the Dunne Girls." *Journal of American Folklore* 118, no. 467 (2005): 54–77.

Mingé, Jeanine M., and Amber Lynn Zimmerman. *Concrete and Dust: Mapping the Sexual Terrains of Los Angeles*. New York: Routledge, 2013.

Moeller, Susan D. *Packaging Terrorism: Co-opting the News for Politics and Profit*. Malden, MA: Wiley-Blackwell, 2009.

Morman, Shane T., and Persona Non Grata. "Learning from and Mentoring the Undocumented AB540 Student: Hearing an Unheard Voice." *Text and Performance Quarterly* 31, no. 3 (2011): 303–320.

Neumann, Mark. *On the Rim: Looking for the Grand Canyon*. Minneapolis, MN: University of Minnesota Press, 1999.

Pascoe, C.J. *Dude, You're a Fag: Masculinity and Sexuality in High School*. Berkeley, CA: University of California Press, 2007.

Pelias, Ronald J. "For Father and Son: An Ethnodrama with No Catharsis." In *Ethnographically Speaking: Autoethnography, Literature, and Aesthetics*, edited by Arthur P. Bochner and Carolyn Ellis, 35–43. Walnut Creek, CA: AltaMira Press, 2002.

——. *Methodology of the Heart: Evoking Academic and Daily Life*. Walnut Creek, CA: AltaMira Press, 2004.

Pezzullo, Phaedra C. *Toxic Tourism: Rhetorics of Pollution, Travel, and Environmental Justice*. Tuscaloosa, AL: University of Alabama Press, 2007.

Poulos, Christopher N. *Accidental Ethnography: An Inquiry into Family Secrecy*. Walnut Creek, CA: Left Coast Press, 2009.

——. "Transgressions." *International Review of Qualitative Research* 3, no. 1 (2010): 67–88.

Reason, Peter. "Three Approaches to Participative Inquiry." In *Handbook of Qualitative Research*, edited by Norman K. Denzin and Yvonna S. Lincoln, 324–339. Thousand Oaks, CA: Sage, 1994.

Reinharz, Shulamit. *Feminist Methods in Social Research*. New York: Oxford University Press, 1992.

Richardson, Laurel. "The Consequences of Poetic Representation: Writing the Other, Rewriting the Self." In *Investigating Subjectivity: Research on Lived Experience*, edited by Carolyn Ellis and Michael G. Flaherty, 125–137. Newbury Park, CA: Sage, 1992.

Ridge, Damien, Victor Minichiello, and David Plummer. "Queer Connections: Community, 'the Scene' and an Epidemic." *Journal of Contemporary Ethnography* 26, no. 2 (1997): 146–181.

Roberts, Helen, ed. *Doing Feminist Research*. London: Routledge, 1990.

Ronai, Carol Rambo. "Multiple Reflections of Child Sex Abuse: An Argument for a Layered Account." *Journal of Contemporary Ethnography* 23, no. 4 (1995): 395–426.

Royce, Edward. *Poverty & Power: The Problem of Structural Inequality*. Lanham, MD: Rowman & Littlefield, 2009.

Schacht, Steven P. "Lesbian Drag Kings and the Feminine Embodiment of the Masculine." *Journal of Homosexuality* 43, no. 3–4 (2002): 75–98.

——— . "Beyond the Boundaries of the Classroom: Teaching about Gender and Sexuality at a Drag Show." *Journal of Homosexuality* 46, no. 3–4 (2004): 225–240.

Sieczkowski, Cavan. "Lake County School Board May Slash All Student Clubs to Blockade Gay-Straight Alliance." *The Huffington Post*, February 7, 2013. Accessed May 25, 2014. http://www.huffingtonpost.com/2013/02/07/florida-school-board-student-clubs-gay-straight-alliance_n_2638124.html.

Smith, George W. "The Ideology of 'Fag': The School Experience of Gay Students." *Sociological Quarterly* 39, no. 2 (1998): 309–335.

"State Nondiscrimination Laws in the U.S." *thetaskforce.org*, May 21, 2014. Accessed June 2, 2014. http://www.thetaskforce.org/downloads/reports/issue_maps/non_discrimination_5_14_color.pdf.

"States." *freedomtomarry.org*, May 21, 2014. Accessed May 25, 2014. http://www.freedomtomarry.org/states/.

"Suicidality and Self-inflicted Injury." *2005 Youth Risk Behavior Survey*, April 18, 2007. Accessed May 25, 2014. http://www.doe.mass.edu/cnp/hprograms/yrbs/05/.

Tillmann, Lisa M. "Ode to Academic Labor." *International Review of Qualitative Research* 2, no. 1 (2009): 61–66.

——— . "Labor Pains in the Academy." *Academe* 97, no. 1 (2011): 30–33.

——— . *Weight Problem* [motion picture]. United States: Cinema Serves Justice, 2014. http://cinemaservesjustice.com/weight-problem.html.

Tillmann, Lisa M., and David Dietz. *Remembering a Cool September* [motion picture]. United States: Cinema Serves Justice, 2014. http://cinemaservesjustice.com/Remembering.html.

Tillmann, Lisa M., Rex Hall, and David Dietz. *Off the Menu: Challenging the Politics and Economics of Body and Food* [motion picture]. United States: Cinema Serves Justice, 2014. http://cinemaservesjustice.com/off-the-menu.html.

Tillmann-Healy, Lisa M. *Life Projects: A Narrative Ethnography of Gay-Straight Friendship*. Ph.D. diss., University of South Florida, 1998.

——— . *Between Gay and Straight: Understanding Friendship across Sexual Orientation*. Walnut Creek, CA: AltaMira Press, 2001.

———. "Friendship as Method." *Qualitative Inquiry* 9 (2003): 729–749.

Waterston, Alisse, and Barbara Rylko-Bauer. "Out of the Shadows of History and Memory: Personal Family Narratives in Ethnographies of Rediscovery." *American Ethnologist* 33, no. 3 (2006): 397–412.

Westhaver, Russell. "Flaunting and Empowerment: Thinking about Circuit Parties, the Body, and Power." *Journal of Contemporary Ethnography* 35, no. 6 (2006): 611–644.

Wolkomir, Michelle. "Emotion Work, Commitment, and the Authentication of the Self: The Case of Gay and Ex-gay Christian Support Groups." *Journal of Contemporary Ethnography* 30, no. 3 (2001): 305–334.

PART I

GOING HOME

GAY MEN'S IDENTITIES, FAMILIES, AND COMMUNITIES

1

DON'T ASK, DON'T TELL

COMING OUT IN AN
ALCOHOLIC FAMILY[1]

Of anything I have written, this piece required the most careful negotiation with participants. At the project's dawn, four siblings (one gay, one lesbian, and two heterosexual) gave permission to use real names and other identifying details. Each spoke at length about coming out in their "Catholic clan" and about coming of age in an environment frequently disrupted by alcohol. In 2003, I visited the family's hometown, shot photographs, and conducted fieldwork and interviews. My key informant, the gay male sibling who had moved away, called the experience "an intervention." Back home, I composed a draft, reviewed and edited the work with my key informant, sent copies to the other three siblings, and attempted to schedule a follow-up visit so that all could workshop the piece collaboratively.

Silence.

The siblings did what members of alcoholic families often do: close ranks. Letters, phone calls, and emails went unanswered. My key inform- ant let me know that his siblings might withdraw consent. There would be no return trip. What would it take, I asked, to salvage our work together?

Potentially revealing elements, such as places and occupations, had to be changed. No photographs could be used. I could write about alcoholism in the family—if I didn't identify the alcoholics. I could reveal general alcohol-related patterns but not specific instances. Perhaps ironically, I could expose previously undisclosed information about the gay and lesbian identities of Matt and Elisabeth Moretti (not their real names, of course), their relationships, and their sexual discovery, so long as I didn't uncover THE family secret. In the years since that fieldwork visit, I have struggled to find a way both to honor my relational responsibilities and to present "lives in a complex and truthful way for readers."[2]

What follows is a compromise fraught with risk. If I have allowed myself to be manipulated and co-opted by this system, I risk undermining the project's potential contributions to the practice of family ethnography and to the understanding of the coming out process and of alcoholic family dynamics. If the work reveals too much, I violate my own research ethics,[3] jeopardize the relationship I have had with my primary informant since 1996, and risk alienating Matt from his family.

Thus, with trepidation, I begin.

On June 22, 2003, Matt and I convene at his place to discuss our planned trip to Tremaine, Massachusetts. Three of his siblings, older sister Elisabeth (Bets), elder brother Paul, and younger sister Ashley, still live in the area and have agreed to be interviewed. At our session, I ask Matt to talk about his family and his life before our paths crossed.

He tells me, "The Morettis are a loving and caring Italian Catholic clan. I was born in New York, 1967, but grew up in Tremaine, home of top Boston executives and children groomed for the Ivy League. My childhood consisted of family, school, neighborhood friends, and athletics. Mainstream America.

"Born in 1929, my mom grew up in Brooklyn: tenement buildings, tough, working-class neighborhood. She is a saint: turn the other cheek; support your family through thick or thin. Strong belief in God and in the Holy Catholic Church.

"My father, born in 1926, was a broker, so I guess we were upper-middle class. I say 'I guess' because both my parents have blue-collar roots, and that sensibility persists. As a child, my dad lost both parents. Still, he got through school and went into the military; the GI bill paid for college. Earned his degree and did well enough to move our family to Massachusetts. Wonderful provider: house in Tremaine, summer home, every toy you could want."

I sit back in the faux-finished antique chair at Matt's dining room table. Looking into his long-lashed blue eyes, I reflect, "Over the years, I've met several Morettis. We had lunch with your mom and sister Patti shortly after you separated from Kirk. The moment you went to the men's room, they peppered me with concerned questions: 'How is he? What can we do?' Your parents and sister came the moment they heard about your emergency appendectomy. They seem exactly as you described: 'loving and caring.' Because of our work together and our friendship, I know that you dated men for years before coming out to anyone in your family, including your sister Elisabeth, herself an out lesbian for more than 20 years. You spent three years with your first male partner, Nick, and were well into your relationship with Kirk before disclosing to Elisabeth and Ashley on your last trip home, in 1996. What kept you so guarded?"

Matt takes a sip of water. "I grew up thinking, as many of us did, that homosexuality was shameful and something to hide."

"How did your family deal with shameful experiences?"

"Don't look at them. Don't talk about them. Step lightly. Move on. Let sleeping dogs lie."

Given what I know of Matt's history, I can guess the roots of this, but I ask anyway: "How did you learn those rules?"

He exhales. "This is tough for me to make public because eventually, family members will read this. I don't want them to feel exposed or hurt. But you've known me long enough to understand that, in my life, many roads lead back to alcohol."[4]

I nod. "My mind replays that birthday party in 1999: your partner, drunk, passes out in a parking lot. You carry Kirk from the car to the house. His breathing becomes irregular. As we contemplate dialing 911, you tell me for the first time about your family and your own history with alcohol."

Matt responds, "Clan gatherings always began as festive celebrations: first holy communions, confirmations. The atmosphere would be light, then boisterous, then raucous. Several relatives could be Jekyll and Hyde.

Sober and slightly drunk, these were pleasant guys. Extremely drunk, they were aggressive and could become combative physically. Ticking bombs. If one of these guys grew agitated about something—say, Notre Dame losing a big game—the sober family members stuck around, because he would go after somebody, and when he did, we needed everybody else there to shut it down. You could see it, feel it: game over; here comes the trouble.

"As a kid, I knew if relatives were out drinking, sometime during the night there would be a major blow-up: yelling, everybody running toward the commotion. I would get out of bed, and my older siblings would order, 'Go back to your room and close the door!' The next morning, everything would be calm. If I tried to bring it up, nobody would talk about it.[5]

"In many ways, clan drinking *was* my childhood. It set the patterns and shaped our identities: peacemakers, enablers, caregivers, survivors. Morettis accept hardship; we know how to handle crises. Someone has need, someone is hurt, Morettis mobilize. We got that from growing up behind enemy lines.

"No choir boy myself, I binge drank in high school and college. I can be the same mean drunk I grew up seeing. You wouldn't believe the bar fights!" I try to imagine my soft-spoken, boyish friend, a lean 5'6", engaged in a scene reminiscent of *Road House*.[6] Matt continues, "Over the years, members of my extended family died of cirrhosis, but most Morettis eventually got our acts together on our own or through AA. I feel uncomfortable sharing this. Being gay is about me; the clan's struggles extend beyond me. We never discussed this outside the family. None of my Tremaine friends knew.

"I love my family. Given their childhoods, my parents did the best they could. I got my needs met, though emotional support tended to come from my siblings. The game plan was 'Grow up and get away, but not too far. Those left at home could be damaged.' My brothers and sisters sacrificed their weekend lives to manage this. In many ways, they raised me,[7] and I have a special connection to each of them.

"Three still live in the Tremaine area: Elisabeth, Paul, and Ashley. When Bets graduated college, she moved in with her first girlfriend. We all made assumptions about her sexual orientation, but it was 'don't ask, don't tell.' In '96, I brought Kirk home to Tremaine but introduced him as 'my friend.' We stayed with Bets and her partner Ruth. When my sister asked if she should make up the couch for Kirk, I said, 'The guest bed's fine for us both.'

"I told Ashley on that same visit. It only confirmed what she already knew. Ashley always was street savvy. Both Elisabeth and Ashley root for the underdog. Ashley's approach: 'Fuck anybody who doesn't like who you are.' My sisters ended up telling my mom, who I assume told my dad, because I've never said anything to him as far as 'I'm gay.'

"Growing up, I ran in Paul's footsteps. My brother was everything I tried to be: strong, independent, blue-collar masculine. Paul excelled at sports, loved working on cars. He ran with a macho crowd. Any homophobic joke—any off-color joke, really—was a riot to them.

"Paul also can be very loving, caring, and nurturing. He's reluctant to let anyone, aside from his wife and children, see that, but I've always known that part of him.

"For a while, I told myself that Paul didn't have to know. I didn't live close. I was happy with our relationship. Why risk that? I didn't want Paul to think of me the way I assumed he thought of gay men: effeminate, maybe even disgusting. I knew he loved me and saw me as a really good guy. I believed that finding out I was gay would shatter that. His wife Faye started suggesting that I could be gay. Finally, he prodded her, 'Stop beating around the bush.' She said, 'Matt's gay and frightened to death to tell you.' Paul called and left the best message: 'I love you more than ever, and you'll never change in my eyes.' What a relief!

"The hardest part of coming out to my family has been the anguish I put myself through. Never did I consider how positive it could be; I focused completely on the risks. An upcoming hurdle will be my nephews and nieces. Some are now young adults, and we'll be interacting on a different level. I've sensed that some of my siblings prefer that I don't say anything to the children. I want to take their lead, but that's a challenge when we don't talk openly.

"Before we embark on this trip, I need to do a lot of work with each of them, especially Paul. We will move past 'go' here. 'Go' was: 'I'm gay.' Moving past 'go' means: 'How do you feel about disclosing to your children? Are you comfortable coming to my home and being around my partner? Will you treat him as we treat your spouse? *What* do you accept? That I said, "I'm gay," or who I truly am and how I live?'"

Going Home

Four p.m., Thursday, November 6, 2003. Phone to his ear, Matt greets me at his front door and ushers me inside. Hurriedly, he dons a brown leather jacket over blue Banana Republic sweater and jeans, sends a fax, answers another call, and programs his email with an out-of-office auto-reply. His frenetic pace pricks at my already-raw nerves. Matt hasn't returned to Tremaine in seven years. I will meet siblings Elisabeth, Paul, and Ashley for the first time. How are they feeling about our visit?

I drive us to the airport through intense rain and swirling fog. Matt stares silently out the clouded window. As we park, check in, and board, we communicate and soothe our personal and shared anxieties through sighs and knowing glances.

We arrive in Boston 15 minutes early: 8:50 p.m. Matt films the baggage claim area with the video camera he purchased for the trip. Our bags emerge, and we head to Alamo for our rented Chevy Cavalier.

I navigate from Mapquest directions while he maneuvers across the slick terrain from I-90 to the expressway leading into Falkland, where Ashley lives. Past their fall prime, clusters of red, orange, and yellow hands cling to maples and oaks. When Matt settles into the drive, I ask, "How do you feel?"

"Nervous. I fear discovering that people I love are not as accepting as I have hoped. I want them to be brutally honest. How else will we learn and grow?"

Around 11:00 p.m., we pull up to the Dunlevy residence, home of Ashley, her husband Kyle, and their daughters Zoe and Ivy. Ashley and Kyle have nearly completed restoration of their colonial house, built in the 1700s. Opening the back door, Ashley welcomes, "Come in from the cold!" When we step into the light, I see that her upswept hair has the same tones as Matt's, varying from sunny blond to sandy brown. The siblings also share high cheekbones and straight white teeth.

Ashley draws Matt close, then turns to me. Perhaps not knowing what else to do, she and I embrace as well. Her gentle touch offers me a sense of home. "The girls already are in bed," she says, "and Kyle's at a jam session. But let me show you around." Original wide-plank floors, exposed beams, gingham and toile curtains, rustic antiques and reproductions, and hand-painted crafts fill the space with warmth.

After the tour, Ashley sets out leftover Halloween treats and wine for Matt and me. Sipping a non-alcoholic beer, she updates her brother about their cousins and former schoolmates. We spend an hour chatting before Ashley directs Matt to an air mattress in the living room. She lets me know that her daughters are bunking together, giving me Zoe's bedroom.

Upstairs, I clear the desk tucked into a dormer and type field notes. Just past 2:00 a.m., I crawl beneath a quilt adorned with stars and fall quickly asleep.

"I Really Need to Leave"

The next morning, Ashley and daughter Ivy decide to accompany Matt and me on our trek to Tremaine. Before heading to town, we drop by Paul Moretti's large two-story farmhouse, about a mile away. An older, slightly redder-haired version of Matt appears at the door. I note the kindred shape of the brothers' noses, jaws, and mouths. Looking stressed and under-slept, Paul lets us know, "I'm late for a meeting." He hustles Matt and me into the kitchen to meet his infant daughter Tyler and around the house for a rapid-fire tour.

"See you tonight," Matt says as we move toward the door.

"Uh," Paul hedges, "I didn't realize you were coming *this* weekend." My stomach sinks. So much for the "work" Matt pledged to do "with each of them, especially Paul."

"I have to go to New Hampshire," Paul explains, "to put our snowmobiles in the shed."

Matt studies his brother's face. "Oh . . . um, when are you leaving?"

"First thing tomorrow."

"I could go with you," Matt suggests.

With a flick of his wrist, Paul says, "Nah, stay here and do your thing."

Time with you IS our thing, I silently muse.

"When will you be back?" Matt asks.

"Not sure," Paul says, drumming his fingers on the counter. "Listen, I really need to leave."

I wonder when—or if—we'll see Paul again.

Holy Family

Damp leaves sprinkle the back roads to Tremaine. Ashley provides the local lore: who moved/lives/works where, who slept with/married/divorced whom.

We stop first at Holy Family Catholic Church, a white chapel with gothic arched windows and doors. Ashley and Ivy wander the grounds while Matt and I venture inside.

Ascending stairs to the choir loft, Matt sees long-handled baskets and smiles. "Paul and I used to hide up here, avoiding offertory duty." Above the altar beams a stained glass window of Jesus on the cross, a radiant substitute for the standard macabre crucifix. "I feel surprisingly comforted," he reports. "Even the smell—candles, incense—is familiar. Eighteen years of my life. Ashley was baptized here. She, Paul, and I had our first communions and were confirmed in this church. Two of my sisters got married here. Being Catholic was our saving grace. No matter what alcohol-induced chaos occurred Friday and Saturday nights, Sunday morning would come. There were the Morettis: all together, all going to Mass. It pulled our family back together."

I ask, "Has religion shaped your family members' responses to your coming out?"

"One of my in-laws said that if I offered up my life to God, He might answer 'my' prayers and make me straight." Matt rolls his eyes. "Mom once told me, 'Your father and I pray every day that you'll be in heaven.' I laughed. I'm like, 'Me and God are tight.' My dad has remarked that some of the best teachers he had in school were priests that, were they not in the clergy, probably would have identified as gay."

"Has coming out affected your faith?" I query.

Matt looks out over the sanctuary. "I have grown more aware of Catholic dogma, but coming out has not affected who I am, who I've always been, to God. The conversations I have with Him are as meaningful now as ever." We linger quietly. Matt closes his eyes for a few moments, perhaps in prayer. He opens them and gestures toward the stairs.

Matt and I find Ashley and Ivy playing on the floor of a classroom in an adjacent building. "Maple Creek?" he suggests. Ashley nods, and the four of us return to the car.

Schooled in Silence

We wind along the horseshoe route to Matt's middle school. Pulling into a parking space, Ashley says, "Ivy and I will wait here."

Matt and I move through metal doors and veer right, down a long cement-block hallway. We pass the office, library, and rows of aging maroon lockers. Suddenly, Matt takes in a breath. His pace slows. Reaching for my sleeve, he says, "I was not a happy kid here." Matt's face goes pale. We stop walking.

"How do you feel?" I ask.

"Sick to my stomach."

"What was it like for you here?"

His brow furls. "Lonely. Awkward. I remember trying to be transparent. I never felt like I fit in. I had no network of friends. The 'real jocks,' who ruled the school, played baseball or football. My sport was gymnastics, and the first comment was always: 'That's a *girl's* sport.'"

"And you understood the underlying message."

"Yeah: 'You're a fag.'" He exhales. "Do you mind if we leave?" The moment I begin shaking my head, Matt grabs my hand and strides toward the door.

Back in the car, a concerned Ashley turns to read Matt's expression. "What happened?"

"A visceral response, like being in seventh grade again."

With a sigh, Ashley says, "At the height of the clan's weekend antics."

Matt nods. "You're right."

"I was still in elementary school," Ashley recalls. "One day, my class discussed alcohol and alcoholics. Kids talked of 'bums' in Manhattan."

Matt says, "I'm sure that's how our family envisioned alcoholics: homeless men of the Bowery. In their minds, our relatives couldn't have been addicts. They were kind, dedicated family men, solid citizens, successful businessmen."

Ashley reports, "That day in school, I said, 'But maybe alcoholics go to church, maybe they like to watch football.' My teacher spoke to the counselor, who called Mom. She came immediately, and I'll never forget the drive home, the silence thick between us. The take-away lesson: 'Don't *ever* talk about that again.'"

"Too Much Disclosure"

After a driving tour of their old neighborhood, we pull up to Tremaine High. Ashley and Ivy wait by the door while Matt and I walk the indoor track. His eyes pan the championship banners hanging from the ceiling. "Only girls had a gymnastics team. I could have competed individually, but it felt like too much disclosure." Matt shakes his head. "In middle school, I threw double backs on floor. Excellent technique, probably on target for a scholarship. When I got here, I was strong enough to do giant swings on high bar, but not strong enough to be the person I was, so I quit gymnastics. I probably regret that more than anything I've ever done or not done in my life."

Finding Their Way Back

That evening, Elisabeth joins us for dinner. Ashley sets the harvest dining table with tavern dishes, serving Cabernet, pizza, and chicken parmesan buffet style. Taking a seat, Elisabeth asks, "How was Tremaine?"

"Exhausting," Matt says. "We walked through Holy Family, the old neighborhood, and our schools. Wading into Maple Creek made me anxious, almost nauseous." Elisabeth leans toward him, wide blue eyes filling with tears.

Matt continues, "In middle school, I didn't connect the pressure to suppressing my sexuality but to being constantly measured: scholastically, athletically, socially."

I turn to Elisabeth. "What were those years like for you?"

"Tremaine . . . not an easy place to be different," she says, nodding toward Matt.

"To be lesbian?" I probe.

She tucks wispy-banged, chin-length hair behind one ear. "When I was 15, our dad caught me with another girl. He yelled at us, demanding to know if we were queer."

Matt sits back. "You never told me that. How'd you answer?"

"I denied it, of course, but I knew otherwise."

"You felt certain at that age?" I query.

"I believe it's inherent. This is who I am. I'm not making a choice."

Matt adds, "Some say it's your upbringing that makes you gay. No way. Paul and I had the same upbringing. He's absolutely heterosexual, and I'm absolutely homosexual."

Elisabeth asks me, "What's your theory on that?"

I turn this over. "My standpoint emerges from studying the history and language of sexuality. The categories 'heterosexual' and 'homosexual' divide us in a single, arbitrary way: according to the sex of those with whom we tend to be intimate.[8] Politically, I think it more strategic to destabilize these terms rather than shore them up:[9] '*absolutely* heterosexual,' '*absolutely* homosexual.' I take seriously your sense that it's inherent. I view same- and cross-sex intimacies as equally natural. But 'natural' is itself a human-made category inseparable from history and culture. I believe that same- and cross-sex intimacies are morally equivalent, and I consider some element of choice important, because it affirms the legitimacy of how we live and whom we love."

Elisabeth asks, "How would you answer a fundamentalist who challenges, 'If you can choose to be gay, why not choose to be straight?'"

"I would explain that, for me, the ethical considerations do not center on the sex of one's partner but on whether the relationship is consensual, non-exploitive, and mutually fulfilling."

"What has been the role of religion in your life?" queries Elisabeth.

"As for the Morettis, Catholicism provided a backdrop for my life and family. We attended Mass every week. I served as a cantor in church. I went to Catholic university. But from an early age, I identified with feminism and struggled with the secondary role of women in the Church."

Elisabeth says, "I haven't been to Mass in forever because I won't be part of something that does not accept me. Even within my own family, I've been approached with 'God's law.' That just floors me. I'm loving, caring, hard-working. One quality cancels out all others? Some of my lesbian friends remain quite spiritual, and I'm very, very envious. I just don't feel it."

"I do," Matt says, "but I don't see the Bible as the unquestionable word. Why would God create rational, inquisitive beings if we're not supposed to exercise our capacities?"

I report, "We have a friend, Nate, whose closest heterosexual male friend just found out that he's gay. The friend's response: 'I love you. I care about you. I can tolerate this. But my faith requires that I implore you to repent.' Nate refused to settle. He said, 'I love you. I care about you. And I'm entitled to more than toleration.' His friend kept trying to shift responsibility back to Nate: 'You must accept my beliefs just as you're saying I must accept your orientation.' The friend relocated the problem from his heterosexism to Nate's same-sex orientation. But we also can employ the friend's logic. Can we love the 'sinner'—our friends, our family members—even as we contest their sin, heterosexism?"

I then ask Elisabeth, "Where do your family members seem to be on these issues?"

She sighs. "It is what it is. My partner Ruth and I are accepted, yet there are boundaries we neither cross nor discuss openly."

Matt responds, "I have perceived that. Ruth seems to become involved or stay removed from our family members according to their ability or inability to accept the relationship."

Elisabeth says, "I know that Ashley supports Matt and me as well as our partners. She's already begun introducing her daughters to Ruth's and my relationship."

I ask Ashley, "How do you navigate these issues with your girls?"

"Without any problem," she says. "Zoe recently asked, 'Is this Aunt Bets' bed?' I said, 'This is Aunt Bets' *and* Aunt Ruth's bed.'" Ashley smiles. "This morning she asked, 'Is Uncle Matt married to Aunt Lisa?'" We all laugh. "I explained that 'Aunt' Lisa and Uncle Matt are friends."

I probe, "As your girls ask more specific questions, you will give more specific answers?"

"Absolutely. Growing up, we never had that. My girls will not be kept in the dark."

"You have two siblings in same-sex relationships," I say. "Does it occur to you that one of your daughters—"

"Sure," Ashley says.

"Have you and your husband talked about that?"

"Yeah. And you know what? I'm glad for our experience with Matt and Bets, because if one of my daughters has that orientation, we'll know how to handle it." She reconsiders her words. "Not 'handle it,' but we'll understand that there's nothing wrong with it."

"If you don't mind," Elisabeth says to me, "I'd like to know more about the project. In your first book, I saw you pushing yourself as a heterosexual woman, pushing your marriage."

Matt says, "Her work also pushes the gay participants, including me. Lisa definitely has helped me examine my internalized homophobia and sexism. As someone who can pass, I learned to suppress my feminine qualities. Femininity projected homosexuality, and that felt threatening. In my relationship with Lisa's husband, I find myself connecting to both his masculinity and femininity. That broadens the range of who we can be for one another."

"What do you hope this new project will do?" asks Ashley.

"You may remember that the first project closed with my dissertation defense. Several of the guys testified about their experiences. Everyone seemed poised for new dialogues and transformed relationships. In some ways, that promise was fulfilled. Everybody came out to his family. Some came out at work; others left jobs where they felt they couldn't."

"When I learned of this project," says Ashley, "I was psyched. Matt had been so private. What a huge step!"

Elisabeth adds, "I remember reading some of your unpublished work and smiling. 'That's my brother.' I brought it to my friends: 'Wow, look at this!' I experienced many revelations. I didn't know Matt had such a large group of friends; I'd never been exposed to those relationships. I found you very perceptive, very caring with him. The way you describe him, the way you feel about him, you get Matthew. I've seen the project's effect on my brother, and it's very positive."

Matt smiles. "A monumental journey: being honest, first with myself, then with others."

"For these guys and their families," I say, "the initial disclosure opened a door, but crossing the threshold remained a challenge. I began to wonder why and what would happen if the don't ask/don't tell dynamic were suspended, which is part of what I've asked you to do this weekend."

Ashley turns to Matt. "Have we been practicing 'don't ask, don't tell'?"

"Well," he says, "I haven't been home in seven years!"

Ashley speaks intently, "Everyone misses you, Matt: your siblings, in-laws, our kids."

"I definitely sense that," he responds. "I see that my own fears and projections played as big a role as any in this process. The ball is in my court now."

I observe, "Interesting that this dynamic came about in a family with a lesbian and a gay male sibling. Matt, you spent years hiding a second life from family members—even Elisabeth!"

He replies, "It sounds strange now, but I feared her disapproval. Even though I knew her orientation, it seemed more acceptable to be female and gay than male and gay."

"To her . . . or to you?" I ask.

"Now I can see it as a projection."

I ask, "Elisabeth, had you suspected that Matt was gay?"

"As we got older, I had a gut-level feeling."

"Why didn't you ask?"

"For the same reason he didn't tell: fear of the other's reaction."

"In high school," recalls Ashley, "I watched him read *Sports Illustrated* cover to back. When I listened to him talk to his male friends, I'd cringe. He sounded so rehearsed.

"Matt came to my wedding reception in '96, and I remember driving with him to the caterer's. I fought with myself. Should I ask? I haven't seen Matt in such a long time. I don't want to make him uncomfortable. And God forbid if he's not!

"When he visited later that year with Kirk, they stayed at Elisabeth's. I called and asked her, 'Did they sleep in the same bed?' When she confirmed that, I felt happy, for him and for us. Maybe we'll get Matthew back. By that point, he really had drifted from the family."

Matt remembers, "Before I left, Bets said, 'You need to tell Ashley. You grew up the closest together, and she's asked the most questions.' I dialed her number and said, 'Ash, I'm gay.'"

Ashley laughs. "And I said, 'Matt, I *know*!'"

The conversation moves from one issue, one level, to the next. The siblings seem hungry to reconnect, like old friends finding their way back to one another.

Act II

Eleven p.m., we hear a car in the drive. Elisabeth heads for the window. Mouth agape she says, "It's *Paul.*" I wonder how best to integrate him into our conversation. Matt and I move toward the side door, greeting Paul as he enters; Ashley remains seated at the table.

"Beer?" Matt offers, steering the group toward the kitchen. Paul, Elisabeth, and I follow. Several minutes pass before Ashley joins us. The additional character and change of scene edit the dialogue. Sexual orientation gets cut from the script as family drama turns to comedy.

"We had a lake house," Matt reminds me. "Our oldest brother Alan served as both family prankster and sadist." He takes a swig of Bud. "When Alan got you on the inner tube or skis, his mission was to give you the wildest ride possible.

"One Sunday morning, everybody's hanging out on the dock, dressed for 10:30 Mass." Grinning, Elisabeth and Paul exchange a glance of recognition. Matt amplifies the suspense: "All the sudden, you feel a sinking sense of *doooom.*"

Paul takes the cue. "We turn around, and who's at the land side of the dock?"

"You just *know* what Alan has in mind," Elisabeth says.

Matt recalls, "Looking down at my good pants and shoes, I realize it's every man for himself. Alan spared no one, not even Mom."

"At the time, he pissed everybody off," says Paul. "Now, of course, it's hilarious."

The brothers and Bets laugh themselves breathless with co-constructed tales from the Moretti childhood: amusing/disturbing adventures on water, snow, and the open road. Ashley, now sitting alone at the kitchen table, beseeches, "Where were our parents?" No one answers.

After another beer, Paul and Elisabeth bid their goodbyes. I later wish I'd taken a photo; this turns out to be the last time on our trip that the four siblings will be together.

"Think I'll head up," I tell Matt and Ashley.

Matt walks across the kitchen and pulls me close. "That conversation with my sisters . . . I just . . . I don't know how to thank you." I kiss my friend's cheek.

An hour of field notes later, I settle into bed, anxious about the next day's agenda: interviews with Elisabeth and Ashley.

"Beyond the Locked Bedroom"

Matt and I drive to the townhouse owned by Elisabeth and Ruth. Both greet us at the door. With her blue eyes, rosy skin, and sandy hair, Ruth could pass for a blood member of the Moretti clan. The décor features antiques set off by crown molding and textured paints in khaki and olive. As we move to the living room, I inquire about its focal point, a shabby chic door with chipping paint and dried flowers.

Taking seats, the group begins discussing relationships. Matt says, "Growing up, I assumed my life would include marriage and children. By the time I entered Boston College, I knew that I might be gay. I told myself that my family—worth more to me than my own happiness— would never approve, so I buried it and immersed myself in my studies.

"I graduated, returned home, and got a great job. All along, I always had a girlfriend. Maybe that helped me fit in. I consider those good relationships as far as respect and caring. Physically, I felt turned on by women, but my heart had yet to be aroused."

I ask, "Would you say that, for you, this is more an emotional than a sexual orientation?"

"Absolutely. As I got older, I became increasingly aware of the imbalance in those relationships. Definitely the women experienced a depth of feeling I didn't.

"By this time, I'd met gay doctors: professional, 'normal' men who showed me that being gay was not as different as I'd imagined. Still, I knew that exploring my sexuality meant leaving Tremaine. I took a job with a traveling healthcare company and made my way to Florida, where I began dating Nick. Sexually, I found it similar to my experiences with women. Emotionally, I felt deeply attached for the first time.

"Very masculine and athletic, Nick attracted me because he so defied the stereotypes. I now see that I also was drawn to his ability to *pass*, and I desperately needed to pass. I still believed that my life would revolve around straight people. Neither of us was out at the time, so our relationship occurred between seven at night and seven in the morning. We appeared to be roommates; we even had two bedrooms set up. In public, we would go to movies and leave an open seat between us. Because Nick was so closeted, I wasn't met with the same caliber person as in my relationships with women. Eventually, I had to end that relationship—or we had to wake up in a more accepting culture!

"When we broke up, I finally told a female friend: 'Nick and I were more than roommates.' I felt as though I would throw up from the stress of saying those words."

Tears come to Elisabeth's eyes. "You went through this relationship and break-up alone."

"We *all* do it alone," observes Ruth.

"That doesn't change how sad I feel." Elisabeth turns to Matt. "After Nick, you met Kirk."

"Yes. Joining his softball team, I discovered a supportive group with whom I could talk about my relationship. I felt as comfortable as with our Italian Catholic clan. With Kirk, I grew beyond the locked bedroom. I plunged into a gay life, which came to feel completely normal. Once I knew that my gay family would be there the rest of my life, I could risk sharing that part of my experience with our family."

Ruth says, "I clearly remember the night you and Kirk stayed here. Elisabeth came in and told me you two were sleeping in the same bed. I said, 'For heaven's sake, Bets, he's *gay*.'"

Elisabeth smiles. "Still I said, 'I don't know. Wouldn't he tell us?' Then a knock on our door. Matthew squeaked, 'May I talk to you?' We went downstairs. My heart pounded. He said, 'I'm ... I'm gay,' and I said, 'I know.' We reached for each other."

Matt recalls, "We cried, we hugged, we told each other 'I love you.'"

Elisabeth ventures, "What happened between you and Kirk?"

"I needed more nurturing. Both of us stretched, a long way and for a long time. We valued our love and our life together, but I found that level of stretching unsustainable."

I think about the plotline Matt omits: Kirk's substance abuse. Early on, Matt and Kirk enjoyed clubbing together: the music, the camaraderie of friends, the lowered inhibitions that allowed them to open to each other in ways they couldn't seem to otherwise. Skating close to a line he'd seen too many relatives cross, Matt eventually pulled back from that scene. On a few occasions, Kirk stayed out all night. Hour after hour, Matt would lie awake, awaiting his partner's return.[10]

Elisabeth asks Matt, "What drew you to your current partner?"

"Josh has the nurturing piece. Our needs and abilities align."

"You Expose Him to the Family"

The four of us visit a while before Matt and Ruth head out for lunch. When they leave, I notice Elisabeth's trembling hands. "I feel really nervous," she admits.

"Should we have some wine?" I suggest.

"Great!" she says, moving to the kitchen to pour two glasses of Merlot. We chat at the library/dining table until Elisabeth seems ready.

"I will start with your background, then ask you to reflect on Matt, your relationship, your and his coming out, and your family's responses. I will transcribe our conversation and send you a copy. If I misheard or misunderstood, if you need to add or clarify, let me know. I also will send you a draft of the manuscript." She nods.

Early in our conversation, I learn that Elisabeth Moretti, born in 1959, graduated from Tremaine High in 1977. She earned a liberal arts B.A. and has worked for a small business since 1989. "Describe your brother Matt," I request.

"Extremely kind, loving, and caring. You can't help but like him. When friends and I visited Orlando, I felt so proud to have them meet him. For a time, we lived together in Tremaine, and we were 'best buds.' Matt understands me and I him."

"What turning points stand out in the history of your relationship?"

"Coming out to him. I could no longer take the pain of both a broken relationship and being unable to talk about it. Matt drew me out in a very non-threatening way. I felt safe. The moment I said 'I'm gay,' he gathered me in his arms and told me how much he loved me.

"Then his coming out. I always pictured my brother as heterosexual, though it had occurred to me that he could be gay. Very different from my other brothers. He didn't play lacrosse or football. From an early age, Matthew had characteristics people stereotype as gay: he was very sensitive; he wasn't athletic."

I write "wasn't athletic" in my notes, knowing that my friend—a former gymnast, lifeguard, and centerfielder—will take issue.[11]

Elisabeth continues, "When Matt confirmed he was gay, I didn't have the same reaction that he had for me, maybe because I knew the difficulties. I felt afraid and protective."

"What do you see as your place in the Moretti family?" I ask.

"It's changed. My older sister and I used to be the core. She thought we would grow up, live around the corner from each other, and have our families together. My coming out burst that bubble. I've gone from being central to peripheral in both my immediate and extended families."

"Last night, I heard you reflect on your family with: 'It is what it is.'"

She nods. "That's come with maturity. I relate to Ashley. I had a lot of anger about the years of clan drama, and I was very confrontational. I now see that as wasted energy."

"What about Matt's role in the system of relationships?" I ask.

"A peacemaker, Matthew wants everybody to be happy and get along."[12]

"Seeing Matt this weekend has been . . . ?"

"Wonderful. He and I have communicated more this weekend than we ever have."

"You grew up in a family your brother describes as 'loving and caring.' Among his friends, he again has found support and compassion. Matt has expressed to me a desire to bring those networks closer together. What would that require?"

"Some family members worry that, without a spouse and children, you'll be alone. They need to see that he's loved. Both Matt and I have 'family' outside our blood family. You may know my brother better than I at certain stages. I don't feel threatened by it."

"Elisabeth, what hopes do you have for the project?"

"I hope that, by coming back, Matt will have this kind of relationship not just with you; you've now brought us into it."

I ask, "Any fears or concerns?"

"No fear whatsoever. I only see the positive. Through this project, I learn about my brother. You expose him to the family, which is very helpful."

"Any questions for me?"

"Tell me about your attachment to my brother. Out of all the guys . . ."

My cheeks rise. "I find Matt warm, giving, understanding, inherently trustworthy. He respects intelligence. He respects women. When I met him, we were making different but parallel journeys. Raised Catholic in upwardly mobile families with blue-collar roots, we both lived geographically distant from our hometowns. Matt had embarked on life as an openly gay man; I was learning to listen and bear witness to, study, and document the group that had become our surrogate family."

Elisabeth asks, "Do you see the project going in a positive direction?"

"I think more in terms of process than direction. I expect that, as in *Between Gay and Straight*, turns of consciousness will occur organically in conversations like the one we had earlier with Ruth and Matt, in interviews such as this one, through fieldwork at key sites, and in our follow-up contacts. Collectively, those insights will become the project."

She then queries, "Have you ever been around gay women?"

"More now than during my dissertation fieldwork. My closest friend and colleague identifies as lesbian. I've grown as attached—emotionally, socially, politically—to Kathryn and her partner Deena as to my family of gay male friends."

"Do you relate to gay men and lesbians differently?" asks Elisabeth.

"I tend to feel more aligned with lesbians. Sexism can be as rife among gay men as heterosexual men. I connect to lesbians both as a woman living in a sexist culture and as a heterosexual ally."

She observes, "In some situations, your voice carries more weight than mine or my brother's."

"Different weight, certainly. In 2002, Kathryn and I joined OADO, the Orlando Anti-Discrimination Ordinance Committee. In Kathryn's and my first OADO initiative, we fought to add sexual orientation to the classes protected by Orlando's city code. Both of us wrote editorials, met with council members, and testified at public hearings. As a member of the dominant group, I felt empowered to confront the opposition directly; I even ridiculed their toxic rhetoric at a public rally. The LGB activists tended to be consummately dignified, respectful, and diplomatic; perhaps they believed they could not afford to be otherwise."

Sensing closure, I place my hands atop hers. "Thank you so much, Elisabeth."

She reflects, "How fascinating to look back on my life, Matthew's life, and how they intertwine. Other than coming out, he and I have not 'gone deep' with each other. You would think two gay family members would do that! I need to get to know him again. I trust what I have to give, and my love for him is . . ." Her voice breaks. "You see, I get so emotional. Excuse the tears. That's it."

"Peeling Back the Layers"

Late afternoon, Matt and I return to Ashley's for today's second sibling session. She directs me to the master bedroom, where I set up for our interview. Afternoon sun pours through multi-paned windows as she settles into an antique rocker. "How do you feel?" I ask.

"Good," she says with a grin. "Not as nervous as Bets."

I take down biographical details. The youngest of the Moretti clan, Ashley was born in 1970. Around her graduation from Tremaine High in 1988, her parents sold the family home and moved away. Ashley characterizes herself during the years that followed as "a lost soul." By age 21, she had relocated to Florida and returned to Massachusetts twice. Ashley and her husband dated four years; they eloped in March 1996 and were pregnant that September. "Do you live the life you imagined?" I ask.

"I never projected that far ahead. Growing up, I was a chameleon. I did what people expected. Never formed opinions."

"I'm a middle child," I tell her, "between two brothers. Has being the youngest impacted you?"

Ashley exhales. "I've been seen as a screw-up, immature." Her voice goes soft. "I was put in a lot of adult situations before I was ready. But, you know, that happened to all of us."

I nod and hold her gaze a moment. "Complete this thought for me: being a member of the Moretti family means . . ."

"Fucked up," Ashley says. "We project an image of this wonderful, happy-go-lucky team. And it's not. For me, it's not."

I respond, "Underneath the stories told last night by Paul, Bets, and Matt, I heard a theme: lack of boundaries, structure, supervision, protection. I sensed that you experienced the conversation differently than the others."

Ashley presses her lips together. "Those stories bring up hurt and resentment, even toward my siblings." Tears well in her large brown eyes. "It took a lot for me just to come into the kitchen. It's always been, 'Ignore it. Don't talk about it. Forgive and forget.'"

"Last night, you, Elisabeth, Matt, and I took a different tack. We talked about your life journeys, the sibling relationships. Then, when Paul arrived, our course reverted. It became— "

"Humorous," Ashley finishes.

"Exactly. Very different from the deeper, more personal exchange we'd been having."

"Our family never engaged in that kind of talk. It was always, 'Wild party!' and, 'Fun, fun, fun!'" Then, almost pleading, "Where was the serious and mature side of everybody?"

I say, "How appropriate that the conversations took place in different rooms. Each group behaved like a different family. We all participated in the shift. None of us said—"

"'Join us, Paul,'" she interjects.

"Right. We could have given Paul an update and invited him to sit down. Instead we accommodated, offering what we thought would keep Paul comfortable: the usual pattern."

We sit in silence a moment before I request, "Tell me about Matt."

"A perfectionist. A people pleaser. Sensitive. A good guy. *Private.* Very private. Does his own thing." Emotions seem to swirl beneath "private" and "does his own thing."

Gingerly I ask, "What about your relationship with him?"

Ashley leans back. "I feel very resentful because he pushed the family—me—away." Her voice cracks. "I . . . I think Matthew might care about his . . ." she glances at me, then looks away, "*friends.* But he doesn't put me in a special place like he does his friends. That hurts."

I wonder how my presence here has called up, even exacerbated, these feelings. "What would you like to see in your relationship?"

"More openness. Bets and I have that. She can tell me anything about her relationship with Ruth or her friends. Maybe, in time, Matthew will feel that he can talk to me. I hadn't spoken to him in, like, a year. That much time passed! I get frustrated and say, 'Oh well, he has his own life. I don't fit into that.' That's fine, you know? I can accept that."

"But it isn't what you want," I reflect.

"It's not what I want, but you can't push yourself on people."

"What might you do to cultivate a different connection?" I ask.

She takes in a breath. "The easiest is to call more. We can say, 'Go visit,' but would that really happen? In my ideal world, we'd talk all the time, and when we did, he would share more, like when he talks about . . . uh . . . Joe, right?"

It takes me a second to understand. "His partner? Josh."

"*Josh*," she slowly repeats. "I've heard Matt mention his name many times." Brow furrowed, Ashley seems distressed by the mistake. She continues, "I asked, 'Are you partners?' but he never said anything, so I wasn't going to ask anymore."

Sensing multiple open wounds, I move to what seems like more neutral ground. "Four of your siblings identify as heterosexual, one as a gay man, one as lesbian. Talk to me about that."

"I don't think much about it. Last night, Matt spoke of your husband's feminine and masculine sides. I later said to Kyle, 'I must be really stupid. Such a simpleton. I don't analyze things like that.'" Hearing her self-descriptions of "really stupid" and "simpleton" stirs my compassion. I consider the edicts under which Ashley grew up: don't be too perceptive, don't talk about what you do perceive—canonical rules in alcoholic family systems. Being or portraying a "simpleton" would have been a survival mechanism.

"Has having gay and lesbian siblings enhanced your life?" I ask.

"It enriches me, helps me appreciate what Bets and Matt—lesbian and gay people—endure. I admire them for believing in and being true to themselves." I bear in mind Ashley's difficult and unfinished journey from "chameleon" toward believing in and being true to herself.

"Seeing Matt this weekend has been . . ." I prompt.

"Great," she says. Then, gently, "Um . . . I miss him. I'm happy he's here. It felt good to talk last night. When speaking to him on the phone, I haven't wanted to pry for fear of pushing him away farther. You keep things on a very surface level. But peeling back the layers and talking, you learn about his journey and what he's gone through . . . which has been a lot of pain."

"For you, too, Ashley. Perhaps now you can share more of that with each other."

"This weekend has opened the door," she says. "This is the first mature weekend we've ever had." Awestruck, I write "first mature weekend" in my notes. She continues, "As stupid as that sounds, but seriously, I don't think we've *ever* been like this. What you're doing . . . I'm really grateful."

"We'll Pass"

After my session with Ashley, Matt and I make our way to Paul's place. The brothers reminisce about Matt's visit with Kirk in 1996. "You were just moving into this house," Matt says, laughing. "I remember you looked at us and said, 'Hey you two *homos*, pick up that sofa.'"

Paul blushes. "At the time, I didn't know you actually were . . . um . . . together."

"Relax. I knew you were kidding, though I later took some heat from Kirk."

Eyes downcast, Paul says, "Sorry about that." He shifts quickly. "Faye and I are going to a pub with friends tonight."

All I can think is: *more avoidance.*

Paul prods, "You should come."

Matt sighs. "Man, I'm beat. We've been going full steam for two days. Could we just stay here and get caught up?"

"We already promised our friends."

"I think . . . we'll pass," Matt says. "We won't really be able to visit at a pub anyway." Paul shrugs.

On the ride back to Ashley's, I ask Matt, "What do you make of that invitation?"

"I don't know. Maybe we'll find out tomorrow."

Excavation

Sunday, November 9, 2003: our last day in Massachusetts. Matt and I head back to Paul's, finding the family gathered in their kitchen.

As Paul feeds baby Tyler, the couple shares foibles from Faye's recent pregnancy and birth, her first in ten years.

"Before we knew Tyler was a girl," Paul says, "Ms. Faye almost went crazy."

She retorts, "One son and a husband already, I was not about to have another boy in this house. Somebody would've had to go!" Faye shoots Paul a look of "Probably you, bud." Paul begins working the griddle, filling the space with scents of bacon and blueberry pancakes.

A car pulls up. "Who's here?" asks Matt.

"Same couple we went out with last night," Paul replies.

I wonder about their presence today. Is Paul diluting the visit? Avoiding our scheduled interview? The couple enters the kitchen. As they cross to shake our hands, Paul says, "This is my brother, Matt, and his friend, Lisa." As her son files in and out of the room, Faye gives their friends a detailed, matter-of-fact history of my work.

After breakfast, the brothers haul from the attic a trunk of Matt memorabilia: school and prom photos, notes from old girlfriends, report cards, and assignments. We marvel at Matt's spelling (e.g., "sheey" instead of "she"). Paul quips, "What was that from, eighth grade?"

Matt banters, "*Neither* of us made the highest reading group." He then uncovers a pamphlet entitled *Examination Prayer*. With a chuckle, Matt says, "Mom's idea of help with test preparation." Then, "Paul is an awesome father, totally involved in schoolwork and activities."

My friend also discovers four paperbacks explaining the rules of football, basketball, baseball, and hockey. "Knowledge of sports was my cover," he recalls.

Like an archeologist, Matt slowly sifts through the artifacts, handling each with reverence. He removes a poem, written longhand, about living in Paul's shadow. Matt reads it aloud, then passes the poem to his brother. "I've never seen this," Paul tells us.

"You two better get going," Matt says, reminding me of the time.

"If You Weren't Here Asking Questions . . ."

Tissue and Bloody Mary in hand, Paul leads me into the den. He seems on edge, so I take extra time going over my list of questions. Early in our session, I learn that Paul Moretti, born in New York in 1964, graduated from Tremaine High and earned a degree in manufacturing. Since 1989, Paul has ascended the ranks of the postal service. He met his wife Faye in college. They married in 1990, had their son in 1992 and their daughter in 2003.

I offer my best comforting smile. "Please describe Matt."

"Very caring. Would never wish harm on anybody."

"How are you similar and different?"

"Similar . . . I feel concern for people. For example, I see a neighbor struggling to rake leaves. I know she has a baby inside, so I help her out. Like Matt, I don't ruffle feathers. I'm more 'Take the easy way around. Don't make a lot of noise. Tread lightly.'

"Different . . . communicating with family. If a month, a year, passes before I talk to somebody, it's okay."

I ask, "What's your relationship with Matt been like over the years?"

"Tight. Growing up, we did everything together. Had the same friends. Didn't compete." Paul grins. "Best man at my wedding."

"What role has Matt played in your family?"

"In the past, the focal point, the glue keeping people together."

"Have you played a particular role?" I ask.

"I didn't think so. I'm more of an outsider. I don't take the initiative, which I know is something I have to work on. Then again, that's just not me. I'm not one who has to be involved in everybody's affairs. But listening to Matthew in the last day, it seemed that I was someone he looked up to. Like the little poem about my shadow. I never felt that way, but I guess I was there to make sure that he was okay and pointed in the right direction."

"How does geographic distance affect your relationship?"

"If you said to Matt, 'What would you change about our childhood?' it would be having more direction, focus. If he lived here, Matt would make sure my kids had that. If he had children, I'd do the same. A family is there to support, to share experiences. If you're not there, you're not sharing experiences." Paul rattles the ice in his glass. "I have two kids. My son and little girl don't know Matt; he doesn't really know them."

I then say, "Complete this thought in reference to your family of origin: being a member of the Moretti family means . . ."

He turns this over. "It means deep down, knowing you have siblings to support you, back you up, assist you in a time of need. The siblings move the boat forward, all oars in the water."

I reflect on this. The Moretti brothers and sisters shared a sometimes-chaotic childhood. Ashley tends to frame events in terms of deficiency, asking, "Where were our parents?" and calling the system "fucked up." Her descriptions express experiential truths, but do they serve her well? Paul uses a more neutral metaphor, a ship. He seems to acknowledge that no parent stands at the helm but praises his siblings for "mov[ing] the boat forward." Would this way of narrating events ring true to Ashley's experience?

Paul goes on, "So what being a member of my family means to me is that even though we're far apart and don't communicate weekly, we're tight deep down. *Tight*. Move that ship forward. So a lot of pride. I'm a Moretti. I *love* Morettis." His eyes well with tears.

We absorb this before I alter our focus: "How did you learn that Matt identifies as gay?"

He sits back. "It was . . . I'm a little cloudy, but I would say ultimately from, I guess, your work. I'm not sure if my wife said something to me."

I'm struck by the contrast between Paul's "cloudy" recollection and the seemingly verbatim account Matt provided of Faye breaking the news, Paul's supportive voicemail, and the brothers' subsequent phone conversation. "Has your siblings' coming out challenged you?"

"It really hasn't. You're only challenged when you face something you're not sure you can handle."

"Has it enhanced your life?"

"It's . . . openness. If I'm channel surfing and come upon a gay parade, I don't just flip by. If you see issues—whether it's legal to wed, if they can get health insurance for each other—you take note. With Elisabeth, we don't converse like: 'What is being a lesbian? How is your relationship?' We've never gone into that. Then with my brother, I've never . . . last night was the first time ever discussing anything about being homosexual with him present."

I write "first time ever" in my notes. "The conversation that unfolded in Ashley's kitchen—laughing, joking, reminiscing about crazy times—is that typical?"

Paul laughs. "*Exactly*. It's always: what happened in the past, how much fun we had, and how incredible that we're still alive."

"Have you and Faye talked about how to navigate issues related to sexual orientation with your kids?"

He processes a moment. "If you weren't here asking questions, I might continue to do what I'm doing. Because you're asking, you start thinking, right? The next step has to be a talk with Elisabeth to see what she's comfortable with. In turn, she might ask what I'm comfortable with. Same with Matthew. We've never scratched the surface beyond: 'Hey Paul, I'm gay.' 'Okay, great.' As far as explaining to the kids, I would have to know more so that I'm not just making stuff up. What would I go to my son with now? 'There's boys and boys, and there's boys and girls.' That's the extent of what I know."

I say, "Two of your siblings have primary relationships with persons of the same sex. Has it occurred to you that one of your kids could identify as gay or lesbian?"

Paul shifts in his chair. "You think homosexuality is genetic?"

"Some evidence suggests—"

"I don't rule it out. I hear all kinds of stuff in the news about this. I think that you're wired, and significant emotional events can cross those wires. You're very delicate as a child. One show I listen to, they drill callers: 'What happened? How were you raised? Your mother and father, were they alcoholics?' Nine times out of ten, the caller doesn't say, 'Oh, my parents were perfect.' If it's genetic, then it is what it is, and you are who you are."

I ask, "Have you ever wished that your siblings weren't gay?"

He stares at his feet. "Elisabeth, not so much. Matthew, definitely. Only because of the fight. It's got to be a tremendous fight." I note Paul's assumption that Elisabeth, who faces both homophobia and sexism, has less to fight. He continues, "I don't think anybody . . . In my mind . . . I don't know. Would you want to take that path? It's got to be extremely difficult. So if you choose . . . If you do take that path, it can't be of your own . . . It can't be. You wouldn't . . . What I'm saying is: you wouldn't choose that path. It's got to be a freaking hard path. So it must be . . . It must be that that's who you are. So it could . . . It could still be the wiring; it could still be genetics. What's done is done at this point, and that's who you are; that's who he is, if we're talking about Matt. So yeah, of course, I wish he wasn't, because I'd like to see him, you know, with a wife and kids—and not to say that he can't have kids; he can adopt if he wants. But his fight has got to be hard." Paul's response is typical of our conversation. He seems to simultaneously discover for himself and express to me what he thinks and feels.

His lips curl into a grin. "Provincetown, P-town. Here's a funny story. Real quick. I know we're time sensitive. I'm walking down the road with a friend, my wife, and his wife. Never been there before, so I don't know it's a whole gay community. All the sudden, my friend slips his hand into mine. Now I feel like everybody's looking, you know what I mean?" Though I imagine that *nobody* in P-town outside their party thought anything of it, I nod, wondering why this memory came to mind. Paul continues, "Really awkward, like, 'What are you doing?' My friend won't let go, and of course, the girls start laughing. They knew where we were. I had no idea. It's Cape Cod. You know, you go up there and surf. Afterwards, it was funny as hell."

Paul returns to his previous point. "But the fight, yeah. It's got to be a tough fight."

Changing gears I say, "Let's talk about the work that preceded this project." I then pose what I assume to be a rhetorical question: "Did you have an opportunity to read—"

"Not front to back," he admits.

During a pre-trip interview, Matt told me that, years ago, Faye and Paul sought out copies of unpublished pieces featuring Matt. Why would Paul forgo the opportunity to learn about his brother's experience, especially after agreeing to participate in *Going Home*? Instead of my real question ("Why not?"), I ask what feels less confrontational: "What was it like to encounter Matt's story that way?"

Paul takes a swig of Bloody Mary. "I was a fly on the wall. In some cases, I wasn't ready for that. I didn't talk to my brother. I don't know anything other than, 'Hey, I'm gay.' Now it's in your face: sitting in a tree kissing a guy—stuff that, to me, is like 'Holy Christ!' Then I'm not reading; I'm flipping through and finding out who he is, what he's doing. I'm looking just for Matt. Because of your work, I'm able to peek into his world. Maybe if I did read the entire book you wrote about his friends, I would see different experiences and how others relate to their families. It could uncover a lot of emotions and what they battle also."

"Do you have any hopes for this project?"

"For the public, to open eyes, to show them who they put down, to build more cognizance of what my brother deals with—the battle. Family wise, there's nothing to be resolved. We just need to communicate more. How do I support him? What does he need? If I don't ask, I'll never know. The ball's in my court on that one. I've now asked those questions; maybe others reading the story will do the same."

"Any concerns or fears?"

"Confronting relatives that I've never spoken to about it. If they read your work, they also can see Matt kissing some guy. That's a little awkward—like getting your pants pulled down in public." I register his simile of shaming but do not interrupt. "You think, 'Didn't know that. Don't *want* to know that.' I'm afraid to look under the bed."

"When someone cracks a gay joke, how do you respond?"

"I'm opposite you on that," he says. "To me, it's funny. I'll tell an Italian joke. It doesn't matter. Bring 'em on. One scene I did read in your book: you were at a restaurant, and the waitress asked, 'Is he flaming?' There *are* flamers, you know? I probably would've said the same thing."

I compare the label "flamer" to Paul's stated hope for the project: "For the public, to open eyes, to show them who they put down, to build more cognizance of what my brother deals with—the battle." Later, while transcribing the tape, I ponder the ethics of my own complicit silence.

"That concludes the questions I have for you," I report. "Do you have any for me?"

Paul clears his throat. "You've talked with three of my siblings. I'm not asking you to tell me what they said, but what do you think needs to take place in order to support Matt and Elisabeth better and then eventually be able to talk to my kids?"

I study his face, trying to ascertain his readiness for my response. "At my dissertation defense, many of our friends talked about how the project increased their self-acceptance and facilitated their coming out. But for some, including Matt, the process stalled after the initial disclosure. Your brother has been away for seven years. He knew that the family loved him but felt afraid that if he scratched the surface, he would find out he wasn't really accepted."

Paul leans forward. "He's accepted. He's loved. Why dig any deeper?" Then, answering his own question, "I guess to make sure I'm there to support him because he does have a tremendous fight. But I don't dig into my sisters' marriages, so what needs to be scratched?"

"Of everybody here," I say, holding his gaze, "you were the one Matt felt most anxious about. He knows that you love him, but he also sees you as a guy's guy who deep down may be disgusted by—"

"I don't need to know the details of his sex life!" My pulse quickens as Paul continues, "I don't perceive it as dirty. I just don't need to know."

We sit in silence a moment as I contemplate how best to address the ways Paul reduces Matt's identity to his sexuality. "His fear of your disgust provokes Matt to censor himself. He knows that you're not going to talk about your sex lives. You're the *last* person with whom he would want to talk about that. But love . . . relationships."

"I suppose that's not a hurdle," he says. Then, perhaps reconsidering, "My brain doesn't work like that. So when he tells me, 'I love Doug or Kirk,' or whoever he's with, it's tough to understand." I listen in disbelief to Paul's search for the name of Matt's partner, the engine generating the names of my husband and of the man from whom Matt separated nearly two years ago. Paul then says, "If I keep it guy/guy, it's like, 'What the hell are you talking about?' I have to tell myself, 'Okay, he means me and Faye.' To get my emotion into it, I have to say, 'Did she . . . he support you? How did she . . . he feel?'"

"You have to translate," I paraphrase.

"Exactly. So my question to you was: what would everybody need to do? For me, it's probably asking him, 'How's it going with . . . uh . . .' Who *is* Matt with? I don't even know."

"Josh," I tell him, remembering the parallel moment in my interview with Ashley.

He admits, "I do know my brother's and my sisters' spouses, so to be fair, I need to treat Matt and his partner the same."

"Do you want to say anything about the process of being interviewed?"

Blood rushes to his cheeks. "I got emotional: 'What does Moretti mean to you?'"

"Well, your sisters both cried."

Returning my smile, he opens his palm, revealing a now-crumpled Kleenex. "I didn't bring this in for a cocktail napkin. You know what I mean?"

I turn off the recorder, and we keep talking. "I've enjoyed getting to know your family."

"Faye and I were sorry you didn't go out with us last night," Paul says. "That couple out there: our best friends. I told them about Matt and about your project—the first time I ever talked to any of my friends about having a gay brother."

My mouth falls open. "I had no idea, Paul. I completely misread. Going to a pub seemed like a way to avoid conversation."

"After you and Matt decided not to go," he explains, "we asked them to come over today. We really wanted them to meet you both. That's why they're here."

"Well, thanks for your persistence on that."

Matt and I return to Ashley's for the last time. As we load the car, everyone looks tired but not quite ready to part. Placing the last bag inside, Matt says, "Ash, an amazing time." He pulls her to him, and they hold on for several seconds.

"Come anytime," she says over Matt's shoulder, reaching out to grasp my hand.

"You Forget What You've Left"

Matt and I debrief for the six hours between Ashley's door and Matt's. Aboard our flight, Matt takes the aisle seat, I the middle. We glance at the young professional occupying the window seat. I wonder what she'll think of our conversation but decide not to censor. Matt asks, "What's your overall impression of my family?"

"Resilient. I felt such respect for the lives they lead and experienced a unique connection to each of them: to Elisabeth's empathy, to Paul's honesty, to Ashley's vulnerability."

"So," he says, "did you find what you were looking for?"

"I think I *figured out* what I was looking for: an understanding of— and potentially, a transformation in—family dynamics. Coming out tends to be narrated as an individual journey, but that journey is situated in larger contexts, including the family of origin. I see roots of the way your family has communicated—and not—about sexual orientation in your history as an alcoholic family. Ashley recalled a fateful ride home from school. Whatever your mother's intentions, Ashley deduced: 'Don't trust your perceptions, and above all, don't talk about them.' Ashley suspected your orientation for years but never asked directly. The question must have felt threatening; picture her in the car with you, torturing herself: 'God forbid if he's not!'"

Matt points out, "Ashley's childhood coincided with the highest levels of clan chaos."

"A message she heard over the years has been: 'Ignore it. Forgive and forget.' That must feel very dismissive. Paul learned related but distinct lessons: 'Take the easy way around. Don't make a lot of noise. Tread lightly.' No wonder your and his communication halted at: 'Hey Paul, I'm gay.' 'Okay, great.' Elisabeth, like Ashley, came to fear others' reactions. She learned to wait for others to open doors; you followed her lead. For you, it began quite literally: 'Go back to your room and close the door!' Today, the adult children frame experiences differently. You, Paul, and Elisabeth narrate through comedy: 'now, of course, it's hilarious,' and resignation: 'it is what it is.' Ashley's darker themes of neglect and abandonment are equally legitimate. Her constructions allow her to face life's brutal facts but may close off opportunities to reframe experiences in more empowering ways."[13]

Matt responds, "Early on, I told you that 'many roads lead back to alcohol.' I've been thinking that this weekend felt like an intervention. You witnessed and disrupted old patterns. You asked questions we skirt. You sparked conversations we've never had. You opened yourself in ways we avoid." He pauses. "You don't get paid nearly enough!" We laugh.

"I'm seeing new merits of friendship as method,"[14] I say, "and its dual role of friend/researcher. Alcoholic families tend to be closed systems. To trust an outsider, your siblings needed to see and experience our authentic connection and to be approached with an ethic of friendship: transparency, validation, support. My researcher role allowed us to accelerate relationship building. It gave me license to ask 'nosy' questions, probe for details, offer reflections." I then turn over his last statement.

"You know, it probably wouldn't have worked had I been a paid counselor. The Morettis have loving sibling relationships. I can hear Paul asking, 'What needs fixing?' With specialized knowledge and experience, a therapist comes to help, potentially putting the family in a one-down position. *Seeking* knowledge and experience, an ethnographer says, 'Please help me understand the complexities of this system.' Hopefully, in making their contributions, participants reap therapeutic rewards, such as self-awareness, mutual understanding, and improved relationships."

Matt nods. "I certainly gained insight into my siblings and myself. I learned that, from their perspective, *I* was the one staying away, not communicating about my partner, my life. My silence was conveying, 'Don't ask me.'"

"In our session today, Paul asked what he could do to open lines of communication. The whole weekend, I sensed avoidance: his hurried pace Friday morning, the 'mix-up' over weekends, his snowmobile trip, the rigid pub plans, his inviting friends over today. But during the interview, Paul explained that, last night, he 'came out' to friends for the first time. Paul told them the purpose of our visit; they talked about it all the way to the bar. Your brother intended to introduce you—his brother, a gay man participating in a research project—to his best friends. That's why they were there today."

Matt's shakes his head. "I had no idea. Gosh, I miss them all so much. You had this whole other life, and you forget what you've left." We talk on, barely noticing the beverage and snack services and our eventual descent into Orlando.

As Matt and I board the tram to the terminal, the woman who had been seated in our row asks, "Okay, what's the name of this book, and where will I be able to buy it?"

I walk him to the door of his darkened house. Hugging me tightly, Matt says in my ear, "This was one of the best things that ever happened to me and my family."

Three days later, Matt calls to say that he spoke to his parents about the trip. Matt explained the project, telling them that I interviewed

Elisabeth, Paul, and Ashley about the family and about his being gay. This was the first conversation of this nature between Matt and his father.

Home Again?

I had hoped to interview the Moretti parents, but Paul, Elisabeth, and Ashley would not consent to sharing this piece with them. I followed the siblings' wishes but have questioned many times: did Mr. and Mrs. Moretti, whose identities I masked but who appear as characters nonetheless, have a right to see the work? Who should decide?

Mrs. Moretti's health declined from stroke and Alzheimer's. She passed away in 2009. According to Matt, his father, born in 1926, would be mentally incapable of reading and responding to this account.

The years since the *Going Home* fieldwork also have been difficult for two other members of the Moretti family. Seeking a life free from alcohol's grasp, each has attended AA. Knowing this, I reflect back on the actual and symbolic presence of alcohol during our visit to Tremaine: wine upon Matt's and my arrival at Ashley's, beer or wine with every lunch and dinner, the sweating Bloody Mary Paul brought to the interview, the Merlot *I suggested* to ease Elisabeth and me into our session. I am conscious today, in a way I wasn't then, that Matt and I drank throughout our time in Tremaine.

I cannot say whether Paul, Elisabeth, or Ashley benefited from participating in this project. Perhaps their initial reactions to the draft reflected their wish to protect not only long-buried family secrets but contemporary struggles as well. I worry that the project stripped them of "the self-protective function of denial"[15] and may have caused emotional harm.

When I began this project, I considered Matt's seven-year absence from Tremaine a family problem. My view today is more complex. I now see Matt as a kind of "adaptive distancer,"[16] someone who struggles to maintain a life organized not around alcohol but around "activities and relationships that allow breathing room for reparative work."

Matt and Josh, together since 2002, still live in central Florida. At their home, the couple has hosted Elisabeth and Ruth; Ashley and her daughters; Paul, Faye, and their kids; and several other relatives. Paul and Faye's son has read my prior work featuring Matt and has written a class paper about having a gay uncle. Matt and Josh both have become active participants in caretaking for Mr. Moretti. According to Matt, Josh has earned full son-in-law, brother-in-law, and uncle status. Despite the couple's otherwise complete integration into the Moretti clan, until 2014, Matt returned to his hometown only once, for a family wedding complete with alcohol-induced drama. In June 2014, Josh will visit the Tremaine area with Matt for the first time.

Notes

1   An earlier version of "Don't Ask, Don't Tell" was published in the *Journal of Contemporary Ethnography* (Tillmann 2009; used with permission, Sage Publications). A webpage for this chapter may be found at: http://www.insolidaritybook.com/don-t-ask.html.
2   See Ellis (2007, 14).
3   See Tillmann-Healy (2001, 2003).
4   Interested readers should consult the large (and often contradictory) literature on growing up in an alcoholic family. Classic texts (e.g., Black 1979) constructed a profile of children of alcoholics (COAs) and adult children of alcoholics (ACOAs). However, several studies (e.g., Alford 1998; Barnard and Spoentgen 1986; Bradley and Schneider 1990; Churchill, Broida, and Nicholson 1990; Hall 2007; Havey, Boswell, and Romans, 1995; Seefeldt and Lyon 1992; Shemwell, Dickey, and Wittig 1995; Werner and Broida 1991) found no statistically significant relationship between A/COA status and the characteristics and roles said to be typical of A/COAs. Much research affirms the heterogeneity of A/COAs and of alcoholic families (e.g., Baker and Stephenson 1995; Calder and Kostyniuk 1989; Kearns-Bodkin and Leonard 2008; Rotunda, Scherer, and Imm 1995; Seefeldt and Lyon 1992; Steinglass 1987) and reveals that children who grow up in alcoholic families develop similar struggles and resiliencies as children who endure other kinds of traumatic experience (Hall, Bolen, and Webster 1994; Hall and Webster 2007).
      One methodological shortcoming is that most research has been conducted either on clinical populations (e.g., Veronie and Fruehstorfer 2001), which likely over-represent psychopathology, or on undergraduate students (e.g., Beesley and Stoltenberg 2002; Hall and Webster 2002; Kelley, Nair, Rawlings, Cash, Steer, and Fals-Stewart 2005; Scharff, Broida, Conway, and Yue 2004), relatively homogenous in age, education, and social class. For exceptions, see Mathew, Wilson, Blazer, and George (1993), who compared 408 participants in a community-based study who reported problem drinking in their mother, father, or both to 1,477 age- and sex-matched subjects who did not report having an alcoholic parent; Watt (2002), who analyzed data from a national sample of over 10,000 adults; Casswell, You, and Huckle (2011), who randomly surveyed 3,068 New Zealand residents; and Berends, Ferris, and Laslett (2012), who conducted a large-

scale (n=2649) survey of randomly selected adults in Australia. Berends et al. (2012) found that over 27 percent of respondents had been negatively impacted in the past 12 months by the drinking of a partner, ex-partner, child, parent, sibling, and/or other relative. Casswell et al. (2011, 1093) correlated exposure to heavy drinking with "reduced personal wellbeing and poorer health status." ACOAs in Mathew et al.'s study (1993, 798) "had more lifetime psychiatric diagnoses than the matched comparison subjects." Among Watt's (2002, 260–261) participants, male ACOAs had lower levels of self-esteem and educational attainment, and female ACOAs had more substance-abuse problems than did non-ACOAs. Mathew et al. (1993) did not find a significant relationship between ACOA status and likelihood to divorce, while Watt's (2002, 260) study concluded that both male and female ACOAs "are less likely to marry, more likely to be unhappy in their marriages, and more likely to divorce."

5 This reflects a pattern identified by Gravitz and Bowden (1985, 29), who have worked with over 1,500 ACOAs. According to their research, children in alcoholic family systems frequently "are told not to believe what their own senses tell them." The findings of Berlin, Davis, and Orenstein (1988, 578) confirm that "in a home where a full-scale battle may rage one night and everyone is expected to act as if nothing happened the following morning, a denial process develops which prevents children from having their perceptions validated by others."

6 *Road House* is a 1989 action film featuring epic brawls.

7 Research suggests that older children frequently parent younger siblings in alcoholic family systems (see, e.g., Kelley, French, Bountress, Keefe, Schroeder, Steer, Fals-Stewart, and Gumienny 2007; Seixas and Youcha 1985).

8 See Sedgwick's (1990) *Epistemology of the Closet.*

9 See Gamson's (2000) "Sexualities, Queer Theory, and Qualitative Research."

10 For the five years following this trip to Tremaine, Kirk vacillated between self-imposed sobriety and heavy drinking. He joined AA in 2008.

11 At a workshop session on June 9, 2009, Matt told me that, after reading the draft, Elisabeth apologized for this remark, admitting that it revealed her own stereotypic assumptions.

12 In her clinical work, Black (1979, 24) encountered numerous children from alcoholic families who take on the role of "placater," the child needing to "smooth over conflicts."

13 See Kiesinger (2002).

14 See the Appendix and Tillmann-Healy (1998, 2001, 2003).

15 See Burk and Sher (1988, 293).

16 See Berlin et al. (1988, 579).

References

Alford, Karola M. "Family Roles, Alcoholism, and Family Dysfunction." *Journal of Mental Health Counseling* 20, no. 3 (1998): 250–260.

Baker, Diane E., and Laura A. Stephenson. "Personality Characteristics of Adult Children of Alcoholics." *Journal of Clinical Psychology* 51, no. 5 (1995): 694–702.

Barnard, Charles P., and Patricia A. Spoentgen. "Children of Alcoholics: Characteristics and Treatment." *Alcoholism Treatment Quarterly* 3, no. 4 (1986): 47–65.

Beesley, Denise, and Cal D. Stoltenberg. "Control, Attachment Style, and Relationship Satisfaction among Adult Children of Alcoholics." *Journal of Mental Health Counseling* 24, no. 4 (2002): 281–298.

Berends, Lynda, Jason Ferris, and Anne-Marie Laslett. "A Problematic Drinker in the Family: Variations in the Level of Negative Impact Experienced by Sex, Relationship and Living Status." *Addiction Research and Theory* 20, no. 4 (2012): 300–306.

Berlin, Richard, Ruth B. Davis, and Alan Orenstein. "Adaptive and Reactive Distancing among Adolescents from Alcoholic Families." *Adolescence* 23, no. 91 (1988): 577–584.

Black, Claudia. "Children of Alcoholics." *Alcohol Health and Research World* (fall 1979): 23–27.

Bradley, L.G., and H.G. Schneider. "Interpersonal Trust, Self-Disclosure and Control in Adult Children of Alcoholics." *Psychological Reports* 67 (1990): 731–737.

Burk, Jeffrey P., and Kenneth J. Sher. "The 'Forgotten Children' Revisited: Neglected Areas of COA Research." *Clinical Psychology Review* 8 (1988): 285–302.

Calder, Peter, and Alan Kostyniuk. "Personality Profiles of Children of Alcoholics." *Professional Psychology: Research and Practice* 20, no. 6 (1989): 417–418.

Casswell, Sally, Ru Quan You, and Taisia Huckle. "Alcohol's Harm to Others: Reduced Wellbeing and Health Status for Those with Heavy Drinkers in Their Lives." *Addiction* 106 (2011): 1087–1094.

Churchill, Janet C., John P. Broida, and Nancy L. Nicholson. "Locus of Control and Self-Esteem of Adult Children of Alcoholics." *Journal of Studies on Alcohol* 51, no. 4 (1990): 373–376.

Ellis, Carolyn. "Telling Secrets, Revealing Lives: Relational Ethics in Research with Intimate Others." *Qualitative Inquiry* 13, no. 1 (2007): 3–29.

Gamson, Joshua. "Sexualities, Queer Theory, and Qualitative Research." In *Handbook of Qualitative Research* (2nd ed.), edited by Norman K. Denzin and Yvonna S. Lincoln, 347–365. Thousand Oaks, CA: Sage, 2000.

Gravitz, Herbert L., and Julie D. Bowden. *Recovery: A Guide for Adult Children of Alcoholics.* New York: Simon & Schuster, 1985.

Hall, Camille J. "An Exploratory Study of Differences in Self-Esteem, Kinship Social Support, and Coping Responses among African American ACOAs and Non-ACOAs." *Journal of American College Health* 56, no. 1 (2007): 49–54.

Hall, Cathy W., Larry M. Bolen, and Raymond E. Webster. "Adjustment Issues with Adult Children of Alcoholics." *Journal of Clinical Psychology* 50, no. 5 (1994): 786–792.

Hall, Cathy W., and Raymond E. Webster. "Traumatic Symptomatology Characteristics of Adult Children of Alcoholics." *Journal of Drug Education* 32, no. 3 (2002): 195–211.

——. "Multiple Stressors and Adjustment among Adult Children of Alcoholics." *Addiction Research and Theory* 15, no. 4 (2007): 425–434.

Havey, J. Michael, Donald L. Boswell, and John S.C. Romans. "The Relationship of Self-Perception and Stress in Adult Children of Alcoholics and Their Peers." *Journal of Drug Education* 25, no. 1 (1995): 23–29.

Kearns-Bodkin, Jill N., and Kenneth E. Leonard. "Relationship Functioning among Adult Children of Alcoholics." *Journal of Studies on Alcohol and Drugs* 69 (2008): 941–950.

Kelley, Michelle L., Alexis French, Kaitlin Bountress, Heather A. Keefe, Valarie Schroeder, Kate Steer, William Fals-Stewart, and Leslie Gumienny. "Parentification and Family Responsibility in the Family of Origin of Adult Children of Alcoholics." *Addictive Behaviors* 32 (2007): 675–685.

Kelley, Michelle L., Veena Nair, Tanaya Rawlings, Thomas F. Cash, Kate Steer, and William Fals-Stewart. "Retrospective Reports of Parenting Received in Their Families of Origin: Relationships to Adult Attachment in Adult Children of Alcoholics." *Addictive Behaviors* 30 (2005): 1479–1495.

Kiesinger, Christine E. "My Father's Shoes: The Therapeutic Value of Narrative Reframing." In *Ethnographically Speaking: Autoethnography, Literature, and Aesthetics*, edited by Arthur P. Bochner and Carolyn Ellis, 95–114. Walnut Creek, CA: AltaMira Press, 2002.

Mathew, Roy J., William H. Wilson, Dan G. Blazer, and Linda K. George. "Psychiatric Disorders in Adult Children of Alcoholics: Data from the Epidemiologic Catchment Area Project." *American Journal of Psychiatry* 150, no. 5 (1993): 793–800.

Rotunda, Robert J., David G. Scherer, and Pamela S. Imm. "Family Systems and Alcohol Misuse: Research on the Effects of Alcoholism on Family Functioning and Effective Family Interventions." *Professional Psychology: Research and Practice* 26, no. 1 (1995): 95–104.

Scharff, Judith L., John P. Broida, Kim Conway, and Alicia Yue. "The Interaction of Parental Alcoholism, Adaptation Role, and Familial Dysfunction." *Addictive Behaviors* 29 (2004): 575–581.

Sedgwick, Eve Kosofsky. *Epistemology of the Closet*. Berkeley, CA: University of California Press, 1990.

Seefeldt, Richard W., and Mark A. Lyon. "Personality Characteristics of Adult Children of Alcoholics." *Journal of Counseling and Development* 70 (1992): 588–593.

Seixas, Judith S., and Geraldine Youcha. *Children of Alcoholism: A Survivor's Manual*. New York: Crown Publishers, Inc., 1985.

Shemwell, G. Henry, Katherine Dooley Dickey, and Timothy A. Wittig. "Adult Children of Alcoholics: An Examination of the Category." *Journal of Alcohol and Drug Education* 40, no. 3 (1995): 109–118.

Steinglass, Peter. *The Alcoholic Family*. New York: Basic Books, 1987.

Tillmann, Lisa M. "Don't Ask/Don't Tell: Coming Out in an Alcoholic Family." *Journal of Contemporary Ethnography* 38, no. 6 (2009): 677–712.

Tillmann-Healy, Lisa M. *Life Projects: A Narrative Ethnography of Gay-Straight Friendship*. Ph.D. diss., University of South Florida, 1998.

——— . *Between Gay and Straight: Understanding Friendship across Sexual Orientation.* Walnut Creek, CA: AltaMira Press, 2001.

——— . "Friendship as Method." *Qualitative Inquiry* 9 (2003): 729–749.

Veronie, Linda, and David B. Fruehstorfer. "Gender, Birth Order and Family Role Identification among Adult Children of Alcoholics." *Current Psychology* 20, no. 1 (2001): 53–67.

Watt, Toni Terling. "Marital and Cohabiting Relationships of Adult Children of Alcoholics: Evidence from the National Survey of Families and Households." *Journal of Family Issues* 23, no. 2 (2002): 246–265.

Werner, Laura J., and John P. Broida. "Adult Self-Esteem and Locus of Control as a Function of Familial Alcoholism and Dysfunction." *Journal of Studies on Alcohol* 52, no. 3 (1991): 249–252.

2

FATHER'S BLESSING

ETHNOGRAPHIC DRAMA, POETRY, AND PROSE[1]

Cast:
  Ray Wise: the son
  Steven Wise: the father
  Lisa Tillmann: the friend/researcher

Staging: three chairs surround a table with drawer facing center stage chair; black boxes sit behind chairs at stage right and left.

Props: tape recorder, note pad, pen, scrapbook, yearbook, necktie.

RAY sits at table in stage right chair. STEVEN sits on black box, stage left. LISA stands stage right of RAY.

LISA: [*to audience*] I met Ray Wise in 1995. The softball team on which he played, a largely gay male group in a mainly gay male league, became the focus of my Ph.D. dissertation[2] and first book, *Between Gay and Straight*,[3] a narrative ethnography[4] of communication and relationships across sexual orientation. In 2003, I began a follow-up project called *Going Home*. This involved collaborating with four gay men (including Ray); conducting life history interviews;

and traveling to the men's hometowns and/or other key sites to conduct fieldwork, shoot photographs and video, and interview family members.

This three-character ethnographic play evokes the process of my work with Ray and his father Steven. I composed this from interview transcripts (four sessions with Ray, two with Steven), field notes from a four-day visit to Buck Hill, California, in May 2004, and follow-up conversations, correspondence, and workshop sessions (three with Ray, one with Steven and Ray).

LISA crosses to middle chair, sits, and takes tape recorder, note pad, and pen from drawer.

LISA: [*to RAY*] Do you want your father to be part of this project?
RAY: My real father? Um . . . sure.
LISA: Would he agree to participate?
RAY: Possibly. Our relationship has been complicated, but that has little to do with my being gay.
LISA: He lives in California?
RAY: Outside Sacramento, Buck Hill.
LISA: When was your last visit?
RAY: Never been there.
LISA: Really? Has he lived in Buck Hill long?
RAY: Since maybe . . . '93.
LISA: Wow. When did you last see him?
RAY: Four years ago, at my brother's wedding.
LISA: Describe your father.
RAY: Type-A American male: workaholic, competitive. I remember him wanting to compare test scores, track times.
LISA: Characterize your relationship.
RAY: Tense, distant. Maybe a card around my birthday. Even that has been hit or miss. There's always some excuse: "I didn't have your new address." Then again, my dad has a lot of kids to keep track of: four sons from his marriage to my mom; two sons, a daughter, and a stepdaughter from his second marriage; and two stepsons from his third.

LISA: Tell me about his family of origin.

RAY: My father descends from one of the Mormon Church's founding families. Solomon Wise served as a bodyguard to Joseph Smith.

Dad's family endured illnesses and early deaths. Two of his siblings developed a rare disease. His oldest sister spent years on dialysis before dying. The oldest brother, who himself had polio as a child, donated a kidney to the youngest brother. In high school, my dad contracted encephalitis. His heart stopped; he slipped into a coma and almost died. I know their mother died young . . . cancer or something.

LISA: [*to audience*] May 15, 2004: our final interview before the journey to Buck Hill.

[*to RAY*] How are you feeling?

RAY: Nervous. This won't be just hanging out. You'll ask questions, and my dad and I will have to address issues we normally wouldn't. I know my dad loves me, and I love my dad, but we just never talk. It's almost like visiting a stranger.

LISA: When did you last have a deep conversation?

RAY: Um . . . well . . . we chatted when I told him our travel plans. Looking back, I don't know if we've *ever* had deep conversation. I think my dad and I both want our relationship to be closer, but we need to move from wanting to making it happen.

LISA: [*to audience*] My mind returns to Ray's description of their relationship as "tense, distant." How might this project alleviate tension and draw them closer? How might it open old wounds and pull father and son further apart? The work feels thick with both opportunity and risk. As an author, I know that a text can be produced regardless of what transpires, and conflict drives narrative. But as a narrative ethnographer, I am committed to collaborative, just, and non-exploitive fieldwork. As Ray's friend and ally, I vow to privilege my relationship with Ray and his with his father over any other goal. If the research, writing, or publication of this work threatens to undermine their communication or relationship, I will offer to abandon it, allowing the Wise men to decide its fate.

LISA returns recorder, note pad, and pen to drawer. She stands, crosses to stage left of table.

LISA: [*to audience*] May 19, 2004: Ray and I fly to Sacramento. He sleeps most of the flight while I look over notes and transcripts. As we descend, I take in the tree-covered mountains, patchwork quilt of farmland, and mirrored irrigation ponds reflecting the spring sky.

I met Steven Wise once before, at Ray's college graduation in 1997. Beyond a brief introduction, I'm not sure we spoke. I have a photograph from that day: Ray in cap and gown, Steven in a grey suit. Their embrace appears more obligatory than exuberant.

At the airport, Ray and I retrieve our bags, rent a Ford Focus, and make our way to the southern suburbs. Five-thirty p.m., we pull up to the family's cottage-style house.

RAY stands, crosses to stage left of Lisa.

LISA: [*to audience*] I take a deep breath. The front door opens before we knock.

STEVEN rises from stage left black box, crosses to greet RAY and LISA.

STEVEN: Welcome! [*embraces RAY*]
RAY: Dad, this is Lisa.
LISA: [*shaking STEVEN's hand*] Pleasure to see you again, sir.
STEVEN: Let me help with your bags.

RAY and STEVEN cross to table; STEVEN stands behind stage left chair, RAY behind stage right chair.

LISA: [*to audience*] The living room has a marble topped vanity, washed oak armoire with painted floral design, curved sectional sofa, and upright piano. As we tour, I note the warm décor: family photographs, prints and paintings of Jesus, and travel mementos: German beer stein, Egyptian tapestry, and Asian furniture. Shelves house computer books, several copies of the Bible and Book of Mormon, as well as tomes on leadership and motivation, including Bill O'Reilly's *Who's Looking Out for You?*

STEVEN: [*to audience*] Hundreds of books, and she singles out that one!

LISA: [*to STEVEN*] Selective, I admit, but also reflective of one genre I saw.

RAY: [*to STEVEN*] She's trying to set the scene, establish your character.

STEVEN: [*to LISA*] Why politicize? I thought the project focused on Ray's and my relationship.

LISA: [*to audience*] In January 2006, Ray, Steven, and I meet to workshop a draft of this play. We use several strategies to address material that provokes discomfort or disagreement. If an excerpt is deemed inessential to the narrative and/or harmful to others in the family, it is removed. Other material, particularly that written from field notes, is clarified and expanded based on Ray's and Steven's recollections. Each of us also takes opportunities to address you, the audience, and therefore each other, answering questions as well as offering further thoughts and feelings. Textual politics consume much of our five-hour workshop. While agreeing that relational dynamics should remain center stage, I find it important to show several character dimensions, including faith, personality, and politics, and to express how each seems to inform the way Steven and Ray interact. Ray's approach to the multiple workshops in which he participated communicates commitment to his father, to the future of their relationship, and to the goals of the project, which include promoting introspection, understanding, and dialogue as well as personal, relational, and social change. The resultant text reflects a balance, achieved mainly through consensus but also through conflict and compromise between Ray's, Steven's, and my often-overlapping but sometimes-differing interpretations of relational and project goals.

LISA crosses to center stage chair; all sit.

LISA: [*to audience*] Our host leads us to the patio. Ray and I admire the garden's apricot trees and foxtail fern. We sit beneath a grey stained arbor, the air perfumed by star jasmine. My gaze shifts between father and son: father's eyes: olive, son's: moss. Father's hair: more salt than pepper, son's: chocolate streaked with caramel. If combed straight back rather than to the side, Steven's receding hair would follow the same contours as Ray's. I note the similar shape of their ears, brow lines, and upper lips.

We talk about many subjects that first night: marriage, conflict, loss.

STEVEN: It was supposed to be a routine hysterectomy.

RAY: I thought Grandma died of cancer.

STEVEN: Cardiac arrest. Before Mom went in for surgery, my brother and I prayed over her. Later, we realized that we asked God for her *comfort*, not recovery. My mother also may have had a premonition, because she wrote letters "to be opened after my death" to each of her children.

RAY: Had I been born?

STEVEN: I hadn't even met your mother. I was fresh out of the Air Force Academy and in pilot training.

RAY: Did you see combat?

LISA: [*to audience*] I am struck that Ray doesn't know the answers to these questions.

STEVEN: A tour in Vietnam as Forward Air Controller. FACs fly ahead of attack aircraft and direct strikes against enemy targets.

RAY: Did friends of yours die?

STEVEN: Oh yes.

RAY: Did you kill anyone?

STEVEN: Many enemy soldiers died in the strikes I directed.

LISA removes scrapbook from drawer.

LISA: [*to audience*] Later that night, we sit at his kitchen table while Steven narrates from a scrapbook. Woven wood encases pages of yellowed newspaper clippings. One reads: "Baptism in Vietnam."

STEVEN: Mormon missionaries teach Christianity across the globe, even in countries at war. I used to help deliver medicine and food to orphans.

LISA: [*to audience*] The album also contains black and white photographs, some with concise yet compelling captions:

RAY: [*reading*] "Bodies." "Dead."

STEVEN: 1968, General Westmoreland ordered air strikes against operations near Khe Sanh. Vietcong soldiers forced civilians to carry ammunition and supplies, using even women and children as human shields.

LISA: [*to audience*] At our workshop session, Steven offers further detail:

STEVEN: I understood our mission. Had the enemy captured Khe Sanh, it could have altered the war's course, but when I saw bombs strike those civilians, I teared up so much I hardly could see out of the aircraft.

RAY: [*reading from scrapbook*] "C-130 Crash: 9 MEN KILLED."

STEVEN: American soldiers. Minutes after, I had to land on a debris-strewn runway. Those pools that look like water are melted aluminum from the burning aircraft. [*pointing*] And look at this: I nearly had my tail shot off! That strip of metal saved my life. [*to RAY*] Yours too, I guess.

I'm concerned about what's going on now in Iraq. The U.S. public is losing resolve, just as it did with Vietnam.

[*to LISA*] Do you come from a military family?

LISA: My grandfather served in World War II. I have career military uncles. In 1970, my father was the last man drafted from his county. He was in basic training when I was born. Our family relocated to Salinas, waiting for his unit to be called. I also fear parallels between Iraq and Vietnam—

[*to audience*] I stop myself there.

Throughout the weekend, Steven initiates spirited exchanges about international policy. Ray seldom enters our current-event crossfire. Steven proves an enthusiastic conversationalist, and I remind myself not to allow the project to become *Stevie and Me*. When I step back from these interactions, I also wonder if each of us unconsciously conspires to avoid talking about the central reason for our visit: Ray and Steven's relationship.

RAY: [*to STEVEN*] You met Mom before or after Vietnam?

STEVEN: Before, in Okinawa. I flew many combat missions while we dated—one with her father, who also was stationed in Japan.

Your mother wanted to marry immediately. I'm not sure I was ready to be a husband, but I did very much want to become a father.

LISA: [*to RAY*] You were born in Florida, Eglin Air Force base?

RAY: Right. Second of four boys.

STEVEN: Ray was a sensitive, tender child. [*fondly*] Didn't always take direction, though. "Ray, don't put your finger in that outlet!" [*mimics RAY doing just that*]

[*to RAY*] What do you remember most about childhood?

RAY: Hmm ... camping trips. I definitely recall one 20-degree adventure. The bottom of my boots melted as I warmed my feet by the fire!

STEVEN: [*laughs*] I'm honored to be a father. I loved zooming the kids around on the riding mower, raking piles of leaves and jumping in them. Every night, I would tell the kids a story, and they always liked ones about me, you know? My glory years, I guess.

[*to RAY*] What do you remember about our home life?

LISA: [*to audience*] Steven seems to be searching for what Charles Cooley might have termed his "looking glass self-as-father."

STEVEN: [*to audience*] Through Ray's eyes, yes. I want to know how I, in the final analysis, will measure up as a father to Ray, despite the trials stemming from the divorce. If all they put on my gravestone is "A Good Father," I will have lived a good life.

RAY: [*to STEVEN*] Home life ... gosh, my early memory is pretty vague.

LISA: [*to audience*] Having heard stories of Ray's childhood for many years, I wonder to what extent he feels pulled in this moment between the dialectical tensions of expression and protection, vulnerability and cruelty.[5]

STEVEN rises, crosses to stage left black box and sits. LISA returns scrapbook to drawer, takes out recorder, note pad, and pen.

RAY: I was nine when my parents divorced. I can't remember feeling sad; we hardly saw my dad anyway.

STEVEN: [*to audience*] I was serving a remote tour in Korea just prior to the divorce.

LISA: What led to the dissolution?

RAY: At the time, I had no idea.

STEVEN rises, crosses to table, and sits on stage left chair, LISA returns recorder, note pad, and pen to drawer.

STEVEN: I returned from Korea, and your mom surprised me with divorce papers.

RAY: How do you make sense of what happened?

STEVEN: A relationship is a three-legged stool: physical, social, and spiritual compatibility. Your mother, a reverent woman who deeply loves God and her children, offered a solid spiritual leg. Physically and socially, a mismatch. On our first date, we had the most ridiculous fight—about flamenco dancers!

LISA: [*to audience*] I wonder how Ray's mother will feel about this assessment. Relations in their blended families have been tenuous at times. I want my account of Steven's account to honor his truths and invite response. These renderings may provoke discomfort and will induce change in the family system. What will be the nature and direction of that change?

STEVEN rises, crosses to stage left black box and sits; LISA and RAY stand and cross to stage right of table.

LISA: [*to audience*] Thursday morning, Ray and I wander the development's tree-lined pathways and discuss the first day of our trip.

[*to RAY*] What have you learned?

RAY: Lots, actually. The cause of and details surrounding my grandmother's death. Dad's Vietnam experience. I knew *nothing* about my parents' courtship: where they met, the fight on their first date. My dad's three-legged stool philosophy, that's new to me, and I've never heard his perspective on my parents' marriage and divorce.

LISA: I've observed a conversational dynamic: you've done far more listening than talking.

RAY: [*smiles*] You've done your share of listening as well.

LISA: Perhaps, but I seem to be interacting with your dad more than you are. He hasn't seen you in four years. I thought he'd be full of questions.

RAY: I think answers come more easily to him.

LISA: What has most surprised you?

RAY: Dad was gone a lot for the military; I *never* imagined he would say his primary motivation for marriage was fatherhood.

LISA and RAY cross to table and sit, LISA on center stage chair, RAY on stage right chair; LISA removes scrapbook and yearbook from drawer.

LISA: [*to audience*] Friday morning, Ray and I sit at the kitchen table with photo albums, genealogy books, and the 1959 *El Diablo's Diary*, his dad's senior yearbook. Fourteen track ribbons are tucked inside. The entry for Steven Darien Wise, "Dare," recognizes him for academic achievement, service as class VP and President, and success in gymnastics and all-state football. Inscriptions deem Dare a "real swell egg" and praise his high moral standards.

Ray and I also find a yearly timeline his dad composed of key events. Knowing the year of Ray's birth, I comment, "1970 was big!" Ray reads the entry aloud. It lists events at Steven's church but makes no mention of Ray's arrival.

RAY: [*flatly*] So much for the primacy of fatherhood.

LISA: [*to audience*] Later that day, Ray teases his dad about the missing information. Steven immediately pencils in: "2nd child (Gay) born: Raymond Wise, 8/20/70."

STEVEN: [*to audience*] At our workshop session, I tell Ray for the first time about a journal I kept after Vietnam. I destroyed it during an argument with his mother, which I deeply regret. I used to write extensively about my children. I am certain I wrote about Ray's birth in that journal.

STEVEN rises from stage left black box, crosses to table, and sits on stage left chair; LISA returns items to drawer.

LISA: How did you meet your current wife?

STEVEN: [*smiles*] My oldest brother teaches dance lessons for our local Strauss Festival.

LISA: [*to audience*] Around their home hang photographs of Vivian Wise wearing ruffled waltz gowns in white, blue, and pink and Steven in tuxedos with coordinating ties and cummerbunds.

STEVEN: [*warmly*] Vivian inquired about joining the dancers. My brother called, saying I *had* to meet this attractive lady. Three times, he assured me that Vivian would attend the night's lesson. I'd drive down, but she wouldn't show. After the third miss, I arrived home to the sound of a ringing phone. My brother: "Steven, she's here for the late session!" Got right back in the car. The moment I saw Vivian, I *knew*: pleasant smile, great legs. I fell in love that instant— not just with the legs, mind you!

LISA: How long have you been together?

STEVEN: Since 1993.

RAY: How's your three-legged stool?

STEVEN: [*laughs*] Balanced! We're true friends; we keep each other laughing. I also enjoy her sons, the perfect boys.

[*to RAY*] Uh . . . not that you're not perfect.

STEVEN rises, walks to stage left black box, and sits; LISA takes out recorder, note pad, and pen.

RAY: Years ago, my dad began referring to Vivian's sons as "my boys." That always felt weird. Though I haven't spent much time with her, my sense of Vivian is that she's really sweet, and it wouldn't surprise me if much of the contact my brothers and I have received from my dad in the last several years has been prompted by her. With each marriage, my father seemed to wipe the slate clean: new family, new life.

LISA: I've known you since 1995 and in four significant relationships. *You* seem to wipe the slate clean: new partner, new life. Was it always like this?

RAY: To varying degrees, yes.

LISA: Tell me about your first love.

RAY: At 17, I noticed this good-looking guy in church. In retrospect, I was totally cruising Luke: 22, just back from his overseas mission.

Our youth group went on a ski trip. Each room at the lodge slept two. Luke immediately piped up, "Ray and I will take this room." Turned out to have only one bed. As we got ready for sleep, Luke undressed down to his Mormon garments. I thought, *Oh my gosh!* I don't recall seeing my *parents* wearing only their garments. Luke asked, "Ever had a back massage?" When he laid his hands on me, adrenalin flooded my body. After several minutes, Luke said, "Why don't you give me one?" I sat atop him, totally turned on.

[*leans in*] Trust me, Lisa, I'm not gonna talk about sex too in-depth.

LISA: [*playfully*] You don't scare me.

RAY: You won't be the only reader.

Luke and I got under the covers. He reached over and touched me, sexually this time. I was nervous, shaking, but I did the same thing back.

Didn't sleep the entire night. Finally at some point, I said, "Luke, we have to promise that we'll never, ever do that again. We could go to hell!" I think I even said we had to repent.

On the ride home, Luke fell asleep on my shoulder. People started to wonder about us. They all went to my church and school, so I became very secretive about Luke.

Two weeks later, I let it progress further—no turning back. This continued for nine months. Luke always gave me handmade cards with messages like: "If you were a woman, I'd marry you."

Around graduation, I shut him out. Wouldn't take his calls. He came to the ceremony anyway, sat in the front row, bought me, like, 15 presents. Later, I felt horrible for rejecting him.

Determined to prove I was straight, I entered a relationship with my friend Nancy, the first girl with whom I had sex. All my life, I'd done everything according to the Church. Didn't smoke, didn't drink. When I'd done what I thought was the worst of all—had sex with a guy—I reasoned that having sex with a girl would make it better. How? I don't know, but it made sense to me at the time. Nancy became the first person in whom I confided about being gay. I'd given her a promise ring. We were engaged; she was planning the wedding, picking the colors. Uh, poor girl! She joined the Mormon Church for me; I baptized her myself—actually dunked her head under the water!

The day after I told Nancy, I sat down with my mom: "I think I'm gay." She said, "I love you. To be honest, I've wondered since you were 16." So my mom knew before *I* did, before anything happened with Luke. At 16, I'd come home flipped out because my swim teammate put his arm around me. This overreaction prompted my mom to send me to a Mormon counselor. After a few visits, the counselor said to her, "Don't worry. There's *no way* that he's gay." It sounds strange, but at the time, *I* didn't know that I was gay. I just thought I liked being around cool guys. It wasn't sexual. I hardly knew what sexuality was; I hadn't even masturbated!

I remember Mom asking, "Were you ever molested as a boy?" I lied. Knowing the betrayals and suffering she had withstood, I wanted to shield her from further grief.

LISA: [*to audience*] I imagine Ray's mom reading these pages. What happens when the shield lifts?

RAY: When I was in primary school, a man exposed himself and touched me sexually—inappropriate, of course, but nothing like the abuse others have suffered. Several important people in my life have been violated horrifically.

LISA: [*to audience*] He asks that I not share details, but Ray talks at length about abuse, in his life and in the lives of those close to him. At the time of our interview, Ray didn't know about his father's experience.

RAY rises, walks to stage right black box, and sits; STEVEN rises from stage left black box, crosses to table, and sits at stage left chair.

STEVEN: This never has been recorded anywhere: as a child, I was abused by a person I trusted.

LISA: [*to audience*] Where do I keep these secrets I learn but do not own?

STEVEN: It was a man, an adult—obviously gay.

LISA: [*to audience*] *No, a pedophile*, I think but do not say. I also don't say, *Your son was abused by a person he trusted, a man, an adult, a person he too described as "gay."*

STEVEN rises, walks to stage left black box, and sits; RAY rises from stage right black box, crosses to table, and sits on stage right chair.

LISA: I don't understand that attribution. A pedophile is an adult with sexual predilections toward children. A pedophile–child relationship is predicated on inequality and the inability to consent. I think it dangerous to conflate that with emotional, spiritual, community, and intimate relationships between consenting adults. Why label your abuser gay rather than a pedophile?

RAY: Though these encounters scared me, I also was intrigued, curious that this man had sexual interest in another male. Maybe I sensed that was my interest as well.

LISA: Sensed, but didn't act on for many years.

RAY: Right. Around the time I came out to my mom, her second husband transferred to Germany. I decided to move with them, in part to free myself from my fiancée.

RAY rises, crosses to stage right black box, and sits; STEVEN rises from stage left black box, crosses to table, and sits in stage left chair.

STEVEN: His mother took the boys to Germany without consulting me. [*painfully*] For years, I felt cut off from my kids. [*brightens*] I did make one trip, and I got to see Ray working for the . . . what was it? He was a salesman at . . . um . . .

LISA: The Polo Store?

STEVEN: That's it. In fact, I got a tie—still one of my favorites. [*goes backstage to retrieve; returns*] Ray recommended it to me.

STEVEN rises, crosses to stage left black box, and sits; RAY rises from stage right black box, crosses to table, and sits on stage right chair.

RAY: I had an easier time coming out in Germany than I likely would have had in the States. Europeans aren't as hung up on Rambo masculinity.

I met Markus at a club in Munich. At the time, I knew enough German to ask where the bathroom was. Markus spoke no English. His female companion had to translate the whole night. Soon after, we went on a dinner date—sans translator. My German vocabulary was still, like, 15 words. I would try speaking German but had to throw in English words to complete a sentence. I left with the worst headache, but somehow Markus thought all this was cute. When we moved in together, I asked all his associates to speak only German in my presence. Three months later, I was nearly fluent.

Traveling in Hungary, I contracted a parasite. Twenty-five pounds poured off. I thought I was dying of AIDS. Missionaries came, anointed my head with oil, and packed my clothes. The Church placed me with a Mormon couple, keeping me cut off from Markus for weeks. I eventually concocted a story and returned to Markus.

Throughout our relationship, I continued going to services, attending counseling with the bishop, and planning my mission. All this time, Markus believed our relationship would end. He'd begun detaching himself, moving on, dating, and having sex, which wracked my nerves when I found out. I told Markus I'd left the Church and bailed on my mission—just two weeks before I was to leave. He took me back, but things were never the same.

I had one other significant relationship in Germany. Christian had agoraphobia stemming from an abusive father, who used to lock him in a closet. Christian would get intensely close, then disappear into meaningless encounters with other men. Eventually I decided to move back to the States. Christian and I fought the night before my departure. We didn't even say goodbye.

Settled in Florida, I entered a relationship with a male couple, one of the more unconventional things I've ever done. Lasted nine months. All these years later, they're still together, and we're still friends.

Started dating Andrew. It was during our relationship that I came out to my dad. Andrew's mom died of cancer, and he got me thinking that none of us has unlimited time. I made the call and simply said, "Dad, I'm gay." He mentioned a yellow bonnet and green bellbottom pants I used to wear. Funny how people make sense of things.

RAY rises, crosses to stage right black box, and sits; STEVEN rises from stage left black box, crosses to table, and sits on stage left chair.

STEVEN: Didn't surprise me. As a child, Ray ran around in a little yellow doll hat.
RAY: [*to audience*] A decade after disclosure, he *still* recalls that damn hat!
STEVEN: Ray always seemed more drawn to the arts than sports. When I visited the boys in Colorado, his mother let me sleep downstairs, where Ray had his room. He had a young man over. They would go into the bedroom, close the door, and stay a long time.
RAY: [*to audience*] *Homework*, I promise you.
STEVEN: I did feel sad, knowing this would challenge him. One of Ray's brothers totally rejects the fact that he's gay.
RAY: [*to audience*] Relationships with all my brothers *improved* after I came out.
STEVEN: His mom's been a wonderful spirit. We both love Ray just as we do the other boys. Personally, I don't view gay-ism as wrong unless it's an ill-conceived choice.
LISA: [*to audience*] I write "gay-ism" and "ill-conceived choice" in my interview notes.
RAY: [*to audience*] "Ill-conceived choice"?
STEVEN: [*to audience*] At our workshop session, I clarify: when it's not physiological.
LISA: [*to audience*] Steven's explanation moves me to reflect on how seldom each of us has the opportunity to revisit, reconsider, and rearticulate our constructions of ourselves, each other, and the social world. The transcript of my interview with Steven allowed Ray to confront "gay-ism" and "ill-conceived choice" (terms he never had heard his father use). An early draft of the play provided space for Ray to question these constructions. The workshop opened a space

for clarification, though perhaps not resolution. Steven's explanation still affirms the hegemonic biology–choice binary, biology associated with "natural" and "immutable" (and therefore more acceptable), choice associated with "arbitrary" and "contingent" (and therefore less acceptable).

STEVEN: [*to LISA*] God created everything about us and about the world. Therefore, God consciously created the circumstances that produced gay-ism, like any other disease.

RAY/LISA: [*together, to audience*] "Disease."

STEVEN: Or malady, deformity, birth defect.

LISA: [*to audience*] Those words also sting, but I say nothing.

RAY: [*to audience*] I read his descriptions and thought: *where do I begin?*

LISA: [*to audience*] During our interview, Steven immediately reconsidered his language.

STEVEN: Maybe those are the wrong words. Differences, I guess. Last month, I drove home from San Francisco listening to a talk show. Parents spoke of rejecting their gay children. I pulled over and called the station, saying, "I've got a gay son. I totally accept him, and he's welcome in our home."

LISA: Has having a gay son enhanced your life?

STEVEN: It's encouraged me to reach out, to make sure he knew that I didn't reject him. I treat his partner as a real partner. I hope that has helped validate Ray.

LISA: What do you think others could learn from your family's experience?

STEVEN: How does that saying go? "Just get over it." Most of us, because of our Christian training, think homosexuality is bad. I think fundamentally it's . . . I'm not going to call it "normal," but what *is* normal? *I'm* not normal. Neither is an autistic person or someone who has his legs blown off in war. I think those who have extra burdens to carry become stronger. My role is to love and accept Ray, and I'm hoping God will do the same for me.

STEVEN rises, crosses to stage left black box, and sits; RAY rises from stage right black box, crosses to table, and sits on stage right chair.

RAY: Coming out to my dad was the lasting positive result of my relationship with Andrew, which turned into another disaster. Even after Markus and Christian, I automatically trusted. Andrew put an end to that. People said, "He cheats on you." I didn't believe it, even though it was *right there*. After we broke up, I became inherently suspicious. Philip was the first target of my mistrust. Determined not to be a victim again, I became the perpetrator of infidelity. I know I've skirted this issue with you before.

LISA: And then . . . Brian, whom we both met in 1996.

RAY: [*sighs*] So honest, committed, giving. What I put him through! I graduated from college and took my first accounting job on the other coast of Florida. We moved but hated living there. I quit my job, took another. We moved again. I quit, took another job. Making good money but so miserable! You used to say, "It's more important to be fulfilled than wealthy." I've always wanted to write. Having to bartend again is a compromise, but it pays the bills and gives me space for artistic pursuits. Brian was there through it all.

LISA: What did you learn from that relationship?

RAY: [*long pause*] I'm not sure this should be in the text.

LISA: That will be your call. Brian will read this material, as will your current partners.

RAY: I'll always have strong feelings for Brian. During our five years together, he was my *life* partner. I wasn't sure I'd find that again, but I definitely feel that way about Morgan now. From the start of our relationship in 2002, we created a safe space in which to express our deepest feelings.

LISA: [*smiles*] We've covered a lot of ground, my friend. What hopes do you have for our work?

RAY: Mmm . . . to rekindle the relationship with my dad. If it turns out to be a good experience, my brothers might better understand him as well. Maybe my dad, my siblings, and I will talk more often and more deeply.

In a larger sense, the project could support readers in their coming out journeys; I certainly would like to see more of us avoid depression and suicide. The work also might help our families understand our struggles.

LISA: [*to audience*] To accomplish Ray's goals, I offer "Father's Blessing" as a counter-narrative, as discourse in opposition to the homophobia and heterosexism that foster depression and suicide as well as prejudice, discrimination, and violence targeted at persons whose identities and relationships challenge dominant ideas and practices. I imagine this work finding a home on syllabi for courses centered on identity, dialogue, relationships, gender and sexualities, and/or qualitative methodologies. I hope that others will stage this work, giving audience members the opportunity to collaborate in making sense of and meaning from the ways that the actors and director make sense of and make meaning from the ways that Ray, Steven, and I make sense of and make meaning from our experiences, a full hermeneutic—and counter-hegemonic—circle!

[*to RAY*] Do you have any fears or concerns about the project?
RAY: I want to represent and serve my community well. More personally, I have decisions to make about what will go in the text. We've talked about secrets, both mine and my family's.

RAY rises, crosses to stage right black box, and sits; STEVEN rises from stage left black box, crosses to table, and sits on stage left chair.

LISA: Any fears or concerns?
STEVEN: People have misrepresented me. Frankly, when I first met you, I sized you up, trying to figure out if you're one of those wacko activists.
LISA: I'll say this: I *am* surprised, given the solidity of your faith, that you have this view of Ray and of same-sex orientation.
STEVEN: Let me explain. If you were to ask our leaders if the Church supported homosexual sex, they would say, "No." I understand that. I also understand that God has given strict instructions about lying, stealing, cheating, murdering, and adultery.

All stand.

LISA: [*to audience*] Hearing "homosexuality" alongside "murdering," I think of two episodes from the day before. Thursday afternoon,

Steven's stepson appeared, dressed for a school function. When his stepson pointed out the white socks between his black pants and shoes, Steven said:

STEVEN: In my day, that meant you were a fairy.

LISA: I waited for Ray to respond. When he didn't, I said to the stepson but *for* Steven, "Depending on your goal, that might be a useful signifier."

STEVEN: [*to audience*] That's how we spoke in those days. I relayed this story to let them know I was *not* hung up, not afraid to be open about the truth—all of it.

LISA: [*to audience*] Thursday evening, Steven talked about seeing a film with Ray's mother.

STEVEN: In the first ten minutes, we saw murder, rape, homosexuality.

LISA: [*to audience*] Neither Ray nor I questioned Steven's inclusion of homosexuality on this list. Later, I asked [*to RAY*], Why do you think we let that pass?

RAY: Just being here is a big step. One at a time, I guess.

STEVEN: [*to audience*] In 1971, all those activities were considered vices. I didn't mean to equate homosexuality with murder.

All sit, STEVEN and LISA at table, RAY on stage right black box.

STEVEN: Are you a Christian?

LISA: [*to audience*] Not sure I want to go down this path, I say, [*to STEVEN*] I was raised Catholic. I believe that we are here for a purpose, that we should live in service to others, and that there is something beyond this world.

STEVEN: What is the gospel of Jesus Christ?

LISA: Jesus is love.

STEVEN: Good. Now, what was the first word Jesus spoke after starting his ministry?

LISA: [*to audience*] Oh my, Christian *Jeopardy*!

[*to STEVEN*] *That* I definitely do not know.

STEVEN: "Repent."

LISA: [*to audience*] My mind flashes back to Ray's description of the initial encounter with his first love, Luke:

RAY: [*to audience, quoting himself*] I think I even said we had to repent.

STEVEN: There isn't anything we can do on this earth for which we can't repent and be forgiven. I read the Bible. I've studied the passages that have to do with gay-ism. They don't, of course, use that term. The Scriptures say, "We don't want you to have sex in the wrong way, from the rear end."

RAY: [*to audience*] "From the rear end"? I must have missed that verse.

STEVEN: [*to RAY*] Lighten up! I was paraphrasing.

[*to LISA*] But it's not something that forever marks a person. God understands the gay problem.

RAY: [*to audience*] "Problem."

STEVEN: I'm sure He's made provisions so that people will figure out, through genetic engineering, how to fix and eliminate the problem.

LISA: Have you considered that it may not be a problem?

STEVEN: It's certainly a problem in terms of how society responds. I consider many things far worse than being gay. Why am I not ostracized for my failings? [*wryly*] One of them is talking too much. I think lack of tolerance a far greater sin than gay-ism. If someone "normal" has been given blessings but turns around and is intolerant of those who have deformities, birth defects, issues, to me *that* person may be in far greater jeopardy in God's eyes than a gay person.

RAY and STEVEN stand; both cross to stage right of table.

LISA: [*to audience*] The Saturday of our visit, I overhear a conversation between Ray and his dad.

STEVEN: Tell me about your faith.

RAY: I don't want to insult your beliefs.

STEVEN: Your beliefs do not insult mine.

RAY: [*hesitantly*] I think . . . organized religion profits some at the expense of many. I believe that when we die our energy disperses into the universe. We become part of something else—a tree—part of everything else.

STEVEN: Is that enough of a belief system for you?

RAY: Actually, it's depressing. It makes it difficult to relate to our family. I'm happy for you. Part of me wishes I still had your belief system.

RAY returns to stage right black box, STEVEN to stage left chair; both sit.

LISA: You reported wondering if I would be a "wacko activist." What conclusions have you drawn?

STEVEN: Definitely you *are* wacko. [*both laugh*] Not really. But this is hard for me to tell you: members of my family forewarned us that your agenda was to expose the ignorance and prejudice of gay people's family members. I predicted blowing your mind because you expected me to be more intolerant.

LISA: [*to audience*] I confess: as much as Steven wondered about the potential "wacko activist" coming to stay, I wondered about the possible "Jesus freak" playing host. How easily we Other each other.

As I revise, I also note places where I comment to the audience on Steven's constructions of same-sex orientation. I want to let readers—including Ray—know when I find something problematic, but I don't want to abuse my role as primary author by always "correcting" my host, allowing myself the last—and "best"—word.

[*to STEVEN*] What's it been like to have us here?

STEVEN: Very enjoyable. I figured, if nothing else, I'll get a chance to see my son. [*quietly*] You know, he wouldn't come here otherwise.

LISA: [*to audience*] I feel the weight of Steven's assessment.

STEVEN: It's been great seeing him, rummaging around in old photos. I really love him. And we've enjoyed having you here. You're a good listener. You've been gracious, kind, and accommodating [*smiles*], sleeping on the hard floor.

LISA: [*to audience*] Thursday morning, I awakened in a crevasse created by a slow leak in the air mattress. That evening, Steven contemplated alternate arrangements.

STEVEN and LISA stand, cross to stage left of table.

STEVEN: Well . . . you could sleep on the couch portion of the sectional, next to the pullout where we have Ray.

LISA: [*to audience*] I wondered if this communicated acceptance of Ray's sexual orientation, because such an offer likely would not be extended to an unmarried *heterosexual* son and his female companion, or if it communicated hope that Ray's sexual orientation was somehow *revisable*. Until a recent back injury, Ray's partner Morgan had planned to make this trip with us. His absence may contribute to my appearance as "the girl Ray has brought home." As a guest in a conservative Christian household, I also wanted to communicate respect for my hosts' beliefs. For these reasons, I said, [*to STEVEN*] Thank you, but the floor in the office is fine.

LISA and STEVEN return to table and sit, STEVEN on stage left chair, LISA on center stage chair.

STEVEN: Um . . . so . . . what is your relationship with Ray like?

LISA: [*smiles*] I see a lot of myself in your son: fiery yet loyal, searching both for justice and for others' acceptance. Ray and his former partner, Brian, became my and my husband's alter egos. My graduation present was a trip to Europe, and Brian and Ray joined us. The dissolution of their relationship in 2002 devastated me. It felt like my brothers got divorced.

[*to audience*] I notice my efforts to deheterosexualize my relationship with Ray: shifting the focus toward couple relationships, referring to him as a brother.

[*to STEVEN*] I am heartened to see that Ray and Brian have moved on to loving relationships with their current partners, for whom I also care deeply. I've known Ray since 1995. We've shared many turning points: graduations, job changes, moves, deaths of those close to us, my dissertation and book projects about our network of gay male friends.

STEVEN: So if Ray were not gay, would you have considered marrying him?

LISA: [*to audience*] Deheterosexualization incomplete.

[*to STEVEN*] I can't answer that. Our playfulness and warmth always have been bounded by partnerships with others. But sure, Ray would be great marriage material for anybody, male or female.

STEVEN: Last night, I noted strong affection between you. I've often thought of Ray as a handsome, nice guy—good qualities for a heterosexual relationship. In a way, it's kind of a shame. But I suppose a gay person might look at me and say, "It's a shame he's heterosexual." I gotta tell you, I am totally 100 percent heterosexual, so non-gay that I don't even like to shake hands with another man.

RAY: [*to audience*] Come again?

STEVEN: I do, 'cause I have to, but it's weird. I don't even like to shake hands with my own brother. I don't know what it is.

LISA: [*to audience*] At the initial interview, I decide not to pursue what it might be.

STEVEN: [*to audience*] When I saw the draft, I realized that I went over the top by including my brother there. I really don't have a problem with that.

[*to LISA*] And what is your opinion about gay-ism being right or wrong, normal or abnormal?

LISA: When I think about your son, his same-sex orientation and primary relationship feel perfectly natu—

STEVEN: Have you had lesbian feelings or desires?

LISA: [*to audience*] I'm starting to see who's really conducting this interview.

[*to STEVEN*] Growing up, I felt connected to a female friend in a deep, embodied, almost psychic way, but my narrow range of experience prevented me from defining our relationship as potentially erotic.

STEVEN: Have you changed to where now you *would* entertain that idea?

LISA: [*to audience*] I wonder what prompts this line of questioning.

[*to STEVEN*] Given all I've experienced, I can imagine myself falling in love with another woman, but in terms of your three-legged stool, the physical leg tends to be attached to men—as it does for your son.

STEVEN: Do you have a strong sexual attraction to your husband?
RAY: [to audience] For heaven's sake, Dad!
STEVEN: [to audience] Probably could have censored myself more there.
LISA: [rises, to audience] As if on cue, Vivian returns home from work. She, Steven, Ray, and I pack for a night in Yosemite, the spectacular conclusion to our trip.

LISA reads poem aloud.

Renewal

Yosemite:
from the Southern Miwok "yehemite,"
meaning "some among us are killers,"
a reference not to White imperialists
but to an older, closer antagonist, the Paiutes.

Our trip home ends—
and begins—
on the trails of Yosemite.

Embracing us are Sierra Nevada's cliffs and canyons,
its meadows, the Merced River, and Mariposa Grove,
home of the Giant Sequoias,
Earth's largest living beings.

Mist Trail to Vernal Fall,
a .8 mile ascent:
the final hike on the final day.

Terrain shifts from steep climbs
to soft sloping curves.
Vision strains from darkened tunnels
and glaring sun.
Dust whirs in the breezes that

both sting our faces
and nudge us gently from behind.

Low rumbling beckons.
Rested from its winter slumber,
the mountain heaves water
over ancient rocks
and under the bridge
between us and our vernal fall.

Smiling, the father and son pause
to capture this moment,
this place.

We descend,
me shuffling cautiously behind.

Figure 2.1 Ray and Steven Wise.

Their movements alternate:
brisk and purposeful,
then leisurely,
contemplative.

Along the trail they come together,
separate,
come together again.
They allow others to pass between them.

Near the mountain's base,
late spring releases melted snow,
washing the trail clean.

Ever so slightly, the father loses his footing,
shifting away from the son.
Instinctively, the son offers his arm,
prepared to catch the father—
or to take their fall
together.

On the return flight,
I cry as I write these words.
If anyone asks,
I will say that my ears hurt from the descent.
And perhaps this is true.

Yosemite:
an etymology of mistrust,
but a history of renewal.
Even the Miwok and Paiutes
released ashes of animosity,
blending history and family.

Reception

I stayed in contact with Steven, sending a thank-you note, transcript of our interview, Christmas card, and draft of the play. A year and a half pass between our trip to Buck Hill and Ray and Steven's next meeting, when Steven travels to Florida for the wedding of Ray's half-brother on January 7, 2006. Steven invites Ray to bring his partner Morgan and me.

As we pull up to the reception site, I see Steven across the lot. We emerge from the car; he smiles and waves us over. Ray steps into Steven's open arms. This time, their embrace seems more expressive than obligatory. "Dad, this is Morgan," Ray says.

"At last," Steven replies. "I've heard so many good things. Please come inside."

Steven sweeps us around the hall, proudly making introductions and reacquainting Ray. Immediately following each, "This is my son, Ray," is a clear, "and this is his *partner*, Morgan." Only one miscommunication: Steven turns his arms and body toward Morgan, but the gaze of the woman receiving us stops on me. She takes my hand. "Nice to meet you, Morgan."

"*This* is Morgan," corrects Steven, directing her attention across the group.

Her mouth falls open a bit as she processes. Finally: "*Oh*, I get it!" Steven grins, seeming pleased to have provided clarification—and perhaps education.

For two hours, Ray excitedly chats with his half-brothers, stepsisters, and stepmother, some of whom he hasn't seen in a decade.

Break/through

At Steven's suggestion, we meet him and Ray's half-brother Chaz at a nearby Panera for a post-reception visit. Steven buys us "kids" a hot beverage and snack. We settle into a corner high-top. I sit closest to the window, Ray to my right, Morgan on the end, Steven across from me, Chaz next to him. I look over at Ray's half-brother, a 22-year-old with eyes as dark as the onyx hair inherited from his Italian mother. "I hear you live in Orlando, Chaz."

"Near the airport," he says, straightening his grey suede coat.

"Working and going to school?"

He nods, finishing a bite of pastry. "I manage a restaurant and go to UCF, engineering."

I ask Steven about his annual trip to Hawaii, the 2006 Strauss Festival, and his new doctoral program. As in California, Steven proves a prolific conversationalist. He explains, for example, how Mormons came to abstain from alcohol, tobacco, tea, and coffee. Though I know he isn't bothered by it, I suddenly wish I'd ordered a hot chocolate instead of the decaf. Morgan, seated furthest from Steven, sits quietly. In retrospect, I should have offered to switch places, making it easier for Morgan to interact with Steven during this—their first—meeting.

My attention diverts from conversational dynamics when Steven begins talking about the draft of the play. Politely but firmly: "I took exception to your inclusion and portrayal of our political exchanges and of my Vietnam experience."

From the corner of my eye, I see Ray shift in his seat. I reply, "As I said in my letter, we will workshop the draft collaboratively."

Ray assures him, "Lisa wants this to be accurate and fair and to help rather than harm."

Steven nods, but his brow remains furrowed. He then talks at length about Vietnam, sharing stories Ray and I heard in California. There and here, Steven takes on the roles of teacher and mentor. His insistent tone suggests it is critically important to him that we understand his understanding of those experiences.

When Steven finishes, the group sits quietly a moment, brushing crumbs around our trays, taking last sips of beverages long gone cold. Into the silence, Steven says to Ray, "In one of your sessions with Lisa, you described our relationship as 'tense.' I wasn't aware you felt that way." Steven looks into Ray's eyes. "After the divorce from your mother," he then turns to Chaz, "and later from yours, I found that talking to my kids called up painful memories. In Lisa's draft, I come off as an absent, irresponsible dad. It's true I had two year-long tours for the military, and I can be a workaholic, but to me, the state of our relationship was not due to tension but to geographic distance and the pain associated with conflict and divorce." He clears his throat and presses on. "When I met Vivian, I was a wreck. Twice divorced. Separated from my children. Drained, emotionally and financially. I lost my job and couldn't find work in my field. Declared bankruptcy. I developed acid reflux so severe that my symptoms mimicked cardiac arrest. After six trips to the ER, I began having panic attacks. I was . . ." Steven's voice breaks; tears fill his now-downcast eyes. Ray reaches across the table for his arm. "I was psychologically incapable of being a father." I struggle to catch my breath, the emotional intensity of this statement well beyond any we heard in California.

Ray responds, "I love you, Dad."

"Me too, Pops," says Chaz.

It takes the group a few moments to absorb what has transpired. I wonder if either Ray or Chaz will address Steven's vulnerable disclosure. Then, Ray looks at Chaz and queries, "You call Dad '*Pops*'?" This shift strikes a note of relief. Steven smiles.

We continue chatting until 10:00 p.m., a half-hour past closing time. I confirm Monday's workshop session as we bid our goodnights.

Ray sits in the front passenger seat for the ride back. "You okay?" I ask.

He exhales. "It's just . . . I've never seen him cry."

Front Stage

The next day, I retrieve a message from Ray saying that Chaz and Steven are considering the 7:00 p.m. drag show at the resort where Ray and Morgan work. When I call for assurance that I heard correctly, Ray indicates that they already are on their way, so I hustle myself together and to the bar.

Sunday t-dance is hopping; I have to park well into the remote gravel lot. At the door, I get a wristband and make my way past the restaurant and disco, which has filled to near capacity. At the back is the adjoining pool bar where Ray tends. I greet my friend with a kiss, Steven and Chaz with hugs, and am introduced to Chaz's girlfriend, an attractive 22-year-old with dark eyes, tan skin, and flowing amber hair. Our conversation is interrupted by Ray calling, "Dad! Chaz! You're being summoned to the stage."

D-Va is an Orlando institution: tall, Black, large, and in charge. The surround sound speakers boom with her theatrical drawl: "I *said*, 'I hear we have family in th' house!'" She gestures toward our group. "Our beloved Ray Wise has been joined by his father and brother tonight. Father and Brother, Come On Up Here!" The crowd roars.

"No way!" says Chaz. Steven smiles but makes no move.

"Go on, *go*," I encourage. "You too, Ray." Pool bar patrons whoop. Slowly, Chaz dismounts his barstool. He and Steven proceed through the door and into the adjoining room. Ray and I follow. When disco patrons see them emerge, wild applause breaks out.

I snap photos as the Wise men make their way to the stage. With a high-heeled quickstep, D-Va sashays toward Steven. "Mister Wise, I presume. Where are you from?"

"Sacramento," he replies, sounding neither strained nor nervous.

"Excellent. Sir, I hear you are a . . . *Mormon*."

Still managing a half-smile, Steven says, "Correct."

An "ooh," perhaps of both surprise and respect, spreads across the room. I cringe a bit, anticipating what follows. "Mister Wise, how many wives do you have?"

Rolling with it, Steven offers, "As many as I want."

"Just teasing you, sir. We are honored to have you. Most of us make peace with our mothers—probably because our mothers *knew* when we were five! It is another matter to receive support from fathers and brothers. So thank you. Let's hear it for Ray's dad!" Ray in tow, a jovial Steven leaves the stage to resounding applause.

D-Va has not finished. Eyeing a doe-eyed Chaz, she says, "Little Steven Junior."

Clearing his throat, he says, "Uh . . . Chaz."

D-Va offers a sultry, "*Chaaaaz*, I will call out numbers."

"Oh no," says Ray, familiar with the routine.

D-Va continues, "You will answer 'higher' or 'lower.'" She glances toward his crotch. Getting her drift, Chaz is defiant: "I'm not answering that."

Undaunted D-Va says, "Five!"

From the crowd bellow calls of "Higher! Higher!"

Chaz rolls his eyes and squeaks, "Higher" into the mike. This is repeated for six and seven.

D-Va purposefully drops her handkerchief. "Oops, I'll get it," she says, bending over. D-Va begins to rise up, stops at the level of Chaz's crotch, and queries, "Eight?" She lets him off the hook—sort of. "Chazzie, I know how you feel amid all these gay boys. I read Scriptures too. Trust me, this *woman* only lies with men."

To the rescue, Chaz's girlfriend ascends the steps with shots for D-Va and Chaz. D-Va asks, "Who are you to him, Missy?"

"Everything," she banters.

D-Va playfully swings her fists in the air, then directs Chaz's girlfriend stage left, where a group of butch women has gathered. "Those ladies have some business with you, girl."

Our hostess gives Chaz a bicep squeeze. "You've been a good sport. Give it up for little Steven Junior!" Chaz descends with a good-natured grin and a wave acknowledging the thunderous response.

Back in the pool bar, I debrief with Chaz and Steven. Chaz smiles and laughs, seeming not to mind having been D-Va's "straight man." Steven takes it in stride. "I wanted to come here tonight," he explains, "to show Ray my support. In the military, we patronized all kinds of establishments, including some gay ones. Camaraderie isn't forged only on battlefields. Some people are surprised that a Mormon who doesn't smoke or drink can still have fun in bars."

Re/vision

The next day, our workshop commences at 6:00 p.m. and continues past 1:45 a.m. Steven has made extensive notes on the draft. He reads both his responses and suggested rewordings aloud. I sit at my laptop, incorporating feedback into the emerging text. Steven and Ray talk through how certain excerpts may be received by the rest of their family. We strive to balance the reader's need for a good story (engaging plot, round characters, dramatic tension) and the family's need to heal and move forward. At several points, Ray and Steven turn to each other and say something like, "I didn't know you felt that way," or "Let me explain." Steven, for the first time, shares with Ray details about the sexual abuse he experienced as a boy. Steven then lets us know, "I also figured it was time to tell my brother; we talked about it just recently."

When we wrap, Steven asks for a few minutes alone with Ray. They retreat to the living room. I later learn that Steven performed a father's blessing, a ritual begun by Joseph Smith in 1834:

[M]y son, I lay my hands upon thy head . . . Thou hast suffered much in thy youth, and the poverty and afflictions of thy father's family have been a grief to thy soul . . . Thou hast stood by thy father, and . . . would have covered his nakedness, rather than see him exposed to shame . . . No weapon formed against [my son] shall prosper, and though the wicked mar him for a little season, he . . . shall be blessed like the fruitful olive, and his memory shall be as sweet as the choice cluster of the first ripe grapes . . . Thy heart shall be enlarged . . . At thy word . . . the deaf shall hear and the blind shall see . . . [6]

Love, Ray

RE: Decision from *Symbolic Interaction*

Date: April 27, 2008, 7:19 p.m.

Hi, Ray:

Attached is my revised version of the article containing a few suggested changes for Lisa to consider. I will defer to her final judgment.

I am not ashamed of my life and what has been depicted, particularly if the piece can be of value to others. I am not ashamed of you as my son, nor of what you have revealed. On the contrary, I am very proud of you. We both, like so many other people, have had our struggles in this life. What matters is that I love you. If you lived closer, Vivian and I would have you and Morgan over for dinner often and be delighted to have you as a close part of our family circle.

Some say that none of us will get out of this world alive. The truth is, we all will certainly get out of this world alive. I want to look forward to having you there by my side as a son and brother, both of us having fought a good fight, kept the faith, and endured to the end, and in the favor of our God who created us.

Love,
Dad

Re: Decision from *Symbolic Interaction*

Date: April 28, 2008, 7:45 p.m.

Hi, Dad:

I won't lie. When I first saw the e-mail response from you, I was scared. Lisa called me because she hadn't received my forward. As I read your e-mail to her, she got to experience— not for the first time—a sobbing child, longing to feel loved. Through your words, I realized that you have never stopped loving me.

If after our earthly bodies die, I am able to be with the people I love (you, Mom, Morgan, Lisa), then I will be there, and I believe that the way to get there is to love each other, no matter our differences.

When I later called you, Dad, we cried and learned more about each other in that hour than we ever have in our entire lives. It is, to date, my favorite memory of you.

Thank you, Dad, and thank you, Lisa.

Love,

Ray

Notes

1   An earlier version of "Father's Blessing" was published in *Symbolic Interaction* (Tillmann 2008; used with permission, John Wiley & Sons, Inc.: http://online library.wiley.com/doi/10.1525/si.2008.31.4.376/abstract). For other ethnographic dramas centered on relationships, see, e.g., Ellis and Bochner (1992), Foster (2002), and Pelias (2002). For additional performance works that reflect both the interpretive and the critical paradigm, see, e.g., Bornstein (1995), Lockford (2004), Moreira and Diversi (2011), Spry (2011), and Chapter 6. A webpage for this chapter may be found at: http://www.insolidaritybook.com/father-blessing.html.

2   See Tillmann-Healy (1998).

3   See Tillmann-Healy (2001).

4   See Tedlock (1991).

5   See Henry (1973) and Rawlins (1992, 2009).

6   See "Patriarchal Blessing" (n.d.).

References

Bornstein, Kate. *Gender Outlaw: On Men, Women, and the Rest of Us*. New York: Vintage Books, 1995.

Ellis, Carolyn, and Arthur P. Bochner. "Telling and Performing Personal Stories: The Constraints of Choice in Abortion." In *Investigating Subjectivity: Research on Lived Experience*, edited by Carolyn Ellis and Michael G. Flaherty, 79–101. Newbury Park, CA: Sage, 1992.

Foster, Elissa. "Storm Tracking: Scenes of Marital Disintegration." *Qualitative Inquiry* 8, no. 6 (2002): 804–819.

Henry, Jules. *Pathways to Madness*. New York: Vintage Books, 1973.

Lockford, Lesa. *Performing Femininity: Rewriting Gender Identity*. Walnut Creek, CA: AltaMira Press, 2004.

Moreira, Claudio, and Marcelo Diversi. "Missing Bodies: Troubling the Colonial Landscape of American Academia." *Text and Performance Quarterly* 31, no. 3 (2011): 229–248.

"Patriarchal Blessing." *Mormon Origins*. Accessed May 16, 2014. http://user.xmission.com/~research/about/patb1.htm.

Pelias, Ronald J. "For Father and Son: An Ethnodrama with No Catharsis." In *Ethnographically Speaking: Autoethnography, Literature, and Aesthetics*, edited by Arthur P. Bochner and Carolyn Ellis, 35–43. Walnut Creek, CA: AltaMira Press, 2002.

Rawlins, William K. *Friendship Matters: Communication, Dialectics, and the Life Course*. New York: Aldine de Gruyter, 1992.

——. *The Compass of Friendship: Narratives, Identities, and Dialogues*. Thousand Oaks, CA: Sage, 2009.

Spry, Tami. "The Accusing Body." *Cultural Studies↔Critical Methodologies* 11, no. 4 (2011): 410–414.

Tedlock, Barbara. "From Participant Observation to the Observation of Participation: The Emergence of Narrative Ethnography." *Journal of Anthropological Research* 47 (1991): 69–94.

Tillmann, Lisa M. "Father's Blessing: Ethnographic Drama, Poetry, and Prose." *Symbolic Interaction* 31, no. 4 (2008): 376–399.

Tillmann-Healy, Lisa M. *Life Projects: A Narrative Ethnography of Gay-Straight Friendship*. Ph.D. diss., University of South Florida, 1998.

——. *Between Gay and Straight: Understanding Friendship across Sexual Orientation*. Walnut Creek, CA: AltaMira Press, 2001.

3

PASSINGS[1]

Gordon Bernstein and I moved to Tampa the same year, 1993. I began the Ph.D. program in Communication at the University of South Florida as Gordon, then 24, embarked on life as a gay man. I met Gordon two years later. He played leftfield for the Cove, the softball team at the center of the gay male friends about whom I wrote my Ph.D. dissertation[2] and first book, *Between Gay and Straight*.[3]

Both the dissertation and book contain a chapter based on a 1996 series of life history interviews with Gordon. At that time, my friend was beginning to explore intimacy and sexuality with other men. Having internalized our culture's conflation of sex, gender expression, and sexual orientation (where male=masculine=heterosexual), Gordon was stumbling toward the integration of his masculine, athletic identity and his emerging gay identity. He had developed a wide network of gay male friends and had come out to colleagues and his sister, but years would pass before his parents knew him as gay. In 1996, Gordon described Mr. and Mrs. Bernstein this way:

> Dad's real name is Morton, but everybody calls him Tex. Only child. Born and raised in South Philly. My dad finished high school, went into the coast guard, then college. He taught history.

Figure 3.1 Lisa Tillmann and Gordon Bernstein.

I'm my dad's boy. Same dreams, same interests: watching a ball game, walking the beach. There's definitely that father–son rivalry. He still thinks he's 25.

Calm. Even-keeled. When he does get mad, you know it. You don't piss my dad off.

Marilyn, my mom, also born and raised in Philadelphia. Her father was quite religious, Jewish, and really stern. Her mother was born in Russia. My grandmother had 12 sisters and one gay brother, my great uncle Gene.

My parents met through her cousin. Mom was seeing somebody else at the time. I guess my dad got her to the altar first. They married in '61, had my brother in '64, me in '69, and my sister in '75.

Typical Jewish mother: super, super nurturing. Want to be involved. Want to know everything. If you were sick, "Oh, let me do this, let me do that for you." Yeah, my mom is NOT one of those. It was: "You'll be fine. Go to school."

Mom is not very emotional. She had a number of mis-
carriages, watched two of her best friends die and both her
parents, but I've never seen her cry. I don't know if she's ever
cried. But always there if you need her. She's actually a friend,
someone I can talk to about a lot of things—but not everything.

I don't come from a "sit and talk" family. We never discuss
relationships. We talk about sports, our days at work, but never
any real outpouring of emotion.

In terms of coming out, I probably will tell Mom first. My
father is clueless. Will this help him know who I really am? I
don't think so. He's not going to ask a thousand questions. My
father wants to know that the weather's nice and the car's driving
well. I'm not gonna spill my guts and cry. I've already done that
a thousand times by myself, going over the conversation in my
head.

* * *

When Gordon and I reconvened for a follow-up session in 2003, he
overviewed the period since our last interview:

Milestones of the last seven years: developed great friendships,
told my parents I was gay, met my boyfriend, Todd, and moved
to Lauderdale.

My mom was diagnosed with Lou Gehrig's, ALS. Before,
we never spent much time talking. We still don't go real deep,
but she has to listen now. Mom can't get up and walk away,
which she did for years—literally!

Coming out happened exactly the way I thought it would.
My mom was in town. I said, "There's something I need to tell
you." Very matter-of-factly: "I'm gay. I hope this doesn't come
as a big surprise." "Nah," she said, "I sort of figured." We didn't
talk much more than that. I probably forced five extra minutes
of conversation, but she really didn't want to delve into it at that
time. When Mom returned home she told my dad.

Couple months later, I visited them. Dad made no mention of it—until he was dropping me off at the airport! Finally he said, "I cried for a week." I probably am not the most sympathetic. I replied, "You cried for one week. I've been dealing with this for years on my own." He said, "I wish you could've come to me." I'm like, "You're having a hard enough time today. If I'd told you in '91, when I was really struggling, you wouldn't have been there." He referred to places I could go "to change." I made sarcastic comments. I don't think anything was resolved, but you know, it did open lines of communication. Dad talked about my parents' marriage. At that time, we never discussed such things.

My parents and I really started talking when I met Todd in 2000. Back in Philadelphia, I laid it on the line: "I want you to meet him and be yourselves but not pass judgment. If you can't do that, you can't come to my house, and I won't come to yours." I suspect I wasn't even as "nice" as I just put it. Fortunately, they like Todd a lot—probably more than they like me! Todd is generous, caring. He cherishes the people in his life. Todd will let my dad ramble on. It's comical: Dad runs up to him, hugs him hello, kisses him goodbye. Todd treats them like gold. I still don't think my parents perceive us as "the gay couple." They see us as best friends, but they know, obviously.

If I could go back in time, I would do a lot of things differently. I'm envious when I see guys in their early 20s comfortable in their own skin. I don't think I hit my stride until about 27, probably when we did the first round of interviews.

I gave the dissertation to my mom. She might've opened it and skimmed through. Didn't read it, which pissed me off, I have to be honest. I don't even know if she read the chapter about me—a way of knowing more about her son. She didn't take advantage of that.

For the *Going Home* project, I could see my parents saying, "I don't want to talk about all that." I have no idea if they'll be receptive to it.

Going Home

Dave Dietz, project videographer, is stuck in the aftermath of a tractor-trailer jackknife on I-4. I met Dave in 1996 through Gordon's extended network of friends, who used to convene every Monday evening for dinner, *Melrose Place*, and *Ally McBeal*. Born in 1959, this son of working-class Democrats has an equally keen eye, wit, and heart.

Three forty-five p.m., four hours and 45 minutes late, Dave pulls into the drive. He emerges from his Jeep with a traffic trauma scowl but smiles when his eyes find mine.

At Orlando International, the checkpoint crew excavates every pocket of Dave's gear. "Don't worry," my friend assures me, "this happens all the time."

Spotting his cameras, a pony-tailed guard speculates, "Romantic getaway?"

I respond, "Documentary about a gay man returning to his hometown." Perhaps feeling outed, Dave shoots me a smirk.

Figure 3.2 David Dietz and Gordon Bernstein.

Inspection complete, we schlep the equipment onto the tram. "What kind of 'romantic getaway' involves a tripod?" I ask, winking at Dave.

He laughs. "The stories I could tell, sister." Then, turning to business, "Let's mike you when we get off."

"Have to pee first," I report, "unless you want audio on that."

"Now *that's* romantic."

Our flight is half boarded before Gordon arrives from his Lauderdale connection. He takes a well-chewed straw from his mouth and embraces each of us. I run my hand over his nearly shaved head. Dave records us walking from the jet way to our seats in row 22.

A lanky flight attendant strides toward us. Sternly he asks, "Do you have permission to operate that?"

Dave lowers the camera but keeps shooting. We attend the attendant: blond locks gelled with precision, teeth suitable for a White Strips ad, uniform crisply pressed. Dave clears his throat. "Gord here is coming out to his folks," he fibs. Gordon rolls his eyes as Dave continues, "We're going to Philly to film it."

"*Oh,*" says the attendant, hushing his voice. "I know all about that."

"Thought you might," Gordon replies.

Relaxing into the flight, we talk about the weekend ahead. Gordon indicates that I may have opportunities to speak with his godfather, Bob, and Bob's wife Eve, the only confidantes of Gordon's parents who know that he's gay.

In Gordon's lap lies a copy of *Tuesdays with Morrie*, Mitch Albom's bestseller about his rekindled relationship with Morrie Schwartz, a former professor dying from complications of ALS. "How is your mom?" asks Dave.

"Spirits are great, but she has no physical strength. Can't move unassisted. I don't know how much longer my dad will be able to care for her at home."

I query, "What would be the best outcome of seeing them this weekend?"

Gordon turns this over. "I'd like my parents to understand more about my last years in Pennsylvania: the struggle, the turmoil, the loneliness."

My mind flashes to 1996. At our first interview, Gordon described the most challenging time in his journey, provoked by reading *Behind the Mask*, the coming out story of former major league baseball umpire Dave Pallone:

> It was May of '91. I'll never forget buying that book—a traumatic experience just picking it up. This hit me harder than anything ever in my life. Here was someone I could identify with: how we grew up and sports. The next week I spent shaking, literally hyperventilating crying, where I couldn't breathe. I would look at myself in the mirror and break down. Couldn't eat. Couldn't sleep. No one knew what was wrong with me. I remember my dad and I went to dinner. He said, "Gord, if there's anything, you can tell me. If you got a girl pregnant, I'm there for you." That shattered me because I thought, *If only it were that easy*. A line in the book basically read, "No direction, no meaning, no life." That really is how I saw myself. I dealt with this for years on my own. Lonely times, desperate thoughts. The hardest part was not being able to talk about it.

I refocus on Gordon as he expresses his wishes for the weekend: "Given how closed my folks have been to anyone outside my immediate family, it would be an achievement if one or both of them consents to being interviewed about having a gay son. Maybe they'll even ask *me* a question or two about my experience, my coming out. They have no idea what I went through."

The next morning, Gordon provides a narrated tour of his Northeast Philadelphia neighborhood. "Had quite a normal childhood here," he tells Dave and me. "I always knew how to act without being seen as different. I did what people expected. If a thought came to me like, *I'm attracted to him*, I would push it away, knowing this is not the time; this is not the place.

"Most parents in this neighborhood had college degrees, were middle- to upper-middle class, White, and Jewish. Not very representative of the world. As you'll see, we lived on a cul-de-sac, every house the same. Almost all the original people reside there today."

Figure 3.3 Lisa Tillmann and Gordon Bernstein.

We stop at his childhood home, one of seven identical siblings of brick and vinyl siding circling a courtyard. Gordon predicts having at least one neighbor encounter. Pulling over, he urges, "Don't share what we're doing with anyone here."

As we step out of the car, a long-haired woman who looks like she could handle herself in a bar fight emerges from the house next door. "Gord?!" The former neighbors walk toward one another, meeting on her side of the street for a hug.

Gordon presents Dave and me to Cathy, explaining, "Lisa is a professor writing a piece on, ah . . . going back." She nods but makes no inquiries.

Instead they commiserate about Yom Kippur, which is today. Gordon asks Cathy, "Do you eat gefilte fish?"

Wincing, she places one hand about 18 inches atop the other to suggest a container's size. "Like fetuses in jars!"

Gordon tells the group, "My family wasn't very religious. We had an annual Passover Seder and celebrated Hanukkah a few years, but it wasn't a big thing. Mom actually put up a Christmas tree a couple times. She got some static but didn't care what people thought."

Cathy chats with Gordon about Florida real estate and their shared passion for gambling before the former neighbors turn their focus to

ALS. Gordon describes Marilyn's wheelchair-bound condition and daily home health care and Tex's struggles to serve as primary caregiver.

"Give my love to your parents," Cathy says tenderly. "Everyone is praying for them." Her tone brightens. "Still not married, Gord?"

"Still . . . not married," he replies, hugging her goodbye.

Inside the car, we take our places: Gordon driving, me in back, Dave shooting from the front passenger seat. Dave says, "I get the feeling that quality people—good souls—live here. Cathy shows compassion for your mother and father. You are embraced as a neighbor even today. Why conceal the real purpose of our visit?"

Gordon exhales. "People here would be polite to my face but once behind closed doors: 'I can't believe it. That's disgusting!' In one second you go from 'great guy' to 'gay guy.' Part of me wants to put it in their faces—be the gay guy. But I don't, mainly for my parents' sake. They choose to be silent."

The three of us head to the Jersey shore, where Gordon's parents now spend their summers. As we pull in front of the Bernsteins' first-floor condo, I note the small wooden ramp leading from their unit to a landing and the longer metal ramp covering the steps. Dave and I wait behind Gordon, who knocks on the door. Tex answers excitedly. "Gord!" His hair has faded to white, but his tanned and trim body belies his 74 years.

Taking Mr. Bernstein's extended hand, I say, "Nice to see you again, sir." My mind whirls to our only other meeting, in 1996. Following a festive weekend at a gay softball tournament, Gordon and I visited his brother, who was hosting the Bernstein clan. As we approached the house, my then-closeted friend warned me not to out him to his parents.

Tex ushers us inside. Gordon's mother, strapped to an electric scooter, beams when she lays eyes on her son. Marilyn begins a barrage of commands and queries: "Come in! How are you? Sit down! How was the drive? Tex, get them a cocktail!" Her husband sets a Tanqueray and tonic on the tray attached to her scooter. She sips it through a long straw as the group banters about sun, sports, and stocks. I am reminded of Gordon's 1996 observation: "My father wants to know that the weather's nice and the car's driving well."

Marilyn turns 62 today, and she requests a casino celebration. The severity of her condition becomes evident during the scooter-to-car transfer. I hold her purse and glasses. Dave steadies the scooter. Tex and Gordon maneuver her body, Tex facing and balancing Marilyn as she attempts to rise, Gordon bear-hugging her from behind. I try to imagine how Tex has been doing this alone. "Watch my shoulder!" she implores.

Straining, Tex responds, "Marilyn, shift!"

"My foot, my right foot!"

"Work with us!" says Tex.

"Don't you think I would if I could?" she fires back.

Later, Gordon reflects, "My parents always bickered, but her disabilities have escalated that. It has to be humiliating for her and frustrating as hell for them both."

I ask, "Any sense of how they experienced Dave and me?"

Gordon scoffs, "Obviously they felt comfortable enough to be themselves!"

At Caesar's Palace, Tex and Gordon set off to play blackjack as Dave and I wheel Marilyn about the quarter slots. When she nods toward a machine, we stop and insert her tokens. The three of us chat sporadically about the active hurricane season and Marilyn and Tex's planned winter in Florida. Most of the time, though, each of us stares silently at the blinking lights and spinning reels. Marilyn asks no questions about Gordon or the project.

Around midnight, the group heads back to the Bernsteins' condo. Dave, Gordon, and I assist Tex in getting Marilyn safely inside and return to the Holiday Inn exhausted. I type field notes into the early morning. My mind buzzes with thoughts of the next day's tasks: video-recorded interviews with Marilyn and Tex.

It is 7:00 a.m. I begin pacing my room, looking over notes, and packing a legal pad, pens, and list of questions. On my way to the door, I spot the audio recorder I brought for field notes. I walk over and grab it, placing it in my bag.

Gordon ventures inside the condo while Dave and I remove equipment bags from the trunk. Our friend halts us at the door. "No camera."

I exhale my disappointment. "Audio?"

"Ma," Gordon shouts inside, "audio recorder okay?"

"Fine," I hear her say.

Tex emerges, and the three men pile in the Impala.

When Marilyn nods toward the living room, I set the recorder on the coffee table, between a copy of *Tuesdays with Morrie* and a pamphlet on ventilator care.

"In Our Family, We Don't Really Discuss This"

She grins when I request, "Tell me how you met Tex."

"Down here at the shore. He was staying with my cousin, who thought Tex was too old for me. Tex went away for the summer, came back Labor Day. We got engaged three months later, married in June. You just know it's the right person. He didn't make my skin crawl." I laugh. "That's exactly what I told him. I'm not a touchy-feely person."

"The day you gave birth to Gordon . . ." I prompt.

"Went into labor around midnight. Very, very hot that day. A blackout. The hospital elevator ran on an alternate generator. I refused to get in. The guy says, 'You *have* to,' so I made *him* go up and down a couple times first. In my room they pushed the button to adjust the bed, but of course, there was no power. When it came on the next morning, the bed's going up, up, up, up, up." Marilyn's animated neck and head compensate for the limp hands that remain folded in her lap. "Gordon was born that morning—very hard labor but the easiest recovery."

"When you remember Gordon as a kid, what comes to mind?"

Blood rushes to her face. "Gordon was my best buddy. The easiest one to raise, said 'yes' to everything. 'Gordon, take the trash out.' 'Sure, Ma.' Very agreeable, never fought, very pleasant kid. Loved him *to pieces*. He was kind, sensitive. Once my mother baked a cake, and she gave Gordon a piece to take home. He told her, 'Oh, it's very good.' When I served it to him, he waved his hands, 'I don't like it.' I asked, 'Why did you tell my mother that you did?' 'Well, she needed that.'"

I absorb the warmth Marilyn exudes before broadening our focus. "I have a thought for you to complete: being a member of our family means . . ."

She processes a moment. "A lot of commotion and noise."

"Would you describe the household you grew up in the same way?"

"No, not at all! I grew up alone, really. My mother and father both worked, and I always worked, from the time I was 13 or 14."

"Gordon has informed me about an important figure in your growing up, your uncle Gene."

Her face illuminates. "*So* good to me, always there for me—more so than my parents. When I was invited to proms and parties, my uncle always took me to the finest shops. From a young age I knew he was gay. I didn't judge him at all. My mother was crazy about her brother. My father was downright rude. If my uncle entered a room, he would get up and leave." Likely thinking of Gordon, she adds, "Imagine what my father would say today!"

Marilyn continues, "We have a lot of gay people in our family. My cousin had two sons: one was murdered; one died of AIDS. If Gordon wanted to talk to my cousin, he could ask about them. I've not told her that my son is gay because Tex has a real problem with this.

"I always thought Gordon was," she reports. "He was a very, very good-looking boy who had very, very strange girlfriends: fat, ugly. I mean, I have pictures. He was *beautiful*. When Gordon was in high school, I made a comment to Eve, the wife of Tex's cousin: 'Gordon probably is gay.' I just can pick up on it sometimes."

A memory sparks a smile. Marilyn tells me, "Years ago, I was doing work for this guy. After meeting him I told a mutual friend, 'That guy is gay.' The friend said, 'That's the most ridiculous thing I ever heard!' But I was right. How did I know? Without sounding vain, I was very, very pretty. I had long, dark hair—striking. I mean, even *pregnant*, I looked good. I got no reaction from this guy, *nothing*. I thought, *He can't be straight*." I feel both charmed by this self-confident account and pained to consider Marilyn's present state: once-manicured hands now unable to style hair or apply make-up, once-head-turning body now adding girth and losing muscle tone.

Shifting our focus, I say, "Gordon disclosed that around the time of his college graduation, he read *Behind the Mask*, the coming out story of a retired baseball umpire. Did he ever share that experience with you?"

"No, but I recall that book in his room." Her nod signifies the recollection. "All right, and I *knew*." Putting the pieces together, Marilyn says, "Then Gordon went to umpire school."

I report, "He indicated that reading that book hit him harder than anything ever in his life. The author, Pallone, is conventionally masculine, athletic—and gay. Encountering his story helped Gordon's experience make sense to him, but it also confirmed his fears."

Marilyn sighs. "I feel very badly about his struggle. In our family, we don't really discuss this. I wouldn't have a problem telling people, but Tex does, so I don't say anything.

"I'm happy Gordon is in a relationship. I did worry about . . . promiscuity, getting a disease and dying. But look, it's all accepted. Todd comes to family events. We *love* Todd. Even Tex loves him. We have a problem with the relationship, but that's the way it is."

I decide to push. "Can you elaborate on that: 'We have a problem . . .'?"

"Well, you don't want your children to be this—to be homosexual. You'd prefer them to get married, to live normal lives." I note both the heteronormativity[4] of this construction and Marilyn's use of second person. In 1996, I observed that Gordon tended to shift from "I" to "you" when distancing himself from an emotional topic. She continues, "That first night, the night he told me, I felt very, very sad to think that he would not have children. We sat in his living room. He said he wanted to talk about something. My response was, 'I'm not surprised.' He'd been agonizing. I suspect it had to do with his father, because he's supposedly like his father, but Tex loves women. I mean, he's *crazy* for women. Mayor of the beach, Tex strolls up and down, kisses all these women. Doesn't run around, though. I know him. Plus I could find him at any point of the day!"

I ask, "When you returned from that visit to Tampa, how did the conversation with your husband unfold?"

"Tex swears something happened to Gordon as a child. He thinks he was . . . molested." This catches me off guard. Marilyn says, "Gordon never said anything to me about that. I don't believe he was, but I . . . I don't really know." Her gaze penetrates.

"I've known Gordon since 1995," I tell her, "and he's never said anything like that." What if that *hadn't* been the case? I wonder. What would I have said?

"Then I'm right!" she exclaims, sounding relieved and resolved. "He was *not* molested!"

Marilyn then reports, "I said to Tex, 'This is our son. We love him. If he had to keep it bottled in, he'd probably kill himself.' I've read a lot about that. I told Tex he had to accept it. He just *had* to! And he does, but he can't talk about it."

I swallow a lump of anxiety. "Will Tex have a hard time speaking with me about this?"

"Probably," she predicts. "He thinks it's a reflection on him: Macho Man!"

I then ask, "Is there anything you hope your family will gain by contributing to this project?"

She shakes her head. "Tex doesn't read a whole lot. It's just like with my disease: not *Tuesdays with Morrie*, not one thing about it. Just buries his head."

"Tell me about living with ALS," I request.

"I was basically a loner," says Marilyn. "Loved going everywhere by myself. All the sudden, I'm relying on people. It's a real struggle. Thank god for Zoloft! When they gave it to me last fall, I said, 'What's this pill for?' 'Anxiety.' 'I don't have anxiety.' 'You will.' I always moved quickly, and Tex is not so quick. I take Zoloft so I don't kill him! Seriously, though, I appreciate everything he does for me. It's very, very hard for him. Tex is *not* a natural caretaker. He never took care of the kids."

"What's the hardest part?" I probe.

"Mmm . . . *arms*. Legs you really can live without." I reach out and touch her arm as Marilyn blinks away tears. "B-but my . . . arms. Oh, man! Can't believe I'm crying. I am *not* a crier. Gordon will tell you."

Gordon has told me, I think but do not say.

"But Lisa, I can't do anything. I can't dress myself. I can barely brush my teeth."

She clears her throat and changes the subject: "Do you think Gordon accepts himself?"

"Much more than when we first collaborated. At that time, he had just come out to your daughter."

Brow furrowed, Marilyn says, "He was comfortable coming out to her?" Marilyn's tone suggests this is new information.

"It's not unusual to tell a sibling first."

"So he *told* her?" Marilyn muses. "She said that she knew; she didn't say how." I wonder if I am fulfilling obligations of my friend/researcher role—or crossing a line. It feels awkward to be the one dispelling a family myth of sexual abuse and clarifying key details of Gordon's coming out. I am reminded of a quote from Thomas Cottle's family ethnography: "In life study research, family members may employ researchers as sounding boards if not unconsciously as quasi-psychotherapists."[5]

We sit in silence a moment. "It's good talking to you," she says, and we exchange smiles that signify the close of our session.

Marilyn requests that I retrieve her cell phone. When I hand it over, she tries to operate the buttons, but her impotent fingers refuse to obey. After several failed attempts, she sighs. "Will you . . . ?" I take the phone, highlight Gordon's number, and press "send."

"The women have solved the world's problems," I tell my friend. "Now we're ready for the men." I retake my seat on the sofa, and we chat pleasantly for several minutes.

Then, sounding apologetic, Marilyn says, "I didn't want you to videotape me because I'm very self-conscious. I'm not a whole person. I've always taken charge of my life. I don't want to live on a ventilator or with a feeding tube. I'd just as soon die, really."

We lock gazes a moment before Dave appears in the doorway. He smiles at Marilyn. "How you feeling today?"

"I feel good *every* day," she insists. "I have no pain. I'm wonderful, terrific." I consider the contrast between these statements and her previous assessments: "I'm not a whole person," and, "I'd just as soon die."

As Gordon crosses the threshold, Marilyn asks, "Did you go to the beach?"

"A gazebo," he replies, then turns to me, "which is where my dad wants to take you."

"Is he willing to be video-recorded?" I ask.

"No. They all the sudden became camera shy."

Tex enters and treads down the hall, making no eye contact. "Give me a minute," he calls over his shoulder. Heart pounding, I try to sense his mood but cannot.

Later, Gordon overviews the time he, Tex, and Dave spent together. "You missed nothing. We walked. We talked—very typical—about food, finances, everything *but* what was going on. I did mention the project: how important it was to me, what an ally you are to my community, but I got no response. Perfect example of an hour with my father."

Tex returns, sporting fresh shorts and shirt. He and I exit the condo for our session. Before putting the key in the ignition, Tex takes out his wallet. He passes me a photo, perhaps 40 years old, of a slender young woman with coal black hair, standing tall and straight. "Marilyn?"

"Beautiful girl," Tex says wistfully. He returns to its pouch this memento of days—and bodies—past.

"Not on My Side"

At the gazebo, we settle into adjacent benches. I turn on the audio recorder. "How much has Gordon told you about the project?"

"I don't know anything," says Tex.

I wonder what roles father and son played in his under-preparation. Clearly Tex has read neither the dissertation nor the book. Did Gordon not explain the purpose of our work? If not, why not? If he did explain, how can Tex not "know anything"?

"Let's start at the beginning," I suggest. "I met Gordon in '95, when he and my husband Doug joined the same softball team in a mostly gay male league."

"At that time," he responds, "I knew nothing."

I then overview my dissertation. "Coming out proved a central issue for many of the men in my research community, including Gordon. He and I did a series of interviews in '96. We devoted more time to that issue—his struggle to accept himself and to share his identity with his family—than any other. The purpose of this project is to understand more about that struggle by understanding more about the families."

Tex and I spend the next several minutes talking about his growing up. He describes his working-poor South Philly neighborhood of corner hangouts and family businesses, including his grandfather's meat market. I then turn our attention to an important meeting: "Do you remember your first impression of Marilyn?"

His eyes brighten. "Gorgeous. You saw that picture. Built beautifully. Very vibrant and very . . . cleansing. I use that term because I once ran around with a lot of women. Enough said." He proceeds to say, "Married women whose husbands had gone for the weekend would come to Skinny D'Amato's 500 Club, where Jerry Lewis and Dean Martin started out. There I was. I thought the whole world was like that."

We chat briefly about the couple's courtship and the births of their first son and of Gordon. The details Tex provides overlap with Gordon's and Marilyn's descriptions. I then request, "Could you please describe Gordon?"

"Growing up, he was a mild-mannered boy—not that he took crap from anybody. I recall one incident. He was playing pinball. A kid came over, tried to push him off the machine. Gordon gave him a shot." I note that this story follows the attribution of "mild-mannered." Did Tex feel a need to counter this softer quality with a harder edge?

Shifting our focus to the extended family, I say, "I spoke to Marilyn about her uncle Gene, and I'm wondering—"

"Yeah, he's gay."

"Do you have a relationship with him?"

Tex narrows his gaze. "Not particularly."

"Did you know the two sons of Marilyn's cousin?"

"I know who they were. They were gay too." Tex then points out, "There are no gay people in my family at all."

What about your son? I think but do not ask.

"Listen," he says, "I don't know Gordon's whole story. I don't know how or when he became gay. I don't know if it was due to any kind of . . . incident."

Our eyes lock. "By incident, do you mean abuse?"

"Somebody molesting him sexually." I suppose Marilyn's query should have prepared me for this. Still, I feel decentered, struck that both parents posed this question to me—a virtual stranger—rather than to their son.

Wouldn't they have wanted Gordon either to confirm their fears or to put them to rest long before now? Tex asks directly, "Did he ever say anything?"

The breeze whistles in my ear. "Never."

"You've spoken to him more times than I have about this," Tex presses.

"He never said anything like that."

Tex turns this over, shaking his head. "Gordon told me that he knew he was gay since age 12 or 13."

I ask, "And did you suspect when he was that age?"

His mouth falls open. "Never, never, *never*." Then, as if pleading a case, "He did take out girls." Tex next observes, "The girls that he took out were not the prettiest girls that I've seen. Maybe he did that deliberately."

I study his face, which appears a bit forlorn. "Has having a gay son changed your life?"

He exhales. "I'm not happy about it. I'll be honest with you. He would have a lot to offer a woman. Look, I like Todd, but both he and Gordon seem like guys who shouldn't be gay. Gordon's not feminine; I don't think Todd is either. But that's my perception of what a gay person is."

Tex's view reflects our culture's dichotomization of sex (male–female), gender (masculine–feminine), and sexual orientation (different sex–same sex) as well as their conflation. I follow up: "Has having a gay son challenged you in any way?"

"I'm a private person. I don't like other people to know my family affairs. I don't particularly like people to know that Gordon is gay." I sit back, wondering why Tex consented to be interviewed. He continues, "I mean, I love Gordon very dearly, but I'm not happy that he's gay. I'd like to change him. I don't know how. Do you know how?"

I swallow hard. "Nope, sure don't."

Tex fishes, "I don't even know if he had affairs with women."

"He did," I say, then wonder why. Did I feel some need to reassure Tex? Of what? I return to my previous line of questioning: "Is there any way that having a gay son has enhanced your life?"

"No," he insists but quickly reconsiders. "I shouldn't say that. Todd is a nice boy. But it's confusing."

"Their . . . romantic connection is confusing?" I query.

He clears his throat. "Yes, yeah, yeah. I mean, it's uncomfortable to me."

I venture, "I can't imagine a better match for Gordon than Todd."

Tex shoots me a quizzical look. "Of anybody, you see him matched . . . with Todd? That doesn't sit well with me. If you said with a woman, yes. But that's me. I'm trying to be honest."

He seems on edge, but I keep going: "How did you learn that Gordon identifies as gay?"

Tex uncrosses and re-crosses his legs. "He told me."

I pause, unsure whether to challenge his recollection with what I've learned from Gordon and Marilyn. "Do you remember where you were, what was happening?"

"I can't recall exactly."

I prompt, "Did you have a conversation with Marilyn before you and Gordon talked?"

"I don't remember that either."

"Gordon told me about a conversation he had with you. I don't know if you're thinking of the same situation: you two were in the car on the way to the airport."

"I honestly don't remember," Tex says. "Maybe I blocked it out."

I nod, pondering the significance of his last statement. "When you first found out, do you recall more generally how you felt, what you thought?"

"I think I was upset."

I note the brevity of his last several answers. "What did you find most upsetting?"

"Him telling me that he's gay," fires Tex, his tone communicating that he finds the question ridiculous. "And telling me that he knew since age 12 or 13. That's why I asked if there was an incident."

"If that had happened to him," I say gently, "would it be more understandable to you?"

"No."

I probe, "Just something you've wondered about?"

Tex leans back. "I had a similar experience when I was 12 or 13. Two boys lived across the street from my grandfather. One of them was 14, the other 15 or 16. They wrestled me to the ground. One tried to put his penis in my mouth." My stomach drops. "And I bit it. I *bit* it. The kid screamed. I jumped up and punched the other one in the mouth. Then I ran. They were both bigger than me. I told my grandfather and my father right away. *Right away*, I told them. They went over to that house. I don't know what happened, but that family moved within six months."

I consider how fresh these details are to Tex, more than 60 years later. "Good for you for fighting back," I tell him.

When he offers no further response, I say, "A piece about Gordon's life and growing up will come of this project. Is there anything about your or your family's experiences—"

"I told you," stresses Tex, "there were no homosexuals in my family at all."

Sensing a raw nerve, I take a different tack. "If you could say something to parents who just found out that their son is gay, what would it be? Any advice?"

"No. I have none for myself. I'm not happy about it, so what can I tell other people? Be tolerant. That's about all I am. I *am* tolerant."

"Is there anything that you hope will come of this project?"

With a wry smile, Tex replies, "Let him find a nice girl."

A bit stunned, I manage to retort, "I don't see that as the most likely outcome."

"I know," he says. "I'm being facetious." Tex then asks, "Ever see the movie *High School*?" I shake my head. "Frederick Wiseman filmed a documentary where I used to teach. It was derogatory. Wiseman would pan in on one feature, like fat ankles. It would look like the person was ugly, and the person wasn't."

I mull over possible subtexts of this recounting. "The film wasn't honest?"

"It was honest, but why make someone look ugly when you don't have to?"

Wondering if Tex fears being portrayed as "ugly," I ask, "Do you have any concerns about this project?"

"I don't like it to be known."

"You're a private person," I say, repeating words he used earlier.

"Beside being private, I'm a macho person. My son knows how I am. I love women."

"I get that," I say with a grin.

"I don't like to be associated with this type of project. I'm trying to tell you the truth."

"I appreciate that, sir. Do you have any questions for me?"

"Well, I asked you a question, but you didn't give me any answers."

I try to recall. "Please ask again."

"I asked you about Gordon, if you knew how he became what he became."

In formulating my answer, I consider the Buddhist criteria for "right speech": is it the truth; is it the right time; will it be helpful? On one hand, no honest response brings Tex closer to Gordon finding "a nice girl." On the other, the family's experience with ALS surely has taught Tex about living with uncertainty. I offer, "Though not the focus of my dissertation or book, the question of what causes someone to be attracted to persons of the same and/or a different sex drives much research on sexual orientation. After more than a century of investigation, nobody really knows."

"There is no answer," he reflects.

"Are certain explanations more acceptable to you than others? If it were genetic, for example, does that—"

"I understand it might be genetic." He pauses before adding, "But not on my side."

After a drive along Tex's jogging route, we return to the condo. Marilyn indicates that the group will reconvene for dinner at 7:15 p.m.

Gordon has arranged a visit with his godfather, Bob, and Bob's second wife, Eve. Eve's daughter lived with Gordon for a time in Tampa, prompting him to disclose to their family before coming out to his own brother or parents. On the drive to their place, I ask Gordon about the time spent with his mom during my session with Tex. "Had a drink. We talked—not about the project, of course. She made *no* reference to the interview."

"I Hope the Family Can Get Back on Track"

We arrive at a small complex of two-story seaside condos. A tall, broad-shouldered bear opens the door. "Hey, Bob!" Gordon greets with a hug.

"Gooordon!" rasps the alto voice of Eve. "Let me show you the remodel." Wide windows and decks take full advantage of the waterfront views. Gordon and Bob decide to stroll the neighborhood while Dave and I set up for a recorded session with Eve in their kitchen. I review my list of questions while Dave troubleshoots Eve's lavaliere microphone.

Once the audio is rectified, I ask, "How long have you known Gordon?"

"For at least 20 years," says Eve. "Gordon's father and my husband are cousins. Bob lost his first wife. He has two boys; I have two girls. Gordon used to schlep all the kids around."

"Once you knew of Gordon's sexual orientation, did you have any thoughts or feelings?"

Eve tugs at a patch of her wispy sun-lightened hair. "I was very concerned because of his father. This is something I would say to Tex. I'm not going behind anybody's back. His father always talked about his sexual prowess. And I thought, Oh my god. Here is a man who liked to talk about how many times a night he could do it!"

To confirm my sense of the family dynamics, I ask, "So you and Tex have never talked about Gordon being gay?"

"No, nor has Marilyn mentioned it to me. We sometimes have good girly talks." Eve deliberates a moment. "Never about issues with her children, though."

"In terms of your family network, what would be the best outcome of the project?"

Eve props her elbows onto the table, resting her chin on folded hands. "Gordon recently came to a wedding—the first time he was amongst other family members with Todd. He had to be nervous. He had to have angst. What I'm hoping is that next time, he will come just as if he was with . . . Karen, his wife. That he feels validated. I think that the family can be changed.

"At the same time," Eve observes, "ALS has caused Gordon's parents to keep very much to themselves. I hope the family can get back on track, especially with the journey that she's on."

When Bob and Gordon return, I check my watch, surprised that it reads five minutes to seven. To Bob, I say, "Looks like you and I will have to postpone until after dinner."

"No problem," Bob replies. "We agreed to drive Gordon's folks. See you at the restaurant."

"You Don't Have to Live Here"

As Gordon swings into a parking space in front of the strip mall Italian restaurant, Tex strides over, approaches my door, and opens it. "We need to talk," he says firmly, leading me by my bicep into the adjacent space.

My mind spins back to 1996 and Gordon's description of Tex: "When he does get mad, you know it. You don't piss my dad off." I brace myself.

Hands clasping my shoulders, he asks, "Why are you speaking with Bob?"

I feel like a teenager two hours past curfew. "Uh . . . G-Gord reported that Bob and Eve were key figures in his growing up. He wanted our time here to include them."

"*Why?*" he demands.

I swallow hard. "Maybe Gordon should answer that." Later, I will read Steven L. Vanderstaay's account of his efforts to aid participants in his family ethnography. "[F]ieldwork is not social work . . ." he counsels, "well-meaning efforts to help can easily go awry."[6]

Face flush, Tex wipes sweat from his brow. "You don't understand what you're stirring up! You don't have to live here. I live here. I may have to get into fights—physical fights!"

I resist the urge to ask why and with whom. *Diffuse the situation.* "Mr. Bernstein, if you don't want me to interview Bob, I won't." I do not cop to the session I just wrapped with Eve.

"That's up to you!" he snaps, walking away.

I follow him. "No, I'm leaving it up to you. You're right. I don't have to live here. Talk to Gordon. The two of you will decide."

Tex paces the sidewalk while I move quickly inside. I find Gordon, Dave, Bob, Eve, and Marilyn surrounding our table. "What's going on?" asks Marilyn. Then, to Gordon, "Where's your father?"

"You need to speak with him," I tell Gordon.

Peering out the front window, Eve observes, "He does look pretty pissed."

With a sigh, Gordon heads outside. He's gone for what feels like half an hour but is probably no more than five minutes. When Gordon rejoins the group, he winks at me from across the table and mouths, *It's okay.*

The mood turns light. Bottles of wine are drunk, jokes cracked, laughter shared. The subject of this project never arises.

As the waitress clears our plates, Marilyn motions to Eve. "I could use a cigarette."

"Join us?" Eve invites. We exit the restaurant, leaving the men at the table.

Eve fishes a pack out of Marilyn's purse. She places a cigarette in Marilyn's mouth and lights it, then takes one for herself. Eve hands me the pack. I haven't had a social smoke since college, but the cumulative impact of the day's events makes the occasion feel right for one. I sit on the sidewalk at Marilyn's feet. "Mrs. Bernstein, is Tex okay?"

"He'll be fine," Marilyn assures me. Then, with her usual cheer, "It's been wonderful! It was great having Gordon here for my birthday."

When the men emerge, our gendered groups converge around the Bernsteins' car. Gordon and Tex help Marilyn into the front seat. "Bye, Ma," he says, kissing her tenderly.

As we walk Tex to the driver's side, he spins around and opens his arms, pulling me close. The sudden contact jars me, but I settle into the warm space between his neck and shoulder. "Thanks so much," I say. "I hope to see you both again soon."

"Maybe down in Florida," he softly suggests. I step out of the way, making room for Gordon. "Gord," Tex says, lips to his son's cheek, "so glad you came."

Fathers Lost and Found

On the way back to Bob and Eve's, Gordon, Dave, and I process the pre-dinner confrontation with Tex. "What happened?" asks Dave.

Gordon reports, "I told my dad, 'You said something to Lisa. Now say it to me.' Obviously he was uncomfortable with the project. He fidgeted, looking at everything but me. My dad worries not about his son but about how my being gay affects *his* life and what other people will think—as if the retired people he knows will be reading an academic work on gay men!"

He pauses. "In his defense, I consider my own experience. When just starting to come out to myself, I would go downtown and try to pick up the gay newspaper. I would drive around, literally for an hour or two, until no one was in sight. I would leave the car running and dart out—as if the whole world were watching me. That's what my dad thinks.

"I talked about being a good son: 'You should feel fortunate. I do as much as I can for you. When my sister struggled, I stepped in. I ask nothing from you.'

"I told him that I believe in this project. He couldn't understand why I involved Bob and Eve. I replied, 'Dad, they accept me—much more than you do.' He said, 'I like Todd.' I told him, 'I know, and Todd likes you a lot. But you don't see us as a couple, and you don't realize the struggles I've been through.' He said, 'I will have to fight people if they say something.'" In what sounds like utter disbelief, Gordon continues, "I set him straight: 'Dad, Bob and Eve have known for *years*. They've known longer than *you* have.' It was an epiphany. Still, my gut feeling is that it will never be discussed."

I absorb Gordon's account. "I feel sad to think that may be true. When writing about friendship as method,[7] I have advocated putting fieldwork relationships on par with the project. That system of relationships has expanded from our network of friends to include your families of origin. I honor the relationships I'm building with your parents. I feel such compassion for them as ALS brings struggle and suffering to their lives. That both consented to be interviewed at this difficult time stuns me.

"Your father proved quite candid in our session, expressing his discomfort with male intimacy . . . and his wish that you could change." Gordon exhales. I hesitate, wondering how best—or even *if*—I should broach what was, for me, the most unexpected common theme of the interviews. Gently, I say, "Gordon . . . your parents probed for sensitive information they could have gotten from you years ago. Both asked me if you'd been sexually abused."

He clenches his jaw. "It shows their assumptions."

"Your father also seems to fear being portrayed negatively. More than anything, I don't want to make the family situation worse for you."

"Don't worry about that," Gordon insists. "Sometimes it's not totally accepted. You have to show that. Hopefully my dad said good things too. I don't know if he talked about Todd—"

"In a very positive light," I say. "But your father also joked that, for him, the best outcome of this project would be: 'Let him find a nice girl.'"

Gordon shakes his head. "That's a slap to both Todd and me. But it's also a great line."

Dave clears his throat and begins speaking quietly. "My father died in 1994. All my adult life, he wanted to get closer, and I pushed him away. As a gay man, I felt like I couldn't identify with him. More than once he told me, 'Don't let that get between us; *I* don't.' Still I resisted. I never had the openness with my father that you have with yours right now. I watched you today, Gord, just walking down the street with him, plucking a hair from his shirt. I never had such intimacy with my dad, and I'll never be able to. He wanted to be close in that way. I couldn't offer him that. So that's something that I learned about you on this trip: you're very forgiving. Your father frustrates you, but you find a way to connect, to enjoy him anyway."

"I Think It Will Stay Exactly the Same"

We arrive at Bob and Eve's condo. Dave resets the video camera while Bob and I take seats in the kitchen. Plugged in and wired up, we begin: "Bob, what are your observations about how Gordon's coming out has unfolded in his immediate family?"

"It's something that really hasn't been spoken about," Bob tells me. "My cousin Tex puts out a macho image. He certainly isn't happy about Gordon being gay, and it's something that both Tex and Marilyn try to hide.

"This changed the dynamics of their family. It pushed Gordon away. With him in Florida, Tex and Marilyn don't have to accept it as much. If he lived here, I'm not sure Tex would want Gordon to come around that much, especially with Todd. Tex wouldn't want other people to know."

"You've never had a conversation with Tex about this?"

"Never."

"Marilyn?"

"Never."

"In your mind, what would be the best outcome of the project?"

Bob shrugs. "So much energy goes into Marilyn's illness. I don't know if this project will make any impact."

I then ask, "Do you have any fears or concerns? I'm thinking about what happened with Tex at the restaurant."

"I don't think it will get worse," Bob speculates. "I don't think it will get better. I think it will stay exactly the same. I doubt Tex will say a word to me about anything that's transpired."

"Ready for a drink?" calls Eve from the deck. Dave, Bob, and I join her and Gordon there.

Eve turns to her husband. "Maybe you should talk to Tex about Gordon."

"I'll follow Tex's lead," he responds.

With resignation, Gordon says, "Then you'll never speak of it."

"That's my prediction," Bob affirms.

"Some Roads Lead to Dead Ends"

Later that night, Dave films Gordon and me on the Atlantic City boardwalk. When I ask for reflections on the day, Gordon reports feeling pained by what arose in my interviews with his parents, especially his father's stated hope that he'll "find a nice girl." Gordon then comments on "the different feeling in the air" at Bob and Eve's, a welcome contrast to that surrounding his parents, whom he characterizes as "so apprehensive, so uncomfortable, so awkward."

I return to his parents' questions about sexual abuse. Then, tentatively, "Your dad told me about an experience he had in adolescence of being attacked in a sexualized way by two older boys. Has he ever shared that with you?"

"Never," Gordon says, no emotion visible on his face. "He won't share what happened *today*, let alone something that happened 60 years ago! I ask questions, and he won't answer. I make observations, and he either won't respond or he'll change the subject to something light." Then, referring to his coming out, "My dad has known for five years, and I've made *zero* progress."

"What would it take to make progress?"

Shaking his head, he says, "I don't think it's possible. He has that right. You can't force acceptance. On my end now, it's *not* don't ask/don't tell. Every time we get together, I'm with my partner. They see our home, pictures of us traveling. That actually makes it more frustrating."

I lean back against the railing, a mass forming in my throat. "If your parents weren't doing the work when your mom was healthy, I'm not sure what will motivate them to do the work now. I feel, not so much surprised, as sad."

"It's very sad. I've really opened my life to them, but I don't see how that dynamic will change. Some roads lead to dead ends."

Ethnographic Grief

Gordon, Dave, and I resume life in Florida. I plan to compose a draft, to provide all participants a copy, and to invite them to workshop it collaboratively, but the new academic year squeezes out time to write, and Marilyn's ALS descent accelerates. In June 2005, Marilyn catches a summer cold, the kind most of us ride out with a box of Kleenex and a couple doses of Nyquil. Her chest and diaphragm muscles lack the strength to cough fluid from her lungs. On Friday, July 1, Marilyn passes away. She was 62, her last birthday the one we celebrated in Atlantic City.

I saw Marilyn on exactly two occasions: following a softball tournament in 1996 and for this project in 2004. We shared two meals, three bottles of wine, one casino visit, and one interview session. In ways that tend to matter, we were not close. Acquaintances at best.

And yet: I know when and where Marilyn Bernstein was born. I know she grew up in tenement housing. I know about her stern father and her beloved gay uncle. I know how she met her husband, Tex. I know that her son, my dear friend, entered this world during a blackout. I know that after Gordon came out to her, she said to her macho husband: "This is our son. We love him. If he had to keep it bottled in, he'd probably kill himself." I know she wanted to die before having to be put on a ventilator, and I know that she did die on her own terms: no nursing home, no machines.

I have been a vicarious member of the Bernstein family since 1995. I have pored over details of Marilyn's life and relationships. Cycle after cycle of conversation, field notes, interviews, transcripts, and drafts.

What do we call a relationship constructed from hours of listening to the recorded voice of a woman's son, of converting tape to transcript and transcript to narrative? Parasocial? In the nine years Marilyn and I "knew" each other, I surely had many more thoughts of her than she of me. Still, when Marilyn died, the loss felt more social than "para."

Who counts—or gets counted—as a legitimate mourner? Family members, even estranged ones, count. Friends count. Friends of family members stand at the periphery of the inner circle of grief. Where does the ethnographer stand? What of her grief?

Tuesday, July 5, 2005, 1:00 p.m. Marilyn's memorial service begins in Atlantic City. Seated at my computer, I ask her for strength: for Gordon and Todd, for Tex, for other family members and friends, and for me. I return to the transcript of my session with Marilyn and embark on writing this piece.

The ethnographer grieves, often alone, in the solitude of writing spaces as she engages and re-engages accounts of lived experience, theirs and hers. Sometimes she shares her sense of loss with fellow travelers: friends, participants, colleagues, readers. And sometimes, fellow travelers take the grieving ethnographer into their arms, inviting her into their inner circle.

Thursday, April 20, 2006: outside the Ft. Lauderdale baggage claim, I spot Gordon's approaching Lexus RX. He pulls over and steps out to load my bag. Enclosing me between his broad shoulders, he says, "I'm really sorry about you and Doug."

I sigh into his chest. "Thirteen years into a relationship, it's a profound experience to wake up in a half-empty house."

After a sandwich and pint of Stella at Hamburger Mary's, we head to Gordon and Todd's place, a typical South Florida home: one level, block construction, built in the 1950s but renovated to reflect their urban style of stone surfaces, metal accents, and modern art. He and I get comfortable in their living room and workshop a draft of this piece. Gordon says, "I had hoped that reading the sections based on my parents' interviews would call up more emotion, but I guess in order for that to happen, they would have had to *express* more emotion."

I ask if he feels ready to share the work with his father, Bob, and Eve. "I feel ready, but I guarantee you'll never convince my father to sit down like this and go through it page by page."

"What about a group session with you, Tex, Bob, and Eve?"

Gordon cocks his head. "You're kidding, right?"

"Do you think your parents spoke of our visit after we left?"

"They may have spoken about the *visit*, but I doubt they talked at all about the project."

"Not with each other? Not with Bob and Eve?"

Throwing up his hands, he exclaims, "Absolutely not!"

"In the months since your mom died, how have things been between you and Tex?"

Gordon rubs the stubble on his chin. "Great, actually. As you know, my dad has an apartment about a half-hour from here. He spends the night almost every Saturday. We drink, have dinner, hang out by the pool. He adores Todd, and Todd already talks about how much he'll miss my dad when he returns to Jersey for the summer."

The next afternoon, Gordon has a closing on one of his listed properties. I am reading in a lounge chair by the pool when Tex arrives looking tan and lean as ever. I stand to hug him, "Mr. Bernstein, I'm sorry to say that, since we last saw each other, we both have lost our spouses, albeit under different circumstances." I tell him that my husband moved out ten days before. "Please know how very sorry I was—and am—about Marilyn's death."

Tex clears his throat and says, "I need to change into my swim trunks."

When he returns, Tex and I talk about the transition to living alone. I report, "I'm now making coffee for one, reading the paper by myself, having no one's return to look forward to in the evenings. If you don't mind: how long before you began getting used to sleeping by yourself?"

"I'm not used to it," he responds. "I like having someone in bed with me. That has less to do with sex than with wanting someone to hold. I've dated a bit since Marilyn passed, but it's not the same. I don't believe I'll ever marry or fall in love again. I get a lump in my throat whenever I think or speak of Marilyn." Changing the subject, he asks, "What brings you down here?"

I hesitate. "Um . . . Gordon and I met to edit a draft of the narrative. Would you be willing to read it and offer us your feedback and suggestions?"

"I'm always happy to talk to you," he says, "but not for an interview."

Tex gives me a once-over. "Ya know, you're a beautiful girl. I don't understand your husband. If you were 35 years older, I'd ask you out myself."

Gordon, having returned home and overheard, calls from inside, "You don't waste any time!"

"What? She's a lovely girl!"

Sarcastically, Gordon banters, "And that's the most important thing right now!"

"You're an expert on women all the sudden?"

Their repartee picks up speed and volume. Both father and son clearly relish the exchange. I lay back in my lounge chair, enjoying them enjoying each other. It is not a Hollywood resolution—Mom recovers from illness, Dad grand marshals gay pride parade—but I'll take humor and love in the face of loss any day.

Notes

1 Material from "Passings" has been adapted from my Ph.D. dissertation, *Life Projects* (Tillmann-Healy 1998), my book *Between Gay and Straight* (Tillmann-Healy 2001; used with permission, AltaMira Press), and an article titled "Coming Out and Going Home," published in *Qualitative Inquiry* (Tillmann 2010; used with permission, Sage Publications: http://qix.sagepub.com/content/16/2/116.abstract). Portions of this chapter were presented at the 2008 meetings of the National Communication Association. Doug Healy and Dave Dietz shot the images in this chapter, whose webpage may be found at: http://www.insolidaritybook.com/passing. html.

2 See Tillmann-Healy (1998).

3 See Tillmann-Healy (2001).

4 Heteronormativity equates heterosexuality with normalcy and defines all other sexualities as deviant.

5 See Cottle (2000, 229).

6 See Vanderstaay (2005, 406).

7 See the Appendix and Tillmann-Healy (1998, 2001, 2003).

References

Albom, Mitch. *Tuesdays with Morrie: An Old Man, a Young Man, and Life's Greatest Lesson.* New York: Bantam Books, 2002.

Cottle, Thomas J. "Mind Shadows: A Suicide in the Family." *Journal of Contemporary Ethnography* 29, no. 2 (2000): 222–255.

Pallone, Dave, with Alan Steinberg. *Behind the Mask: My Double Life in Baseball.* New York: Viking, 1990.

Tillmann, Lisa M. "Coming Out and Going Home: A Family Ethnography." *Qualitative Inquiry* 16, no. 2 (2010): 116–129.

Tillmann-Healy, Lisa M. *Life Projects: A Narrative Ethnography of Gay-Straight Friendship.* Ph.D. diss., University of South Florida, 1998.

——. *Between Gay and Straight: Understanding Friendship across Sexual Orientation.* Walnut Creek, CA: AltaMira Press, 2001.

——. "Friendship as Method." *Qualitative Inquiry* 9 (2003): 729–749.

Vanderstaay, Steven L. "One Hundred Dollars and a Dead Man: Ethical Decision Making in Ethnographic Fieldwork." *Journal of Contemporary Ethnography* 34, no. 4 (2005): 371–409.

4
REVISITING DON/OVAN[1]

A note about voice: the first-person voices of the sections to follow belong to the study's participants.[2] Donovan narrates the opening and closing sections.

My friend Stacy got married in 2002. For singing at the wedding, she gave me *Between Gay and Straight*, a book written by a graduate of Lincoln High School in Lake City, Minnesota, where I grew up. Blown away by the journey described, I felt touched by the author's openness to and unconditional love for her gay male friends and proud that she came from my small, rural hometown.

In the first chapter, "Before," the author chronicles experiences from the 1980s that show the silences around same-sex orientation and the heterosexism she witnessed and, in some cases, enacted. How surreal to see a straight person describe Lake City—and herself—in these terms! As I read, I kept trying to place her. "Lisa Tillmann. I know that name; I *know* that name." "Before" includes a scene called "Something in Common," about a crush the author had on a guy named Dev, someone rumored to be gay. *In Lake City?* I thought.

On February 7, 2003, I sent an email to the address provided in the book to thank the author for writing it and to introduce myself, Donovan Marshall. I told her that I came out near the end of my senior year, quit school abruptly, and left town, just shy of graduation in 1986.

The response stunned me! Lisa had not known me as Donovan, but she had known *Don* Marshall, the boy I was in high school. She remembered me from track, choir, and theater. In 1985, Lisa reminded me, she had been the youngest cast member in the school's one-act play, *That's It, Folks*; I played Otis, a satanic bartender. Lisa also remembered my younger brother and my father, then a janitor at the high school. I explained that my folks now owned a vineyard on the edge of town and that I had returned to Lake City to help them manage it and to live with my partner since 1997, Jackson Jones.

She informed me of her follow-up project, *Going Home*, collaborations with gay men that involved traveling to important sites and interviewing family members. Lisa indicated that each of her participants now lived more than a thousand miles from where he came of age. She wondered if I might be interested in exploring my experience of living in, leaving, and returning to Lake City. I was totally interested!

Lisa asked me to check with Jackson, my parents, and my brother to find out if anyone would consent to be interviewed. My parents signed on immediately. I'm not yet sure if my brother will participate. With a hawk-like protectiveness, he prefers not to expose the family to outsiders.

Similarly private, Jackson expressed reservations. Raised in the small town of Three Rivers, Minnesota, Jackson suffered constant harassment throughout his school years and was assaulted in a gay bashing near his college campus. Life for us in Lake City, population 5,300, had been quiet. Jackson wondered, *What might the project stir up?* Though I am fully committed to this work, I also have fears. How many people in Lake City will see the published work? Will we encounter backlash?

Lisa and I scheduled our reunion for September 2005. Her husband Doug joined her for the first part of the trip. Jackson and I agreed to meet them for breakfast in Lake City on Wednesday the 21st, the first time I would see Lisa in 19 years. Walking up to the Galley restaurant, Jackson asked how I would know them. I reminded him that the Galley's midmorning clientele skewed retired. I surmised that Lisa and Doug would be the hippest couple in the diner. Later, I learned that Lisa and Doug came to a parallel conclusion about how to spot Jackson and me. Lisa and I made eye contact. She and Doug stood up and stepped away from the table. Like an old friend, Lisa hugged me, then

Figure 4.1 Donovan Marshall and Lisa Tillmann.

Jackson. I don't recall the details of our conversation, only that it flowed freely and we laughed a lot.

That weekend, Lisa brought her videographer, Dave Dietz, to Lake City. We spent Saturday shooting footage at Jackson's and my home, Bluff View Elementary, Roschen Park, St. Mark's Church, and Lincoln High. On Sunday, Lisa conducted a "life history interview" (her words) on our deck. That afternoon, she spoke with my father in the vineyard and my mom at their house.

During our session, Lisa revealed that the person she called Dev in her book had, in fact, been me. That scene did feel familiar: an autumn night, an old car, a kiss between 14-year-old Lisa and an older boy whose sexual orientation others questioned. While reading, I dismissed my initial reaction: *Could this be me?* I am famous for thinking, *"It's all about me."* But apparently, sometimes it really IS!

Lisa let me know that, to create the first draft of "Revisiting Don/ovan," she drew from seven hours of video-recorded footage, from a transcript of her audio-recorded session with Jackson and me, and from field notes of her trip to Lake City. To center my experiences, Lisa wrote the opening of this piece as first-person vignettes in my voice. Next appears what she calls a "dialogic poem" featuring the voices of my parents, Barb and John Marshall. This she compiled from reflections each offered in a separate interview. A single-voiced poem from Jackson's standpoint follows. Lisa closes the piece by portraying a "focus group session" she facilitated in April 2006 with my parents, Jackson, and me.

The Beginning

Lisa asked me to "begin at the beginning." I was born in St. Paul in 1968. We lived on Londin Lane, site of my happiest childhood memories. Our house sat on a seven-acre hobby farm complete with apple orchard, barn, and chicken coop. We had horses, cows, a pig, rabbits, a dog, and like 16 cats.

I'm a lot like my mom, Barb Marshall. Fun, energetic, she could be a Carol Burnett or Lucille Ball. Many talents, especially musical. She'll see somebody playing a mandolin, get her own, and learn to play. Then she moves on to something else: "Oh, I should have a banjo."

On my mom's side, I have cousins who are like my brother and sister. Years ago, I periodically would pack up my life and move 1,000, 2,000 miles away. As much as I loved living on the west coast and in D.C., I would get so homesick for family that I'd end up moving back.

John Marshall, my dad, is the only surviving member of his immediate family. His mother died young, leaving him and his sister Judy in the care of their strict, stern father. Both my grandfather and my Auntie Judy have been gone many years now.

John is not my biological father; that guy left when I was two. Mom and I lived on our own for a little while, then she met John. They got married, and he adopted me. John is the only dad I remember, the only dad I know, so he is my *dad*.

I have a mixed ethnic heritage: Irish, French, German, Polish, and a little Native American. I don't know my birth father's ethnicity. Based on his last name, I would guess it's German.[3]

Early on, Mom told me that if I wanted to meet my birth father, she would bring me to him when I turned 16. A very emotional meeting.

He started crying and apologizing. We spent the afternoon together and kept in periodic contact. At 18, I saw him again and disclosed that I was gay. He had no problem with it. We maintained a connection, but at some point, I said to myself, *I have a father; I don't need a second family.* I haven't spoken to him in years. Lately I've been wanting to, because I heard he's not doing well health-wise, and because he has three other children. Two of them I've seen only once; one I've never met. I look at old photos of my biological father, and we could be twins. I would love to see my half-brother and my two half-sisters—if anything, just to know what they look like. But I don't want to disrupt their lives; they may not even *know* about me.

I was five when my brother, John's biological son, was born. We became constant and sometimes wild playmates. I remember the occasional flying ski pole and butter knife! We were each other's best friend. Even today, I do not consider him my *half*-brother; he is my *brother*.

The New Kid

My dad got a job in Lake City in the middle of my fifth-grade year. I was devastated, traumatized, ripped out of my comfort zone and thrown into a small town. Everybody knew everybody. The other kids were like family; their *parents* had gone to school together. I felt like the new kid for years.

As far as my orientation, nobody discussed it—this was the late '70s— but I always knew. Second grade, I had a crush on a sixth grader who resembled Leif Garrett, and of course, I was totally into Shaun Cassidy and Parker Stevenson, the Hardy Boys. Not so much sexual (I hadn't gone through puberty), just: *I really like them.* Other guys were all about Farrah Fawcett. I dug Farrah too, but for a different reason: fabulous hair!

In St. Paul, I'd gone to Lutheran school. Thirty-two kids in my class. I had my niche; my cousins went there. Coming to Lake City, I wondered, *Will they figure out who I really am?* I knew others would see that part of me as different, but to me, it simply *was*. I've always been comfortable with my sexuality.

Running, Rising, Falling

Lisa asked for a tour of key sites from my past, so I drove us to the school track. My dad recalls my sprinting—the 100, the 200, the 4x100 relay—but the long and triple jumps were my main events. In eighth grade, I placed first in region and made varsity. Two nights before my sophomore year district championship, I took a practice jump, thinking the pit had been raked. My foot caught a divot, snapped up and under. I tore everything in my ankle and spent two-and-a-half months in a cast. Doctors told me I'd never walk the same again. Also a competitive swimmer, I headed straight to the pool as soon as the cast came off. The next year, I went to state in triple jump.

Though I had locker room crushes (older guys, athletic guys, *naked* guys), track was never really sexual. The experience centered more on the physicality, the team bonding, the total acceptance I felt.

If not for track, theater, and singing . . . I don't know. I don't know if I would be here. I was a cutter, a self-mutilator, in high school. You still can see the scars. It always happened between: between track and swimming, between the one-act and all-school plays, between the holiday and spring concerts. I felt as if others' approval hinged on my performance in track, my portrayal of a character, my rendition of a song.

Watching friends cycle through crushes, dating, and breaking up, I felt desperate to experience that. Boy/boy *sex* was available, even in this small town. I had sex for the first time in the summer between fifth and sixth grades. But those occasional encounters *never* involved intimacy, never even kissing. You get hot, you get off, and: "What about that history test tomorrow?" Then you pretend it never happened.

I had a lot of friends, wonderful friends, but I felt completely alone. The pain sometimes cut so deep that I would slash myself with a razor blade. I would see the blood and feel the stinging release. I could channel the agony from my heart into visible, physical pain.

A Source of Comfort

I drive past St. Mark's Church all the time, but until Lisa's visit, I hadn't even walked the grounds since I left Lake City at age 18. I was baptized

Figure 4.2 Donovan Marshall and Lisa Tillmann.

Catholic, raised Lutheran, and confirmed Episcopalian. Choir, Sunday school, church camp. Small community, small congregation—always a source of comfort.

After my confirmation, the priest invited me to become a lay reader. Ordained by the bishop, I could conduct non-communion prayer services. Ladies in the church said I should consider seminary. One Sunday, I was 16 or 17, while giving the sermon I realized: *It's just like being on stage.* People watch me, praise me—and *that's* the pull. I sat down with my parents. "I can't do this anymore. Spirituality, not self-fulfillment, should inspire service to the church."

That experience led me to question my faith. I began reading about world religions as well as energy, crystals, goddesses, paganism, Wicca. I came to draw a bit from each of those.

I go to church on holidays with my parents. Over the years, there have been times when I considered attending more regularly. Part of me aches for that sense of belonging in a church family, but another part recoils from church politics. My coming out sent shock waves through St. Mark's.

"At the Height of It All"

Around ninth grade, emotions began to boil. Everything felt raw. My dad and I constantly butted heads: hair, clothes, music. I didn't know my "real dad" at all, but I would lash out at John: "My biological father wouldn't treat me like this!" We drove my mom crazy.

Senior year, everything fell apart. I started closet drinking, even at school. I would steal alcohol if necessary. When my grandmother passed away, I took tranquilizers from her medicine cabinet.

At the height of it all, drunk and stoned on pills, I went back to my locker and cut myself on both wrists. Blood all over the floor. Olivia O'Connor, my sweet, timid classmate, passed by, eyes wide. In front of her, I took the razor blade and again sliced my wrist. Friends dragged me kicking and screaming to the counselor's office. Someone notified my parents. In the car on the way home, Mom chided, "I can't believe you did this to us. So embarrassing!" I thought, *Can't you see that I hurt? Help me. Listen to me.*

There Are Other People

Every time I pass Roschen Park, I think of Mr. Pratt, who suggested we meet there one afternoon. I had known Mr. Pratt for many years; he worked in Lake City. Mr. Pratt said that he and his *partner* had lived together for a long time in a neighboring small town. They weren't out, though I had heard speculation. As he talked, this feeling came over me: *It will be okay. There are other people.* Very, very powerful.

Coming Out/Dropping Out

Never internal, my struggle to come out centered on others. Will I be accepted? Will my family still love me? You didn't hear much about being gay back then. You didn't have gay average Joe living next door. You saw how they portrayed it on TV (if at all): effeminate, flamboyant, promiscuous. I thought, *How am I going to fit into that? That's not me at all.* I had strong moral and family backgrounds. I didn't want to sleep around. I wanted one partner, a home, kids.

I began telling female friends in seventh or eighth grade. I didn't say "gay"; I said, "I really like this guy. No, I mean I *really* like this guy." Senior year, I told a male classmate. He was totally cool about it.

Figure 4.3 Donovan Marshall.

I regret that I came out to my parents in anger. My mom listened in on a phone conversation with Scott, who became my first boyfriend. When she confronted me, I fired, "Yes, I'm gay, and there's nothing you can do about it!" My parents said they had no problem with me, but I couldn't date a guy while living under their roof.

I had dated girls in high school. Thank god, back in the '80s, you weren't expected to have sex with everybody you took to the movies. I connected with girls, but when I met Scott, I recognized my first chance for a real relationship.

All forces converged: in love, not speaking to my parents, and finishing high school. I can't say for sure how everything went down. All I know is that it felt like I came into school one day, everybody staring, nobody talking to me. Total alienation.

I decided that day. Went to the school office and said, "I want to drop out." Fourth quarter, senior year, just about to graduate top of the B honor roll. One administrator, Ms. Allen, replied, "Okay. Your teachers need to sign this drop slip." Great support, right? When I appeared outside his door, my English teacher stopped class, pulled me aside, and said, "You have a bright future. You're better than this." I made the rounds and went back to Ms. Allen. "Nobody would sign." "Not a problem," she told me. Boom, boom, boom. Ten minutes later, out of high school.

I do beat myself up about that. So close! I received scholarship offers from the U of M Duluth and Viterbo University. UCLA expressed interest for track and swimming.

A degree I would pursue now: psychology. The best therapists have "been there, done that." I would counsel gay youth. The suicide rate breaks my heart. Every day, young people kill themselves, and folks around them say, "We can't imagine why!" The majority of gay people I know have experienced a level of pain that culminated in a brush with suicide or a problem with alcohol and/or drugs.

Leaving

Another one-day decision: leaving home. My parents had gone out. I sat down with my brother, then in seventh grade, and said, "I can't deal with this." Didn't speak to my family for a year. I thought, *You can't fully accept me? That's it.*

I moved to Rochester and lived with my friend, Tammy. She helped me stop the self-mutilation. Home drinking one afternoon, I cut myself. Tammy found me and slapped me up verbally, saying, "Enough! Your life is not that bad." Tammy and the city became my hub for the next ten years. I would relocate to far-flung places, then back to Rochester.

The early years in Rochester also centered around Scott, my first boyfriend, whom I grew to love deeply. Three years into our relationship, and five years older than I, Scott wanted to settle down. Coming out of Lake City, I needed to see and experience more, so I ventured to San Francisco. The scene there turned me off. It's a long way from Rochester to the Castro!

Eventually, I made my way to Minneapolis. Took courses through the U of M to get my GED but never finished. A closed chapter; time to go on.

Reconnecting

Over the years, I came to appreciate and understand my dad. Serving in Vietnam messed him up emotionally. Never talked about it. He wrote a book but kept it from my brother and me. When I finally read the book, I saw him so much more clearly. We started talking on an adult level. One day, we saw each other as . . . friends. We respected each other. We left the past behind. Now we hug every day. A different man, he laughs all the time. He's very loving.

My brother has undergone his own transformation, from wild young man to husband, father, provider. He remains intense and passionate, like our dad, especially about family. Beyond seeing each other at holidays and "How you doin'?" we didn't speak for a long time. Finally he shared how deeply my leaving had pained and angered him, not only because his brother abandoned him, but also because he paid the public consequences. While I embarked on a new life, he went through small town junior high and high school being teased about my identity. I think both of us would like to be even closer, but we're very different. We love each other so much, and we do talk, but we have our own lives now. Also, there still may be unresolved issues. I'm not sure his wounds have healed fully. I don't know how my brother will react when he sees all of this. Very open, he tells everyone that his brother lives with a partner. His protectiveness may come out. He won't fear backlash for himself. He'll worry about me, about Jackson.

Bumpa

My extended family never had a problem with me being gay. Early on, I invited a boyfriend home for Thanksgiving. My grandpa, Bumpa, took him aside: "What are your intentions? If you're not good to my grandson, you'll have to deal with me." Fantastic!

Lisa asked about "turning point experiences" in my family, and the details surrounding Bumpa's death in 1995 came rushing back. Though our life history sessions called up many painful memories, I broke down only once during Lisa's visit, while telling her of losing Bumpa.

Figure 4.4 Donovan Marshall.

After his quadruple bypass, we learned he had cancer. Beat it once, but when the cancer came back, Bumpa said, "No more chemo. I've lived a full life." He got sicker and sicker, and they brought him home. Every other family member had gone to Forest Lake and said goodbye. I couldn't do it. He held on, and he held on, and he held on. Finally, my mom insisted, "You *have* to go."

I made the trip and entered the bedroom where he lay dying, totally emaciated, curled up in the fetal position. I sat down and took his hand. Crying, I told my grandma I didn't know what to say. She said, "Honey, he just needs you here." When Bumpa died the next day, I felt like I couldn't breathe.

Jackson

Before I met Jackson, I'd taken a year off from dating. I lived in Rochester with my best friend, Sue. Her closest friend from college was Jackson's best friend, Lana. Those two girls had been scheming. They arranged a meeting at the Smiling Moose, where I later bartended. I told Sue, "If he comes in, and I feel no vibe, stay there, sitting between us. If I'm interested, we'll switch places." I saw Jackson walk in: Mr. Boy Toy, Ken Doll, 90210. "Switch places! Switch places!"

Qualities that define Jackson: devoted, patient, loving, open, accepting. Very lighthearted. A catchphrase of ours: "I can still make you laugh after all these years." He understands when I need him and when I need to be alone. I trust Jackson completely. I am more myself with him than I've ever been with anyone.

Many challenges of our relationship stem from my self-centeredness: "It's all about me." Like any couple, we've had our major fights, but we always make it through because we know that we want to be together forever. I can't see myself without him. He is my best friend.

Return

Jackson and I had a place in Burnsville. Living in the city, and especially my working in a bar, made for crazy times. I knew every server in Uptown. Free drinks every night, everywhere we went. After partying, Jackson and I would have these "white trash fights" (Lisa bristles at the term, but that's what we called them): high volume, high drama followed by hangovers and hazy recollections. Eventually, we felt ready for a change.

By this time, my parents had bought the vineyard and offered me a part-time job. I worried about Jackson's transition from the Twin Cities to a small town. He had a flood of bad memories from Three Rivers. Would this feel like treading back into those waters? We talked long and hard before deciding to move.

I planned to supplement work at the vineyard by commuting to Uptown a couple nights a week. Then the Smiling Moose closed with no notice. My parents generously hired me full time. The nursery is *very* hard work. In the dead of winter, you'll find me in the snow-covered fields, pruning stock and grooving to my favorite tunes. Never expected I would fall into this, but I really enjoy it.

The return felt comfortable. Jackson and I had been together five years. Because I came out at such a young age, when I returned to Lake City, it wasn't like, "How are we going to explain it?"

Jackson and I like seeing familiar faces at the grocery store. People know us as a couple. Never had any problem here. I can't think of anything in Lake City that undermines our relationship. Lake City is small town but not small town. I see this place as green, growing, accepting. It's got a great energy. I think we'll be here a long time.

Biggest highlight recently: buying a house. Even dealing with the realtor and loan officer was a non-issue. They weren't aloof, and they didn't tiptoe around or go overboard to show their acceptance.

I'm happy with our life. My family loves Jackson intensely, *intensely*. Our families have become close; that's very, very important to me.

Emerging Politics

For a long time, I didn't get involved. Didn't know anything, and I never talked politics. Didn't even vote until 2004, so who was I to condemn the president or governor? Then I joined the Human Rights Campaign, started getting newsletters and action alerts. In 2004, Jackson and I marched with our parents on the capitol in support of same-sex unions and against a proposed amendment to the state constitution.

I don't know enough yet about the parties to label myself a Democrat. Definitely not a Republican. No Bush for me!

Though I'm angered by anti-gay, so-called Christians, I saw the backlash coming. Queer Nation and ACT UP made headlines just as I was coming out. Perhaps their tactics were necessary to get AIDS on the national agenda, but kiss-ins? Did those really change anyone's mind? Let people digest. Be out in your neighborhoods. Let people see you on a day-to-day basis. I have hope that the climate will get better.

"If Only We Could Have Talked about It"

I passed on my five- and ten-year class reunions. *Too soon*, I thought. When the 15-year came along in 2001: *Okay, I'm in a secure, loving relationship. Ready to go back.*

Terrified to walk in, I assumed that certain people would be uncomfortable; maybe they wouldn't even talk to me. But everyone seemed genuinely excited to see me, and they welcomed Jackson as much as anyone's spouse. I asked, "What happened after I came out and left school?" They said, "We missed you and wanted to graduate with you."

The reunion normalized the experience of feeling separate, which can stem from almost anything: skin color, acne, body size, being an effeminate guy or an athletic butch girl. What differentiates being gay is lack of visibility and the ways you closet yourself. I got into conversations: "How did you see your high school years? Mine sucked." "Oh my god," I heard, "mine too!" I found out that some people believed *I* had the charmed life. I realized that I wasn't the outsider that I thought I was. All of us felt the same things, only about different issues. We were *all* confused, sad, lonely, and angry—if only we could have talked about it.

Synchronicity

After the first day of interviews, Jackson, Lisa, cameraman Dave, and I had dinner. At Bronk's restaurant, our table was approached by someone who graduated from Lincoln a few years before I would have, someone who also returned to live in Lake City. He'd seen us filming by the high school and asked Lisa about it. She deferred to me. Though I appreciated the respect Lisa showed, I had almost no hesitation telling him about the project. I did wonder how he would handle it, but what's the alternative to being open?

I once ran into another Lincoln grad at Minneapolis Pride. Blood drained from his face when he recognized me. I asked how he maintained his double life. "Total separation," he told me. I can't imagine living like that.

People either will like me or they won't. If they dislike me for that reason, their loss. I've been down this road many times. All my life, I associated mainly with straight people. In Burnsville, Jackson and I had very few gay friends—not by choice, just how things worked out.

In many cases, we've been the first openly gay couple our straight friends have known, so they ask a lot of questions. In one sense, great; we all need to learn. But for a long time, that was all they wanted to talk about. You know what? Sexuality is a small part of my life. I'm a lot of other things; *we're* a lot of other things. I don't want to talk about being gay all the time.

I really valued Lisa's approach to the project. She sought the full scope, the depth, not just about gay issues but about my whole life, my family, my feelings.

For me, this process reflects, in a word, synchronicity. There is a reason Lisa and I crossed paths in high school, a reason we reconnected, and a reason for doing this work together. At first, I just wanted to be part of something that might promote acceptance and understanding. I didn't realize that talking about my past would be so therapeutic. This has helped me to see the good things about my past and to heal and grow from all the pain. I wonder how it might do the same for my family, especially my dad. Over the years, our relationship has become so open and loving. I don't know how he will feel about calling up the tension and strain we endured, especially when I was in high school and when I first came out.

As Lisa and I have revisited my past, I've been thinking about the relationship between Donovan, the man I am now, and Don, the boy who grew up in Lake City, who clashed with his father, who felt so alone he cut his wrists, who tried to numb the pain with alcohol and drugs, who abandoned his education and his family. I've been reflecting on Don—not *myself* as Don, but Don, the boy over there. I still feel detached from him. Lisa says she wonders if this project will more fully integrate Don into Donovan. I guess we'll see.

"A Stepping Stone":
Barb Marshall[4]

Figure 4.5
Barb Marshall.

"A Great Blessing":
John Marshall

Figure 4.6
John Marshall.

I was born in St. Paul, May 12, 1945. My family came from the east, Pennsylvania and Nova Scotia.

I was born in St. Paul, 1947. I grew up there, various locations around the east side.

I went to grade school in East St. Paul.

Sheila Rawls: my grade school best friend. Fun and outgoing. We pitched fast pitch, elementary through ninth grade. Not a clue that she was gay. When I found out, no big deal.

Graduated from Harding High School in 1963.

I graduated from Harding. Drama and band all through high school.

I went to the University of Minnesota for one year. Wasn't ready for college. Way too immature at the time. Bored me stiff, frankly.

Registered for classes at the U of M. I planned to be a renegade: get women into the marching band and be a comedian on Carson. Instead, I got my tuition money back and bought a 1957 yellow Ford—the end of my formal education.

Joined the army for three-and-a-half years. I'm fortunate to be here. Vietnam showed me how

bad things can get. I know a lot
of guys who came back scarred,
feeling terrible. I have no regrets.
I went to Vietnam because I
believed communism was trying
to take over a defenseless country.

Basically worked in St. Paul,
various places, electronic assembly
mostly.

For years I played softball
with—I know now—a lot of gay
women. Because I was such a
tomboy, some people made
assumptions about me. I worked
at Thermal Options, and as it
turned out, one of my best
friends there was gay. Not
something I thought about until
my boss said, "She follows you
into the bathroom." So naïve at
age 18, I asked, "Why?" Duh!
That opened my eyes. I thought,
*Well, I really like her. Great sense of
humor.* I went to her desk and
said, "So, you're gay." She looked
at me. "Well, just say it right
out!" I said, "I *did.* So you are?"
"Yeah. I thought you knew." It
didn't make any difference.

I spent two-and-a-half years in
college in Colorado. Never
graduated. In the summer I
would work for my sister's
husband, who owned a
construction company. I learned
to be a carpenter and was being

groomed to become one of the owners.

I met my first husband in 1967. He was going out with some tramp. My girlfriend and I flipped a coin to see who would try to take him away from her. I don't know if I won or lost, but I ended up with him, and we got married. I guess I would call it winning, because without that, Don wouldn't be here.

Don was born on Groundhog Day. I went bowling the night before. I slipped and bounced, like three times. They said that's why he came three weeks early. A small baby: six pounds, 12 ounces. We called him Donny. The first grandchild. That's where "It's all about me" comes from. It was ALL about him!

I call it my "practice marriage," lasted three-and-a-half years. What can I say? Two Scorpios.

As things worked out, I met my wife back here in Minnesota. She was having trouble with her husband. Eventually their relationship broke up, so I became interested.

Don was two years old. As a young boy, he had a very unusual personality. He'd say stuff nobody else could think up. One time, Barb said that he could answer the phone. I thought he was too young. He goes over, picks it up, and says, "Whobody?" It just cracked me up!

Don kept everybody laughing with his comments. He didn't know he was funny. He came home from Sunday school: "Quinn tried to get me to do something not nice, and I said, 'Get thee behind me, Satan!'" In kindergarten, his teacher called me up. "Where did he learn words like 'ludicrous,' and how does he know how to use that?" That was Don, always animated and outgoing.

Growing up, he wasn't serious about anything of substance. His hair became enormously important. I would try to explain the superficiality. He would feel cut to the core. His values were so different from mine. We clashed all the time. I was way too hard on him. If I had it to do again, I'd just let him be who he was. I didn't appreciate that he had a very unconventional personality and a great sense of humor.

A drama queen—no pun intended—since day one. By four or five, he would put on a wig and make-up; anything to be the star of the show.

His best friends were always girls. He was athletic, but he didn't like team sports. Then again, neither did my other son. Yeah, I can look back at high school: the singing and the acting. There was always a hint, and I think Don knew a long time before that.

I didn't think he was gay, just rebellious, always wearing bizarre clothing and listening to music that I don't think he enjoyed, frankly.

It wasn't that big of a deal until a 35-year-old man called our house. I told him exactly what I thought and made Don hang up. I don't know if he remembers that or not. Don tends to block out unpleasant things.

It crossed my mind many times that he'd pull something like announcing, "I'm gay!" When that happened, I thought of it as just another stunt.

He always played the part. He would be whoever people thought he should be. That goes back to my ex-husband, to the rejection at age two. Don was very smart, very aware.

Counselors didn't help at all. They asked, "Does Don do drugs or alcohol?" I knew he smoked pot, but that wasn't the problem. He couldn't share anything. He was crying out for help—but not from Mom and Dad. He would stay in his room for two, three days at a time.

His pattern of deceit led us to counseling. The counselor suggested a contract. Seemed like a good idea, so we wrote one. He stomped on that the very next day; he did every single thing we asked him not to do—the very next day! At that point, I realized it was hopeless. The alienation was complete.

He was in a play at school. I don't know if we've ever talked about this. It was very traumatic. His character had blood on his shirt. Unbeknownst to us, Don actually had cut his wrists. He didn't know how else to deal with his pain. A classmate went to the Catholic priest. He contacted our priest, who called us and said, "Don has drugs and booze at school, and his wrists are all cut up." I went to his room, and he had a suicide note with blood on it and almost the exact words from the play. The gay part was never a problem for us. The problem was how Don struggled to cope.

He'd been going to Rochester, saying it was to see "a girl" or "some friends." We suspected that wasn't true. His mother confronted him. "It's a guy. He's my boyfriend. I'm gay."

I don't know if he ever said, "I'm gay." Did Don remember that? I must have blocked that out. I wonder where he gets that tendency.

He came out. Told everybody in a small town that he was gay. Adolescents just can't deal with that. They're insecure with their own sexuality. They harassed the devil out of him. Humiliated him. Harassed him right out of school. He quit, even though he had completed every requirement. He *had* graduated high school; he just didn't stay long enough. The kids drove him out, essentially. It's the saddest thing you can imagine. Maybe in a big city, it would have been different. I thought the school was at least neutral. Ms. Allen tried her damndest: "Keep your butt in that chair, and you'll graduate. Show up one day a week." But he couldn't bring himself to do it.

I worked at a gossipy local business when he quit school in '86. I did not want to make up stories. I told them, "Don is gay.

He came out in physics class. His friends have turned against him. He could have attended one day a week to graduate, but he quit school."

Many people came up to me after all this happened. Walking by the drug store, I felt an arm come around my shoulder. This person said, "Don't feel bad. My son left his wife for a stripper." Another person said, "Ha! That's no big deal. I got a brother who went from Harry to Hailey, and we all accept him/her."

Shortly after that, he left home. That was awful. We never had the choice of accepting or rejecting. Just like that—gone.

Don was angry at me, but he was angry at everybody then. He felt he had to get away.

I felt confused. That he would just walk out on us like that, just leave us behind. Weeks turned into months, and he made no attempt to get in touch with us.

But we were still in touch; we still talked.

Barb seems to recall being in touch with him from time to time. I remember *months* of not knowing where he was. Literally *years* of knowing very little.

A painful process. I think if Don hadn't run off like that, we

My younger son had a hard time with it. He got the backlash at school. He said, "Anytime anything was mentioned about gay, everybody looked at me like I was some authority on it."

Don went to "live the dream" in San Francisco. All I could see was a very naïve young man going into a very dangerous situation.

A week before Thanksgiving, I told my father, "Don is gay." Totally accepting.

could have dealt with it more quickly. He wasn't ready to do that; maybe we weren't either.

Eventually Don moved with some momentary boyfriend to San Francisco. Thought sure he'd get AIDS. It was awful. Terrible.

We always kept the door open. His grandfather, whom he thought a great deal of, wanted to get in touch, to let Don talk. "You and me are buddies. What you got to say?" His grandfather never had any problem with it.

From time to time, Don would show up dressed in outlandish gay clothing. We wouldn't have conversations; he'd just be there. I think he expected us to moralize. We never did—never *would*, frankly. Some people *are* gay. When the family would get together for holidays, he always received an invitation. After a while, he started to come.

We brought a gay friend of Don's—it could have been the next Christmas—to my parents' place. This young man's family would not allow him home because he was gay. I never thought to call my dad and stepmother beforehand. They put another plate on the table, Evie played the organ, and we sang Christmas carols. The gay Norman Rockwell!

He slowly realized that it wasn't going to be a problem being part of the family again. Little by little, the wounds healed. They're not totally healed, though it may seem that way to the eye. As I said, I regret being so hard on him.

We introduced Jackson to the family at Easter. Probably 24 people in the living room. After the blessing, I said, "Oh, by the way, we have someone new here: Don's boyfriend Jackson from Three Rivers." Everybody began to eat. I heard: "Oh, Three Rivers. Remember that vacation we took?" But poor Jackson, white as a ghost, sat hyper-ventilating, like someone should give him a bag. He didn't know

what to make of it, but that's
how the family accepted it. And
everybody just loves Jackson now.

Having a gay son absolutely
has enhanced my life. If Don
wasn't gay, we wouldn't know
Jackson and Jackson's family.
What would we do without
Jackson? Oh goodness, he's a
stitch. He's very loving, very
affectionate.

The biggest surprise to date is
the way Lake City has accepted
Don and Jackson. That astonishes
me. No harassment, no
machismo. According to Jackson,
if they were up in Three Rivers,
they would not be living this
lifestyle. But Lake City feels
almost like *we* feel about it, like
what's the big deal? What *is* the
big deal?

Don and Jackson complement
each other remarkably. What
would you call it? Symbiotic.
Don's weaknesses are Jackson's
strengths. I find Jackson
meticulous, self-disciplined,
mature.

Those two are perfect for each
other. I'm very lucky. I have two
wonderful sons, a daughter-in-
law, and a son-in-law. I couldn't
have handpicked a better partner
for Don.

My life is an open book: "This is my son Don and his boyfriend Jackson." Any negativity that comes in, I send it back. Send it back positive.

His mother makes a point of saying, "Don and his boyfriend Jackson." I usually don't do that. If it comes up, I'll say, "Yeah, they're gay." If it doesn't, I let it pass. People have asked me, "If you could make him heterosexual, would you?" I say, "*He* doesn't want to be heterosexual, so why would I even enter into that?" I know at St. Mark's they were talking about the fact that Don had come out.

I practice Reiki, and that's helped me respond to negativity. When word got out that Don was gay, folks at St. Mark's immediately assumed that he had AIDS. "He cannot take communion anymore. No more communal cup." I had it out with them.

The deacon told them, "Well, the *other* gay people in this community don't feel that way." "Really?" the church gossips responded. "Who would they be?" Like we're looking for communists.

On a personal level, having Don and Jackson here has been

wonderful, a great blessing. We get to see them all the time.

Since working together, we've become a great deal closer, and we understand each other a great deal better. Don has so much ability. He's very talented.

When I think of Don, the first word that comes to mind is compassion. Awareness of other people and how they feel.

A lot smarter than he gives himself credit for, Don never feels like he's proven himself. I'm as proud of him as I can be. But he's always struggling to feel good enough, even though he's much better than virtually anybody I know at most things. Much better at most everything than *I* am.

Did he tell you that we don't use Donald Wayne anymore, that it's Donovan John?

I still can't call him Donovan, frankly. To me, he's Don. He accepts the fact that I got to call him Don. I don't think he'd know what to make of it if I started calling him Donovan.

Donald Wayne was a different person than Donovan John is.

My advice? If you have a gay child, accept that fact. It's not that big a deal. It seems like it's going to be because society has

engrained us with that. Now it
just seems like a very normal part
of life. I hope that the project will
help parents accept their children
and gay people to accept
themselves.

This project is a stepping
stone. My hope is that someday
Don can walk down the street
and hold Jackson's hand.

"It's Not My Whole Life":
Jackson Jones

I was born in northern Minnesota.
  My family lived outside of town.
  We had a river running through our backyard.
  I would take nature walks, blaze cross-country ski trails,
    snow-shoe, swim, fish
—the whole bit.

"Close-knit family" is probably an understatement.
  What more do you need to know:
    we're in the middle of the woods;
        three generations of family as neighbors?
  At the same time, it's not like a . . .
cult.

I'm basically Polack and Svede.
  We went to see my great grandma in the nursing home;
    I was probably five.
  First words out of her mouth: "Now, ooo 'er yew?"
  "I'm Jackson." "*Yack*son ooo?"
  "I'm Jenny's son." "Oh, yer
*Yen*ny's son!"

Confirmed Lutheran
    and haven't been to church much since.
    Religiously, like Donovan, I will pull a bit from
everything.

One older sister.
    I followed in her footsteps: swimming, track.
    Always there for me if I need her.
    We call each other for major life issues
        and every Thursday during *Survivor*.
    She had my nephew;
        that's been a joy
for Donovan and me.

My mom taught elementary school.
    Did everything for those kids,
        would put in her own money
            for things they needed.
    She's very much the caretaker
of the whole family.

Dad was a union rep, gone a lot.
    Standoffish in my childhood.
    Not so emotionally attached.
    When I went to college, it was a big deal
        for my dad to hug me goodbye.
    As with Donovan and his dad,
        we became closer and closer over the years.
    Now the hugs, the "I love you"s are just . . .
natural.

In my hometown, kids called me "gay," "queer."
　　Walking the halls, I'd get that the whole time.
　　Every day.
　　Beginning in sixth grade,
　　　　I would count the days
　　　　　　until the school year was
over.

Middle school seemed like it would be better.
　　I was making all these friends.
　　Then one guy started it
all over again.

Somebody came to our house
　　—I was probably 15—
　　　　and wrote "fag"
　　　　　　in shaving cream
　　　　　　　　underneath my window.
　　When I cleaned it,
it took the paint off our house.

For prom, we submitted predictions for classmates:
　　what they would be doing in 10 years.
　　These were read aloud.
　　They came to my name . . .
　　　　and skipped it.
　　Weird, because everybody was on the list.
　　Years later, I found out that everything
　　　　that had come in about me
　　　　　　was bad.
　　And so, rather than make up something,
they skipped my name.

I kept all this from my parents and sister.
   I'd take my walk in the woods
      and vent.
   When I finally had a breakdown in high school
      my mom was heartbroken
         that I hadn't shared those feelings,
those problems.

I do think all this made me stronger.
   At a high school dance,
      one of the harassers came in and yelled,
         from one end of the cafeteria to the other,
            "Jackson, are you gay?"
   Before I could stop, it came out:
      "No, but I'm sure if you keep looking,
         you'll find one to suit your tastes."
   That was really the first time
      I bucked back.
   Normally, I'd just ignore them.
   That was how Mom raised me:
      "Ignore them, and they'll go away."
   Well, they weren't
going away.

I ran into another harasser after my first year of college.
   For some reason, he showed up at my workplace.
   He's like, "Hey, Jackson. How's it goin'?"
   It was all I could do not to say,
      "Fuck you"
         and punch him.
   I looked him straight in the eye. "You know what?
   I have absolutely nothing to say to you;
      you made my life
         a living hell."
   I turned around
and walked away.

Once out of high school, I wanted no contact
    with the people
        or that town.
    Years later, I got a call.
    "They're going to tear down our school.
    I'm in charge of contacting former students
        and asking them to come for a reunion."
    I said, "I have *no* interest
whatsoever."

Donovan has said that when people refer to him as "Don,"
    it brings him back.
    I have the same thing, because some people
        —being that I'm Jackson Jones—
        used to call me J.J.
    Whenever I hear that, I immediately will be like,
"*Noooo.*"

Prior to college, I thought of *gays* the same way
    many up-North people did.
    I didn't kiss a man full-on until age 20.
    I *wanted* to,
        but the first time,
            I found it almost
repulsive.

I dated girls, even into college.
    While coming out, I actually had a girlfriend.
    I finally reached that point where:
        "This is totally unfair to her."
    I was suicidal, I guess;
        I mean, I was ready to jump off a bridge,
you know?

I hadn't planned to come out to my parents when I did.
   It would have been right before I turned 21.
   They called me at college
      and asked where I'd spend the summer.
   "With Peter and Terry";
      I explained that they were together.
   My mom's like, "What do you mean 'together'?"
   "They're gay."
   She said, "You'll be guilty by association."
   My dad piped up: "That's not something
      you can see *yourself* doing,
         is it?"
   At that point, I was coming out to all my friends,
      so I just said, "Yeah, it is;
         I am gay."
   Mom started crying,
      couldn't really talk anymore.
   Dad didn't say a whole lot.
   And the phone call
was over.

I called my dad the next day.
   He said, "Come home so I can set up an appointment;
      we need to get you in for counseling."
   "Dad, for one time in my life,
      I *don't* need counseling;
         I think I've finally gotten it
together."

They've come through like troopers.
    I think it helped both of them to get involved.
    Mom went to a couple PFLAG meetings,
        met some other parents.
    They've even marched with us.
    My dad, the union rep, had signs ready
        —further than *I* go with it, almost like,
          "Pull back a little here;
            you're overdoing."
    At one march we turned around.
    A former student came running up to my mom:
        "Mrs. Jones?!"
    He burst into tears.
    That was a big, big step for my mom
        —just to see that her son's
not the only one.

When I first came out
    my mom had to face the things
        that I'd been facing.
    She would be in the back room with all the teachers,
        and someone would crack a gay joke.
    My mom would get furious
        but wouldn't say anything;
          she'd walk out.
    Eventually, she started saying,
        "I don't appreciate that."
    Now, she's like, "Yeah, my son's gay."
Point blank.

My mom had a gal from our church pestering her:
    "So what's Jackson doing?
    Is he dating anyone?
    Is he dating anyone?"
    "Yeah, a *boyfriend*
—since 1997!"

I went to college in Wisconsin.
    Was in the main choir and the chamber singers;
        I could sight-read like no tomorrow.
    Degree in biology; that's the nature boy in me.
    After college, the best pay I could find in my field,
        medical research,
        was about eight bucks an hour.
    I took the first job offered that paid over ten an hour
        and have worked my way up ever since.
    I design webpages and work from home
        —where else can you get a smoke break
right at your desk?

Lana and Sue had been trying to set up Donovan and me.
    We both figured: it's the two straight girls
        who know exactly one gay guy.
    "So they must be *perfect* for each other!!"
    One night, Lana said, "We're going to the Moose to see Sue.
        Donovan's there too,
            and he's single."
    I'm like, "Oh, god! Do I need to go home
        and try to look pretty?"
    But then I thought, "Screw it.
    Let's see what the guy's all about."
    We walked in,
        I saw Donovan,
            and that was pretty much
it.

Outgoing, always laughing, always pleasant:
    those were the main things that attracted me, I think.
    Not that he wasn't pretty,
        but it was mainly personality,
            the public display of "holy buckets,
               here he goes
again."

Donovan's and my coming out journeys
   are pretty different.
   One of the primary differences:
      I got gay bashed in college.
   Hanging out with a friend at a bar,
      I heard someone in the back:
         "That guy over there
            is a fag."
   I ignored it;
      he got louder and louder.
   I'm like, "Let's head out."
   We got about a block down.
   Behind me, I heard,
      "Hey!"
   As I turned around, I got sucker punched by,
      I later learned, one of the football players.
   My glasses went flying;
      I went down on the concrete.
   Five or six other guys stood there calling me names.
   The disempowering thing: there was no way
      I could have defended myself.
   It was just, "Hey!" Smack!
   All of a sudden,
      I'm the "fag" that got beat up.
   I ended up in the emergency room
      thinking I had a broken nose,
         blood gushing everywhere.
   We did track down the football player
      and took him to court.
   But my nose wasn't *technically* "broken"—
      the reason officials gave
         for charging the guy who assaulted me
            only with "disorderly conduct."
   I still have all that documentation filed away
somewhere.

Getting bashed changed my whole view of the world.
    Donovan is much more "Go for it."
    I'm more "Got to know the facts."
    I had just come out in college;
        everything was great;
            all my friends were still my friends.
    Then . . . smack!
    It made me realize that,
        no matter where I go, this could still
happen.

Moving to Lake City was scary at first.
    To me, small town life meant Three Rivers
        and the place I got bashed.
    I immediately thought: rednecks.
    Same kind of people,
same kind of views.

People in Lake City may know about us,
    but it's not in their face.
    A lot of people harbor feelings that you *don't* know about,
        you *don't* hear about,
            you *don't* see.
    Of course, after this project,
        a lot more people are going to know.
    What happens when Joe Schmuck down the street,
        who hates fags,
finds out about us?

I think the best outcome for this project
    is not to need this project.
    Just to have kids be who they are
        and not have to explain,
            not have to worry,
                not have to
hide.

This is like therapy!
    The project has made us step back and examine things
        that we haven't thought about for years
            and draw on the experiences that we've had since.
    You can look back and have a more grown-up approach
    versus this frightened kid
you once were.

Still, to be interviewed about being gay . . .
    to me, it's such a small part.
    It's weird to zoom in on it;
        it's not my whole life,
you know?

Family Meeting

The close of this chapter marks both endings and new beginnings. Shortly after Lisa's visit in September 2005, Jackson and I began talking seriously about our relationship. We had developed a dynamic similar to one I have had with my family: avoidance of underlying issues. A lot of emotions surfaced through our participation in this project. I don't think we initially saw our work with Lisa as a catalyst for change in our relationship, but it may have been. I came to understand that I had a lot of work to do on myself. Just before Thanksgiving, I moved from our home to my parents' place. At first, everything in my body pulled me back toward the relationship, but it now seems like both of us are the happiest we've been in a long time.

When I emailed her, Lisa responded with shock and sadness. I knew that she and Doug had been in counseling themselves and that Lisa was struggling to hold onto her own long-term relationship. Then, a week before her scheduled follow-up visit, Lisa contacted Jackson and me with an announcement: she and Doug also had separated. Lisa declined my offer to postpone the workshop. She mailed me a draft, and we collaborated by phone and email. Lisa sent a slightly revised version to my parents and to Jackson. On Monday, April 24, 2006, Jackson agreed to rejoin the Marshall clan so we could discuss our reflections on the project.

I return to the vineyard from running errands to find my mother making coffee and Lisa setting up her laptop and recorder in the dining room. When I pull Lisa in for a hug, I notice how weary she looks. She says in my ear, "Lots of change since we last crossed paths."

"*Lots*," I affirm.

My dad arrives, smiling warmly. "How *are* you?" he asks Lisa.

"Hanging in," she says.

We take seats around the oval table, Lisa and Mom at the ends, Dad and I at the sides. Mom sets down a tray of cheese, crackers, and fruit. Lisa refuses when I pass this to her. "Are you eating?" Mom asks.

Lisa quips, "The loss-and-grief diet: more effective than Atkins or South Beach!"

"Take care of yourself," Mom warns. "When my first husband and I separated, I lost so much weight I wound up in the hospital."

After a pause, I ask, "Is Jackson coming?"

Checking her watch, Lisa says, "He should be here in a few minutes."

"It's been a while since I talked to him," I report, swallowing hard. "We haven't spoken about the chapter at all."

"Did reading this call up any thoughts or feelings about Jackson or about your relationship?" Lisa asks gently.

I reply, "I wouldn't change anything I said. I still feel that he is my best friend."

"It was a good nine years," Mom says. "Even though Jackson is not part of Don's life in that way anymore, he'll always be part of our family."

Lisa nods. "Did you speak as a family about what transpired during my visit?"

In her usual style, Mom recalls, "After you took us to dinner, I think I said, 'Wasn't that nice that she bought us chicken?'" Lisa laughs.

I say, "I held back on quizzing my parents: 'What did you tell her?' I wanted to read the narrative first."

Mom offers her serious response: "I prayed that it wouldn't cause trauma."

I tell the group, "I had that fear too."

"And did the visit or the document cause trauma or conflict?" Lisa asks.

"Conversation," I tell her, "not conflict. For example, I remember an extended period of being away and not talking to the family."

"I do too," says Dad.

"But Mom remembers differently; she recalls seeing me in Rochester."

"Frankly, I don't think that happened," Dad insists.

Mom says, "We had at least three dinners at Red Lobster, and we met twice for lunch."

"I remember those meetings," I respond, "but *after* a long separation."

"You're probably right," she quietly concedes. "In his section, Don also commented on the day that we picked him up at school. He recalls that I said, 'I can't believe you did this to us. So embarrassing!' Reading that pained me. I can't imagine myself saying that. I don't care what people think. But he remembers it that way."

Lisa points out, "You certainly had different perceptions of Ms. Allen. John remembered her trying to get Don to stay in school—"

Mom interjects, "She said, 'Six weeks to go. If he comes on Mondays, he'll get a diploma.'"

"That may have been what she told *you*," I say.

Jackson appears at the door and teases, "What are you trying to retract?" All of us rise and cross to greet him. Lisa comments on how healthy he looks and how she likes the vibrant henna rinse in his hair. He takes a seat between my parents.

Lisa reports, "We were sharing experiences of reading the narrative."

"Very enlightening," says Mom.

"Incredibly moving," I add. "I feared it would come across as detached, cold, but I actually cried several times. To see my life, and the lives of people who are important to me, on paper . . . you took care of us so well. I found the way that you wrote really safe and loving."

Jackson offers a wry smile. "I marveled at how you condensed Donovan into so few pages and how smooth you made him sound. Quite a feat of editing!"

Returning his grin, Lisa asks, "Jackson, have you had any conversations about the manuscript?"

"I did call my mom and read my section to her over the phone. I'd forgotten how much I had, in prior conversations, downplayed the harassment at school and the gay bashing in college."

Mom responds, "I felt so angry when I read that!"

Jackson continues, "My mom got all sad again: 'I didn't know so many things.'"

"I don't think you told *me*," I point out. "Nine years together, and even I didn't realize how often and how severely your peers bullied you."

Jackson sighs. "It was like, 'Oh god, just get me out of this town!'"

"Given that," Lisa says, "how brave of you to live again in a small town, to stay even after your separation from Donovan. My project's other three participants live with their partners in urban environments. Their friendship networks consist almost entirely of other gay men. This has a protective yet isolating impact on their lives. One recently told me he felt 'alone'—politically, spiritually—in his family. You two are much more integrated into non-gay community networks, and you have far more day-to-day contact with family members."

Lisa then asks Jackson, "Have you talked to your dad about the manuscript?"

"My dad actually answered the phone. I said, 'I got Lisa's work in the mail and wanted to go over it with you and Mom.' He hedged, 'Uh . . . you've talked to your mom more about that, so I'll hand you over.'"

"Your parents could read our part too," Mom offers, "if they want to."

Jackson tells us, "My mom asked me to read aloud Donovan's section as well. I'm like, 'I don't have that much time!'" We all laugh.

"Anything you would add about what you've learned as a result of our work together?" Lisa asks the group.

Jackson speaks first. "I learned to keep growing. You look back and see things in a different light. You say, 'That thing that got me so upset was dumb.'"

"You endured years of experiences I wouldn't classify as 'dumb,'" Lisa responds. "In our time together, I found you warm, pleasant, funny—even while telling me about the harassment and the bashing." Her voice breaks as she continues, "Terrible things happened to you. I felt a lot of compassion while hearing you speak of them and in the process of writing about you."

Eyes downcast, Jackson quietly offers a one-word reply: "Thanks."

Into the silence that follows, I say, "I found interesting the question Lisa posed at the end of my section: will Don and Donovan become one? I don't know. I know I need to continue dealing with what happened, but I don't know if I want that person to become part of who I am now. This project changed me. I don't keep emotions as bottled up, and our work helped me see how others remember experiences differently."

Mom responds, "It's not so much, in the end, what you remember as fact; everyone sees the 'facts' differently. It's the feelings you had, how you can look back and re-experience those feelings, and grow from that. Whether I'm totally accurate doesn't matter. I still felt that way."

"That's part of it, too," I say. "The important thing is how I cope with what I feel. I was angry; it was okay to be angry. I was hurt; it was okay to be hurt. But it's now time for different *responses* to those feelings."

Dad tells the group, "In those days, the three of us spoke words, but we didn't communicate. Barb and I were too angry. He was totally withdrawn. Even now, I see that sometimes. You shut yourself off, Don, and that's really, really bad for all of us."

I nod. "I know I do that. At least now I'm aware of it."

Dad says to Lisa, "Over the years, our communication evolved, but some of the same crap is still there. Your project brought that out in our minds. That's a big deal."

We continue talking about the draft. Jackson and my mom correct a couple factual errors and offer a few clarifications. We spend the most time joshing my ex about his chosen pseudonym: Jackson Jones. Afterward, over pizza and beer, the group sits down to a less-than-conventional "family" dinner (with mother, stepfather, son, former partner, and researcher). When coping with separation, loss, and grief, and moving toward healing and reconciliation, we small town folks find it best to work—and eat—together.

Notes

1 Dave Dietz shot the images in this chapter, whose webpage may be found at: http://www.insolidaritybook.com/revisiting.html.

2 For other narrative works containing first-person prose from participants' perspectives, see Kiesinger (1998) and Cherry (1996).

3   When we met with Lisa on April 24, 2006 to workshop a draft of this piece, my
    mom confirmed my assumption, letting me know my birth father is half-German,
    half-Polish.
4   This poem brings together overlapping and differing perspectives on family events.
    Constructed from interview transcripts, the text may be read either one column at
    a time or back and forth.

References

Cherry, Keith. "Ain't No Grave Deep Enough." *Journal of Contemporary Ethnography*
    25 (1996): 22–57.
Kiesinger, Christine E. "From Interview to Story: Writing Abbie's Life." *Qualitative
    Inquiry* 4 (1998): 71–95.
Tillmann-Healy, Lisa M. *Between Gay and Straight: Understanding Friendship across
    Sexual Orientation.* Walnut Creek, CA: AltaMira Press, 2001.

PART II

LOVING FRIENDS, JUST FRIENDS

EMOTIONS, ETHICS, AND POLITICS OF ALLY–LGBTQ+ RELATIONSHIPS

5

REMEMBERING A COOL SEPTEMBER

PAIN, PREJUDICE, AND PATRIOTISM[1]

On September 11, 2001 and for weeks thereafter, the nation cries. Waves of anguish wash over me—but not *into* me. Buried alive, I suffocate under a shroud, unable to move or breathe. Clawing through the tangled webs of everyday existence, I wander the liminal neverland between consciousness and sleep.

CNN coma: 3:00 a.m., 4:00 a.m., 5:00 a.m. Planes exploding, towers burning, folding, burning, folding, burning, folding.

"This just in": new shot, new angle, same angle, North, South, Trade Center, Pentagon, New York, Shanksville, D.C. Workplaces to graves. People to ash.

On the mornings of our nation's mourning, I am wracked without sobbing, brimming with no tears. I *study* the images: a man with outstretched arms and legs—reaching, falling. I cannot see his face. Are his eyes open? I cannot hear his voice. Does he call out? For whom?

At ground zero, a desperate, candlelit collective—waiting, hoping. "Missing: Paul Ortiz." "Looking for: Scott Hazelcom." "Vanessa Kolpak, 5'3", hair: blonde, eyes: blue/green. Please call with information." Wall of tears. Portraits of grief. I can only . . . gasp.

On September 11, and for months thereafter, the nation howls. Act of War. Terrorists. Infinite Justice. Even my usually subdued husband Doug seems perched, ready to "do something."

I do nothing. I write no letters, send no emails, call no one—not even my parents. Aside from my students at Rollins College, I don't ask if anyone's okay, if anyone has lost someone. Nobody. Nowhere. I am embalmed yet awake at my own wake.

And then it happens, not with a cataclysmic bang but with a whisper of humanity.

Tim and Rob, two of my closest friends, have been together for five years. One October evening, I visit their new apartment. As I step onto the sidewalk, I see their two trucks parked in tandem. Everything seems normal: Rob's Isuzu Rodeo, Tim's Ford Ranger, both aging but holding.

As I move my line of sight toward the door, my peripheral vision catches a glimmer. I turn toward it. The hazy glow of an orange-yellow streetlamp sends silver sparks from the corners of their trucks. At first,

Figure 5.1 Tim Mahn and Rob Ryan.

Figure 5.2 Lisa Tillmann and Rob Ryan.

I think it a reflection off their taillights. But when I move closer, I see the source of this illumination: the stars and stripes of two matching American flag decals.

I have seen thousands of these in the last month: on billboards, in store windows, on cars speeding down I-4. I have watched the landscape fill with red, white, and blue ribbons, shoes, t-shirts, ball caps, lapel pins, earrings, scarves, pendants, ties, and tie tacks.

But, for the first time, something pierces my skin.

I think of my two friends. Natural athletes with middle-America good looks, both pass easily, offering both a touch of safety and a shove toward the closet.

Rob is two years older but more boyish looking, an Irish Catholic (like me), the sixth of seven children, a physical therapist by training with a gentle voice and comforting hands.

Tim comes from a large blended Mormon family. After putting himself through private school, this cost accountant abandoned corporate America because it bled his soul dry.

Figure 5.3 Tim Mahn and Lisa Tillmann.

I recall our travels together: South Beach, Ft. Lauderdale, Atlanta, Paris.

I think of shared milestones: Doug's and my wedding, Tim's graduation, my graduation, their move to Orlando, our move to Orlando, the publication of my book *Between Gay and Straight* (whose cover the four of us grace), birthdays, anniversaries, separations, reconciliations, injuries, illnesses, deaths.

As I move toward the reflection, I think of Jerry bin Falwell, verbal terrorist. Following the attacks on the Trade Center and Pentagon, he said of Tim and Rob (and of all of us who identify as queer and/or feminist), "I point a finger in their face and say, 'You helped this happen.'"

I consider the many churches in which my friends are not recognized as a couple. Spiritual ties bind Tim and Rob, but not to each other. A fellow Mormon once told Tim that his homosexuality was "a cross to bear," like cancer. Under Catholic doctrine, the pathway out of their relationship's "sin" is paved with celibacy, a practice some priests cannot sustain.

I think of pop culture's normalization of homophobia. On *The Marshall Mathers LP*, Eminem refers to men like Rob and Tim as "fags" or "faggots" 13 times. *Marshall Mathers* debuted at number one, sold millions of copies, and won three Grammys. Eminem got to sing with Sir Elton John.

When I reach Rob's Rodeo, a truck imprinted with 200,000 miles of inside jokes and family outings, I think of the thousand ways, large and small, that our nation tells them, "We don't see you. We wish you didn't exist." Their companies' health insurance and bereavement leave do not cover domestic partners. Rob and Tim cannot file joint income taxes and are not entitled to survivor benefits.[2] In most states (including Florida, where we live), it is perfectly legal to refuse Tim and Rob service in a shop or restaurant; to deny them a hotel room, house, or apartment; even to fire Tim and Rob for no other reason than being gay.[3] At the time of the attacks, they could be prosecuted in 14 states (including Florida) for having consensual sex in the privacy of their own home;[4] Tim and Rob could not adopt children, even those who were sick, abandoned, unwanted;[5] and Tim and Rob could not serve openly in the military.[6]

But, they could—and can—be targeted, bashed, and left to die. Because sexual orientation was not a protected status on September 11, 2001, this would not have met the federal criteria for a hate crime.[7]

I pause and take in the image of this shimmering flag adorning Rob's truck. When I run my hand across the decal, I feel my lower lip pull away from its twin. Breath leaves my body. I ponder all the philosophical, political, and material reasons for these two men *not* to display these flags—as I consciously have not.

And then I ponder these two men: compassionate, proud, loving. My hand covers my mouth, and my eyes fill with their first tears since that terrible September Tuesday.

Notes

1   Earlier versions of "Remembering a Cool September" were presented at the 2002 National Communication Association meetings and published in *Cultural Studies↔Critical Methodologies* (Tillmann-Healy 2004; used with permission, Sage Publications: http://csc.sagepub.com/content/4/2/198.abstract). Also see the film by this title (Tillmann and Dietz 2014) on the website for *In Solidarity*: http://www.insolidaritybook.com/index.html#film. Rick Merrifield and Doug

Healy shot images in this chapter, whose webpage may be found at: http://www.
insolidaritybook.com/remembering.html.

2   The Obama administration has interpreted the 2013 Supreme Court decision in
United States v. Windsor, which struck down the Defense of Marriage Act (DOMA),
to mean that legally married same-sex couples are entitled to the same federal rights
and benefits as married different-sex couples.

3   Still true as of this writing.

4   On June 26, 2003, the U.S. Supreme Court in *Lawrence v. Texas* struck down all
state sodomy laws.

5   At the time of the attacks, Florida was one of three states to bar adoption by gay
and lesbian individuals and/or couples. On September 22, 2010, the 3rd District
Court of Appeal struck down Florida's ban, in place since 1977.

6   On September 20, 2011, President Obama signed the repeal of "Don't Ask, Don't
Tell," ending the military's ban.

7   President Obama on October 28, 2009 signed the Matthew Shepard and James
Byrd, Jr. Hate Crimes Prevention Act, enhancing penalties for crimes motivated
by the victim's actual or perceived sexual orientation, gender, or gender identity.

References

Tillmann, Lisa M., and David Dietz. *Remembering a Cool September* [motion picture].
United States: Cinema Serves Justice, 2014. http://cinemaservesjustice.com/
Remembering.html.

Tillmann-Healy, Lisa M. *Between Gay and Straight: Understanding Friendship across
Sexual Orientation*. Walnut Creek, CA: AltaMira Press, 2001.

—— ."Remembering a Cool September: Pain, Prejudice, and Patriotism." *Cultural
Studies↔Critical Methodologies* 4 (2004): 198–200.

6

STATE OF UNIONS

POLITICS AND POETICS OF PERFORMANCE[1]

It is Friday, May 6, 2005, day two of the First International Congress of Qualitative Inquiry. I arrive at room 210 in the Illini Union, 25 minutes early for our 1:30 session. The room immediately strikes me as less than ideal: aging ventilation system blowing and clanking, narrow rows of seats stretching back, podium several paces from the LCD projector. I must choose: use the mike but forgo the slides I have spent untold hours preparing or show the slides and project my voice much louder than I have practiced. I choose the slides.

I connect my Dell laptop to its brethren projector, boot up, and double click the PowerPoint file on my desktop. The title slide illuminates. With an exhale, I press the projector remote's "Black Screen" button and take a seat. My piece is scheduled last.

Barbara Jago, fellow USF alum, approaches from behind. Eyeing my black sweater, jeans, and boots, she fondly greets, "Conference wear for the newly *tenured* professor." I stand to hug her. The reunion continues as we wave over Christine Kiesinger. Then arrive our academic parents, Art Bochner (Barbara's, Christine's, and my graduate advisor) and Carolyn Ellis (member of our doctoral committees and chair of this panel). As the room fills, sweat beads at the base of my skull.

The quality of the other presentations leaves little space to worry about my own. Mary Poole describes her activist work with MoveOn during the 2004 presidential election; Abby Arnold and Wren Colker's co-constructed narrative chronicles the conflicted relationship between a stepdaughter and stepmother; and Robin Boylorn confronts the largely White audience with her experiences as a graduate student of color. When the applause for Robin subsides, I move to the front of the room.

I turn off "Black Screen," but my slide appears neither on my computer nor overhead. I push the button again. Nothing. Someone moves to turn off the heater, but its fan keeps whirring loudly. I power everything down and reboot, turning on the projector, then the computer. Shaking my head in Art's direction, I know exactly what he's thinking: *This is why I never use PowerPoint.* Audience members begin opening windows; it may be my nerves, but the room feels over 80 degrees. I decide to reboot one more time (computer, then projector). Alas! My slide appears on the laptop. I turn around: nothing on the screen. Function F4. Now the slide appears on the screen but not on my computer. Several repetitions later, I still can't get the image onto both. I decide to proceed with a blank monitor.

I take a deep breath and smile at the three-quarters full room. With a nod toward Mary Poole: "Let me first honor a fellow precinct leader." I peel off my sweater to reveal a grey retro muscle shirt reading "John Kerry for President." Planting my feet shoulder-width apart, I embark.

Warning:
      though I am a postmodernist,
            an anti-essentialist,
    and an aspiring queer theorist,
      I will be making capital-T
                  Truth statements
  in this political
      poetic
      polemic.
  I invite you to offer your own truths
  in response.

I spent the autumn of 2004 as many did:
  walking,
knocking, and what bordered on
  stalking, [Mary offers a knowing laugh.]
all to prevent the result we now have:
Four
More
Years.

[I cue a photo of George W. Bush, eyes ablaze, finger pointed accusingly,
with the sort of expression Jon Stewart mocks with a "Heh, heh!" on
The Daily Show.]

Four
More
Years:
the refrain
lodges
in my throat.

I swallow
and begin to speak,
my words flowing
from despair,
          fear,
and hope.

I address this
  address
to men like those
in my research community.

Men with whom I have been collaborating
          for 10 years on a project exploring
communicative and relational opportunities and challenges
of friendship across sexual orientation.

Men who have shared
their stories,
   struggles,
and families
with me.

Men who identify (privately)
as gay (not queer).

Men who also tend to be
White,
healthy (at least for now),
middle-, upper-middle, or upper-class,
educated (not academic),
professional (not overly political).
Men who can
and do
pass.

That audience, the "you"
in the commentary
   to come,
is probably not the "you" in this room.

But I suspect I am not alone
in counting such men
among my closest friends,
my family.

My friends,
every day I question the ethics
of my participation
in an exclusionary "program of privilege":[2]
heterosexual marriage.

I remind myself that I never can understand fully
the constraints under which
you live,
    love,
    move,
and work.

But as a woman who teaches gender and queer studies,
I know a thing or two about
constraints.
I have slogged my way through
the year-long academic hazing we call
tenure.

[Laughter spreads as I post a slide of a yellow and black road sign reading, "Danger: Men at Work."]

The senior members of my department:
all White,
middle-aged,
heterosexual,
upper-middle and upper-class
men.

The Faculty Evaluation Committee:
six White,
middle-aged,
heterosexual,
upper-middle and upper-class
men.

[I advance to a photograph of me, at perhaps six years old, pressing a tiny iron to my toy ironing board.]

Figure 6.1

Deans,
President,
Chairman of the Board
—need I go on?

So yes, I know a thing or two
about constraints,
about repression,
about rage,
about the performance of
good
little
self
in everyday life.

Here is my question:
my friends,
where were you
in this election cycle?

The stakes were so high:
the remaking of the Supreme Court
in the images of Scalia and Thomas,[3]
the overturn of *Lawrence v. Texas*[4]
and *Roe v. Wade*.

Remember that night at Margaret Cho?
We howled,
fists raised,
when she railed against homophobia in schools.
But when she questioned
why old men still control
the reproductive freedom of women,
I applauded,
nearly alone,
in that "family"[5]-filled auditorium.

Later, in the car,
I asked what you made of this nonresponse.
You didn't respond.
I asked again.
Silence.
Ache.
More silence.

Let me tell you a story.
A young mother dies, as thousands did,
after a back-alley abortion.
Social services RI PS an orphaned boy from his home,
placing him where he will be shamed and struck
throughout his childhood.
The boy grows up and inflicts this violence
onto his son.
A friend of yours inherited this legacy.
His father is the boy whose mother bled to death.
Such was "life" in America
before *Roe v. Wade.*

[I advance to the next slide. As nine other smiling White men in suits
look on, George W. Bush signs the inflammatorily named "Partial Birth
Abortion Act."[6]]

Did you see that piece in the *New York Times*
featuring gay male Republicans for life?[7]
Not "for life" as in forever gay
                or forever Republican.
As in: Anti-Abortion
        Gay
        Male
        Republicans.
When I get my head around this,
I will report back.

My friends, can you not see
that your fate as a gay man
is intertwined with mine,
with all women's?
In *Gender Outlaw*,
Kate Bornstein credits Craig Lucas with the statement:
"Homophobia and misogyny are not related.
THEY ARE THE SAME!"
I don't know about "the same,"
but surely two sides of a
reversible coat.

It could be said that,
of all members of your—our—community,
you have the most to lose
by making yourself vulnerable.
Passing brings privilege,
however temporary
and unstable.

I also see,
     hear,
      feel—
but never understand fully—
the economic,
     social, and even
     bodily consequences you might bear
should things go terribly,
       even violently,
awry.

[I display an image of protesters from the Westboro Baptist Church
with signs reading: "GOD HATES FAGS" and "GOD SAID KILL
FAGS." The next slide features a young woman who has been bashed.
Her right eye is swollen shut, her mouth bloody.]

On the other hand, my friends,
compared to your non-White,
working-class,
lesbian,
and transgender brothers and sisters,
<u>you stand on firmer ground.</u>

In this election cycle,
so many others *did* make themselves
vulnerable,
canvassing for Kerry,
                MoveOn, or most visibly,
                HRC.[8]
Why not you?

I realize that it's heresy for someone
with heterosexual
        and marital PRIVILEGE
to excoriate you for what are, at least in part,
responses to homophobia and heterosexism.
But I am afraid of your—our—
complacency.

We share many enemies,
and they are organized,
                on-message,
                well-financed.
Emboldened by "mandate,"
they earned, according to Bush,
        "capital in the campaign—
political capital"—
and they
"intend to spend it."

If their heterosexist amendment[9]
was not that final moment of clarity,
what will it take?

You tell me you're not a single-issue voter.
But this federal amendment,
these state initiatives,[10]
strip your humanity
and undermine your most significant relationship:
one *hell* of a single issue.

What will it take to get
a little more of your—our—discretionary income
into the nonprofit sector?
A little more of your—our—
time,
energy,
spirit into grassroots efforts?
What will it take?
I am afraid of the answer.

[Advancing to a black and white image of Matthew Shepard,[11] I turn
to meet his gaze for a few seconds before continuing.]

You and I knew that Kerry wasn't Kucinich
or even Dean
(not that you voted for Kucinich
or even Dean).
You did vote in the primary,
right?

You and I had read the Kerry-Edwards (re)position paper.
Against the heterosexism amendment
AND same-sex marriage.[12]
For civil unions
AND state determination.
Those saucy Republicans:
always cooking up
charges of inconsistency!

And who could forget the 2004 "debates"?
Kerry's remark
(was it off the cuff;
was it calculated?):
"If you were to talk to Dick Cheney's daughter,
who is a lesbian . . ."
Or Edward's condescension-qua-compassion,
his "respect" for Dick's "embrace"
of his none-too-proud Mary,
as if she had contracted leprosy
while spreading the Gospel of abstinence-only.

But
don't get me started
on Daughter Halliburton either.
I'm more ambivalent about outing
than about *selling* out.
Marginalized status does not automatically confer
raised consciousness,
but neither is it a free pass
for undermining others' human rights.

So yeah,
Kerry was not the second coming,
but how can you simply throw up your hands
and not vote?[13]

And *you*.
You came to my "Take Back Our Country" barbecue
on September the 11th.
You ate pulled pork,
drank beer,
wrote a check for MoveOn.
Now I hear you were part
of the 23% of GLB folks who voted for Bush,[14]
whom you believed would be "better for business."
Whose business?

And *you*, Mr. Representation without Taxation.
What do you think financed
our public educations,
including our state-subsidized college degrees?

And you two.
Did you have to buy your new
and your certified pre-owned BMWs
from the only dealer in town
whose towering billboard read:
"We Support the Troops and President Bush"?
Yes,
I did see the Kerry-Edwards sign
in your yard.

And to all those
with neither the time nor the energy
to canvass and phone bank:
let's cut the crap!
Don't think
I don't know where you were
on Friday and Saturday nights.
My sources go clubbing too.

You're right.
I haven't told the whole truth:
four long years ago,
I saw Al Gore as the hollow man,
              the stuffed man.[15]
It sickens me to report
that my only contribution in 2000 was
my vote.

I felt indignant when dubious voter rolls,
voter intimidation,
and the Supreme Court
delivered the White House.
Indignant,
but not enraged,
not militant.
That would come later:
the quid pro quo tax cuts,
the fox-guarding-henhouse environmental policies,
the five million more without health insurance,
the heterosexism amendment,
the war,
the war,
THE WAR.

[I barely can speak each repetition as I post images of flag-draped coffins
and of wounded and dead children.]

Florida, *our* state, my friends,
was "lost" by 537 votes.
537!
One person,
one team,
could have mobilized that many.
Why not me?
Why not *us?*

Yes, I admit,
this report has been neither fair nor balanced.
I know that after voting for Reagan, Reagan,
                    Bush, Bush,
                    Dole,
            and Bush,
you sucked in your breath
and cast this one
for Kerry.

Figure 6.2 Tim Mahn.

Figure 6.3 Mike Fried.

And you folks:
where do I begin?
Fundraisers,
action alerts,
get-out-the-vote drives.
To hit the streets
and work the phones,
you sacrificed extra shifts
and overtime pay.
You talked politics with your customers,
perhaps at some cost to your small business.
To facilitate your activism your partners
arose even earlier,
worked even harder,
stayed even later.

[Slides feature photographs of MoveOn team members and their partners.]

> So, my friends,
> *wherever* you were in this election cycle,
> here is my question:
> *where*
> do we go
> from here?

[I advance to the last slide, telling the audience, "I took this photograph two blocks from my house." I leave the image on the screen.]

Figure 6.4

The room remains silent for several seconds. At last, a man a few rows from the back says, "Like you and Mary Poole, I was a MoveOn precinct captain. I'm also a gay man. I know you said the 'you' in your commentary is probably not the 'you' in this room. But even I felt implicated by some of the lines." He clears his throat. "Several times during your performance I asked myself: *did* I do all that I could?"

Feeling pain in his question, I respond, "I try to show myself grappling with that as well. Whatever any of us did individually and collectively, it was not enough.

"You said you felt 'implicated.' I've thought a lot about interpellation: who is the 'you,' the subject, hailed by this piece? The poem emerged from everyday experience among my network of gay male friends. Those lines stem from actual events, real conversations; I am not being hyperbolic. I speak to these men and about them, but in the process, I speak to larger social forces and hail a broader audience."

He asks, "More specifically, what—and whom—is the poem for?"

"It's a call to action for all of us. We may be marginalized in one or more ways: me as a woman, you as a gay man. But we also have the privilege that comes with our dominant statuses: my heterosexual privilege, your male privilege, our White privilege, educational and class privilege. The question is: how do we use that for liberatory and just ends?"

Keith Berry asks, "How has your research community responded to the piece?"[16]

With the back of my left hand, I wipe sweat from my brow. "Everyone was invited to a performance at Rollins College, though only my friend Mike could attend. I also read it to my friend Tim over the phone. Both responded with something akin to: 'Right on!' But both Mike and Tim served on my MoveOn team, so they were less likely to feel challenged by the more critical lines."

Keith presses, "Why didn't you include, as you have in past work, your participants' voices?" His brown eyes lock on mine.

"I take your question very seriously. Such inclusion would have made the piece more dialogic, as would have greater efforts to ensure that my participants had prior access. Perhaps not doing so makes me something of an ethnographic 'fink,' to use Goffman's[17] term."

Silence again falls. Just as the audience seems poised to move on, Art Bochner says, "I'm wondering about . . . tone. I didn't have the same reaction to reading this as a text as I did hearing you perform it today. My graduate advisor used to say, 'We shouldn't alienate those we're trying to persuade.' I'm wondering if anyone would like to talk about that."

Keith responds, "I think of autoethnography in Goodall's[18] terms: as relationship and conversation. I am perplexed by your decision to scold those whose liberation you claim to support."

A man I don't recognize immediately follows up. His voice shakes as he says, "To me, your performance felt like gay bashing."

My stomach drops. Before speaking, I find my center. "I said early in the piece, 'I invite you to offer your own truths in response.' Thank you for doing so. I cannot dispute that, to you, it *felt* like 'gay bashing.'" My spirit connects to the hurt and despair he embodies. Gingerly, I add, "To me, the piece is radically *anti*-heterosexist, a longtime friend and ally speaking from her heart, her gut."

"A *'friend,'*" he retorts, clearly marking the word with vocal quotation marks, "speaking to members of an already-marginalized group to which she doesn't belong."

The ground beneath my feet seems to quake a bit, but I retain my balance of passion and compassion. "That description is accurate but incomplete. Again, each of us has both marginalized and dominant identities. I 'live, love, move, and work' under different, but related, constraints. When I speak to or about these particular men, I see myself as speaking across the table to my peers.

"You might experience such a dynamic if your fieldwork involved a community of women. Your experience as a gay man could move you to empathize with women's struggles, to work for gender equality in your everyday life, *and* to critique ways that *women's* actions and inactions further our own oppression. For example, my piece doesn't mention, but you could in fairness raise, the fact that 48 percent of women—more than twice the percentage of GLB persons—voted for George W. Bush.[19] I do think it important to distinguish between hegemonic critiques that reproduce oppressive practices and structures and anti-domination critiques aimed at undermining and dismantling those."

Keith says, "That seems to place responsibility for understanding the researcher/performer's intent in participants' and audience members' hands. What do you see as *your* role in that process?"

Lesa Lockford interjects, "Perhaps it is, as Art mentioned earlier, a question of tone. I wonder how the piece would be received differently if the central emotion you communicated were fear instead of anger."

A woman seated behind Lesa queries, "What's the implication, though? That autoethnography rightfully expresses sadness and fear but not anger?"

Bud Goodall says, "I met Lisa through her autoethnographic account of bulimia[20] and followed her journey into this fieldwork community in *Between Gay and Straight*. What does it say if we embrace her as a 'girl' struggling with an eating disorder or as the consummate gay man's gal pal but resist her speaking from the truth of her lived *political* experience?"

"There does seem to be something gendered about that," observes Lesa.

I respond, "I made a deliberate, rhetorical choice to write and speak in second person, to be direct and confrontational—a style reflective of my research community's conventionally masculine gender expression."

"Plus," Bud says, "the poem is an open text. I heard this coming not from anger but from pain, perhaps even betrayal. Think of the interaction she describes after Margaret Cho and the failure to achieve inter-subjectivity over women's rights.

"Perhaps it is a sign of autoethnography's maturation that scholars using the same methodology, and likely sharing similar politics, have such divergent opinions about how to accomplish their goals."

As the conversation shifts to the other presentations, I take my seat and begin turning over the responses, a process that continues to this day.

Ethical "State of Unions"?

I believe in judging research practices as Keith Berry suggests: "by their impact and efficacy."[21] My performance at the Qualitative Congress sparked a lively, layered discussion, but at what cost and to whom? I still pause when re-engaging the responses of gay male audience members who felt "implicated," "scolded," even "gay bashed."

What of my friends' responses? In "State of Unions," were the men in my research community "participants" in any meaningful sense?

At the very least, I should have ensured that these men had access to the poem prior to my first public delivery. I did distribute copies and solicit feedback before submitting the piece for publication—a step in the right direction but still ethically insufficient.

My friend and colleague Kathryn Norsworthy and her research collaborator Ouyporn Khuankaew,[22] following Buddhist practices of "right speech," offer three criteria for judging "rightness": Is it the truth? Is it the right time? Will it be helpful? Regarding the first question: I wrote and spoke my truths but explicitly marked them as "capital-T Truth statements." Though I invited others' truths, and Congress attendees offered them, I could have marked my truths as provisional and contingent. Such rhetoric likely would have evoked less alienation and pain. At the same time, as I expressed, the stakes felt so high: on the line were my friends' basic human rights—if not their very lives. Indeed, during the eight years of his administration, President Bush signed no legislation or executive order that advanced rights on the basis of sexual orientation or gender identity, and Bush's Supreme Court nominees (especially Samuel Alito, preceded by Sandra Day O'Connor) maintained a body well to the right of the general population—an impact that may last decades.

This relates to the question of "right time." To me, the situation felt urgent, desperate. The time had to be *now*; I wrote the piece within days of the 2004 election.

Readers and audience members enter an intellectual and/or performance space with a range of lived experience and at different places in their own identity developments. Therefore, no text or speech—and certainly no polemic—will feel "right" to everyone. My first performance of "State of Unions," part of a panel sponsored by the GLBTQ Caucus of the National Communication Association (NCA), occurred barely two weeks after the election. No audience member there expressed feeling gay bashed or even implicated, but that offers no vindication. For those prone to being triggered by the poem, the election may have been so fresh that they shut down emotionally. In addition, no one explicitly invited members to respond to the piece's tone, as Art Bochner did at the Congress.

Environmental differences also may have contributed to how audiences received "State of Unions." The NCA room was much quieter and smaller, and I had access to a microphone. My NCA delivery likely sounded much closer to my normal speaking style than to the near shouting I thought I needed to reach Congress attendees seated in the back of a long room with a loud fan.

Returning to the notion of "right time," my performance at the Congress occurred just over six months after Election Day. Some audience members may have had enough emotional distance from the election to engage the ideas and even the tone of "State of Unions"; for others, the election still may have felt like an open wound.

As with the other two questions, "Will it be helpful?" cannot be answered, only processed. Helpful how and to whom? I could not stand by quietly while the ruling party used and stoked fear and hatred of LGBTQ+ persons as a distraction to what seemed to be its real agenda: the upward distribution of wealth and the communication of U.S. military dominance. At the same time, I recognize now that, even when I feel frightened or angry, I must stay focused on the major *sources* of oppression. I must ensure that I do not relocate the problem and blame the targets of oppression. When I perceive that someone—even a member of a marginalized group to which I do not belong—contributes to her or his own and/or to others' oppression, it is my duty as an ally to try to interrupt that. To the greatest degree possible, my interruption should convey "*loving* honesty," a phrase offered by a member of my research community. "State of Unions," while honest, is insufficiently loving. The poem, even as published in 2009, was too much an ethnographic monologue, too little an ethnographic dialogue.

In "Friendship as Method,"[23] I indicated that researching with an ethic of friendship requires a reflexive stance of mutuality, empathy, and understanding. I take seriously feedback indicating that my poem and/or my performance failed to embody that stance. My responsibility now includes moving forward with heightened and better-informed commitments to equality and justice for my friends, for their communities, and for everyone.

Notes

1 Earlier versions of "State of Unions" were presented at the 2004 meetings of the National Communication Association and the 2005 International Congress of Qualitative Inquiry and published in *Qualitative Inquiry* (Tillmann 2009; used with permission, Sage Publications: http://qix.sagepub.com/content/15/3/545.abstract). John and Beth Tillmann contributed the photograph of me as a little girl. A webpage for this chapter may be found at: http://www.insolidaritybook.com/state.html.

2 See Warner (1999).

3 In his second term, George W. Bush appointed two Supreme Court Justices, Samuel Alito and John Roberts. Both were among the dissenting judges (along with Scalia and Thomas) in *United States v. Windsor*, the case that overturned the Defense of Marriage Act.

4 The 2003 U.S. Supreme Court decision in *Lawrence v. Texas* struck down sodomy laws in 14 states. Scalia and Thomas dissented, as did then-chief justice Rehnquist.

5 In this context, "family" refers to people who identify as LGBT.

6 The medical term for this exceedingly rare procedure is "intact dilation and extraction."

7 See Kirkpatrick (March 9, 2004).

8 The Human Rights Campaign, a civil rights advocacy organization.

9 The Federal Marriage Amendment seeks to define marriage in the U.S. Constitution as a union between one man and one woman. The Republican platform of 2012 reaffirmed the party's support for this amendment.

10 In 2004 alone, 14 states passed statutes and/or constitutional amendments banning same-sex marriage; see "State Laws Prohibiting Recognition of Same-Sex Relationships" (May 15, 2013). By the end of 2008, 37 states had passed such legislation. In 21 states, prohibitions went beyond marriage to include recognition of, e.g., civil unions and domestic partnerships.

11 A 21-year-old student at the University of Wyoming murdered by Russell Henderson and Aaron McKinney in 1998.

12 John Kerry altered his stance and expressed support for same-sex marriage seven years later, in 2011.

13 Across sexual orientations, nearly 57 million eligible voters did not participate in the November 2004 elections. Sixty-two million votes were cast, 38 million less than in the spring 2009 finale of *American Idol* (see Berman, May 20, 2009).

14 See "CNN.com Election 2004" (n.d.).

15 A nod to T.S. Eliot (1988).

16 For an extensive discussion of Keith's reactions to "The State of Unions," see Berry (2006).

17 See Goffman (1989).

18 See Goodall (2000).

19 See "CNN.com Election 2004" (n.d.).

20 See Tillmann-Healy (1996).

21 See Berry (2006, 3).

22 For examples of their work, see Khuankaew and Norsworthy (2000), Norsworthy
    with Khuankaew (2005), and Norsworthy and Khuankaew (2012).
23 See the Appendix and Tillmann-Healy (1998, 2001, 2003).

References

Berman, Craig. "100 Million Votes Cast on *American Idol.*" *Associated Press Archives*,
    May 20, 2009. Accessed May 16, 2014. http://www.newsvine.com/_news/2009/
    05/20/2844665-100-million-votes-cast-on-american-idol.
Berry, Keith. "Implicated Audience Member Seeks Understanding: Reexamining the
    'Gift' of Autoethnography." *International Journal of Qualitative Methods* 5, no. 3
    (2006). Accessed May 16, 2014. http://ejournals.library.ualberta.ca/index.php/
    IJQM/article/view/4372/3502.
Bornstein, Kate. *Gender Outlaw: On Men, Women, and the Rest of Us.* New York: Vintage
    Books, 1995.
"CNN.com Election 2004." *cnn.com.* Accessed May 21, 2014. http://www.cnn.com/
    ELECTION/2004/pages/results/states/US/P/00/epolls.0.html.
Eliot, T.S. "The Hollow Men." In *T.S. Eliot: Selected Poems*, 77–80. San Diego: Harcourt
    Brace Jovanovich Publishers, 1988.
Goffman, Erving. "On Field Work." *Journal of Contemporary Ethnography* 18 (1989):
    123–132.
Goodall, H.L. Jr. *Writing the New Ethnography.* Walnut Creek, CA: AltaMira Press,
    2000.
Khuankaew, Ouyporn, and Kathryn L. Norsworthy. "Struggles for Peace, Justice,
    Unity and Freedom: Stories of the Women of Burma." *Seeds of Peace* 16 (2000):
    16–18.
Kirkpatrick, David D. "Gay and Republican, But Not Necessarily Disloyal to President."
    New York Times, March 9, 2004.
Norsworthy, Kathryn L., with Ouyporn Khuankaew. "Bringing Social Justice to
    International Practices of Counseling Psychology." In *Handbook for Social Justice
    in Counseling Psychology: Leadership, Vision, and Action*, edited by Rebecca L.
    Toporek, Lawrence Gerstein, Nadya Fouad, Gargi Roysircar-Sodowsky, and
    Tania Israel, 421–441. Thousand Oaks, CA: Sage, 2005.
Norsworthy, Kathryn L., and Ouyporn Khuankaew. "Feminist Border Crossings:
    Our Transnational Partnership in Peace and Justice Work." In *Helping Beyond
    the 50-Minute Hour: Therapists Involved in Meaningful Social Action*, edited by
    Jeffrey A. Kottler, Matt Englar-Carlson, and Jon Carlson, 222–233. New York:
    Routledge, 2012.
"State Laws Prohibiting Recognition of Same-Sex Relationships." *thetaskforce.org*, May
    15, 2013. Accessed June 4, 2014. http://www.thetaskforce.org/downloads/reports/
    issue_maps/samesex_relationships_5_15_13.pdf.
Tillmann, Lisa M. "The State of Unions: Politics and Poetics of Performance."
    Qualitative Inquiry 15 (2009): 545–560.
Tillmann-Healy, Lisa M. "A Secret Life in a Culture of Thinness: Reflections on Body,
    Food, and Bulimia." In *Composing Ethnography: Alternative Forms of Qualitative*

Writing, edited by Carolyn Ellis and Arthur P. Bochner, 77–109. Walnut Creek, CA: AltaMira Press, 1996.

——. *Life Projects: A Narrative Ethnography of Gay-Straight Friendship*. Ph.D. diss., University of South Florida, 1998.

——. *Between Gay and Straight: Understanding Friendship across Sexual Orientation*. Walnut Creek, CA: AltaMira Press, 2001.

——. "Friendship as Method." *Qualitative Inquiry* 9 (2003): 729–749.

Warner, Michael. *The Trouble with Normal: Sex, Politics, and the Ethics of Queer Life*. New York: The Free Press, 1999.

7

DEADLINE

ETHICS AND THE ETHNOGRAPHIC DIVORCE[1]

Stretching back in my home office chair, I access the college voicemail. The system lets me know, "You have one new message."

A friendly but unfamiliar male voice: "Hi, Dr. Tillmann. I'm writing a story about gay–straight friendships."

This triggers my PTPD (Post-Traumatic *Presidency* Disorder). Eight years of beating back threats to civil rights. Under Gore or Kerry, would friendship across sexual orientation—the topic of my dissertation and first book—have passed from social justice crusade to "so 20th century"?

Other feelings flood my body: hope for the change Obama promised; pride that a reporter views my work as potentially useful; and fear. Raw fear.

"I found your book, *Between Gay and Straight*, on Amazon," says the voice.

Shit. Can I talk about that in light of—

"My piece is for the Sunday Style section . . ."

I cringe at the cliché. Fifteen years of friendship, teaching, research, and activism relegated to the Style section. *Queer Eye* and the great sigh.

". . . of the *New York Times*."

The *Times*? Eight years too late, this call. In 2001, publicity for my newly released book had accelerated: features in the *Milwaukee Journal* and the *St. Paul Pioneer Press*, a one-hour discussion on Minnesota Public Radio, then . . . 9/11. With the Cheney cabal hawking WMD mythology, who had space for a heartfelt, uplifting story of my husband's and my integration into a network of gay male friends? Who cared that a heterosexual South Dakota farm boy grew up to play right centerfield for a predominantly gay male team in a queer softball league? We were at war, goddamn it!

The voice again: "I'd like to ask you a couple of questions."

Tension grips my neck. I have *responses*, I think, but few answers. You may not like the answers I do have. *I* don't like them. They are not *good* answers to questions flowing naturally from what had been a good story. The Afterword is a fucking downer.

I imagine our interview opening with, "So, Lisa, do you and your husband still keep in contact with members of the Cove team?"

"Yes," I would tell you honestly, "I still count these men among my closest friends."

An astute Sunday Style reporter would note: "You said 'I' and 'my.' What about your husband?"

Struggling to swallow, I suppose I would have to let you know, "He and I divorced in 2006."

"Your-husband-came-out-as-gay," you might blurt out, as many did, the inflection on "gay" straddling question and declaration.

To be fair, I did live, write, and publish a border-crossing ethnography. In it, I discussed ongoing speculation about my husband's sexual orientation. But I would answer, "No. The project, our friends, had nothing to do with the divorce."

Your humanity might prevent you from probing, "What then? In the book, you two seemed so perf—"

"Call it a period piece" would be my wry reply.

Even if asked, I would not tell a reporter about the grueling Tuesdays. Session after session, he and I claw through the muck of our pasts. I frantically dig for the buried trunk of his unhappiness.

I surely would not speak of that April Tuesday. Seemingly, we had gained ground. London in March. Vegas the previous Thursday to Sunday. We arrive for the week's session. He uses the restroom while I chat up our counselor about slots, Cirque du Soleil, and Pai Gow poker. He returns with a near-empty bottle of water, sits down, and announces, "I had an affair."

I would not disclose how many people have stopped me at this point to interject: "With a man?"

Therefore, I would not have to repeat my standby reply: "If my husband had come out as gay, that may have been infinitely *easier*—unless that too had involved infidelity, then I suspect it would have felt exactly the same: *personal*." I refuse to debate origins of sexual orientation. With sexual indiscretion, there is no debate. Irrefutably, it's a choice. In his case, two and a half *years* of choices.

I would leave out his leaving that Tuesday night, his secession from the "daringly honest union" I wrote about in *Between Gay and Straight*.

To my disclosure of divorce, you might offer, "I'm sorry. I had noticed you dropped the hyphenated name."

I'm not sure "dropped" captures it, I would think but not say. Cast? No . . . *severed.*

Gingerly you might ask: "Does your husband—" You would catch yourself. "Your *ex*-husband . . . does he still play in a gay league?"

"No," I would reply. "He has . . . uh . . . other commitments."

I would not tell you that my ex-husband abandoned his mistress and called next to the stand a Jehovah's Witness. He converted so they could marry in 2008. He indeed "came out"—not of the closet but into the Watchtower.

Yeah, I realize those are not mutually exclusive spaces.

See, if I did tell you of his conversion, you likely would say incredulously, "According to Watchtower dogma, homosexuality is an abomination and may be caused by demon possession!"

To this, I would have to admit, "I did read that."

"B-but," you might sputter, "does your ex, the protagonist from *Between Gay and Straight* . . . does he believe that?"

"I don't know," I would have to answer. Maybe I never knew.

If I told you all this, you would be within your rights to say, "This story sucks!"

Which is exactly why I hesitate to report to reporters on this subject. Exactly why "Deadline" was the *pre*-narrative spelunking in my belly for more than three years, unable to stand and walk to the page.

Perhaps, Mr. Sunday Style Reporter, these are *not* the questions you wanted to ask. Perhaps you wanted academic reflections on media portrayals or on intersections between the political climate and interpersonal relationships. "Your" questions are really my projections— *my* questions.

A few more: was *Between Gay and Straight* only a story, only *my* story? Was this character—this relationship—that I constructed merely a *con*struct? What happens when the characters we create stop saying their lines, when the people on whom we base these characters cut us from their scripts?

Into my voicemail, you say, "I'm on a really tight deadline."

Dead, I think. Exhausted. Extinguished. Barren. Buried.

Line. Line of dialogue. Line of text. Research line. *Life*line.

Dead Line.

"I would need to speak to you in the next hour. If you do get this, the name is Doug."

Of course it is. That's the name of his character too.

Characters need no ethical protections, but what of the *humans* whose love, ambivalence, and/or cruelty inspire our renderings? As a researcher—as a professor who *teaches* research ethics—I am obligated to ensure accuracy, to uphold confidentiality, to secure informed consent, to use deception only as a last resort, and to promote beneficence.

In terms of accuracy, I could stand behind public record. My ex-husband confessed to the affair in open court, and both the county and the church sanctioned his remarriage. Public record provides legal cover, but what of my "relational ethics"?[2]

Confidentiality would be impossible to offer. This account only makes sense in connection to my book, which I published under my real name and in which I used his real name. Even if I wrote under a pseudonym and altered every identity marker, his character remains identifiable— to him, to his second wife, to the children he now helps raise.

To perform and/or publish this piece, am I obligated to inform *all* of them? To secure their permission?

Would proceeding without informed consent constitute a form of deception? What of *his* deception? Am I obligated to hold myself to a higher ethical standard as a researcher than he embodied as my husband?

Part of me wants to say, "If he didn't want to be typecast as a cad, he shouldn't have played the part so convincingly!" But "cad" oversimplifies and flattens.[3] He deceived me about the affair but acted honorably in many other ways throughout our 13 years together. I did not have an affair but surely inflicted harm with my words, my actions, my inactions.

In *Between Gay and Straight*, I advocated "friendship as method," researching with the practices, at the pace, in the natural contexts, and with an ethic of friendship—a stance of caring, hope, and love.[4] To promote understanding and combat injustice, I suggested using this approach to research perpetrators of hate crimes, such as the men who assassinated Matthew Shepard. Surely my ex-husband deserves at least the ethical consideration I thought appropriate for *murderers.*

Finally, beneficence calls me to minimize the risks and maximize the benefits of research. He has moved on to another family, another life. How might revisiting our dissolution and understanding more about its impact on me and on my work facilitate his learning and growth? Is it arrogant and self-serving to think that such revisiting would provoke anything beyond shame and pain?

What of my ex-husband's journey? How does *he* frame our life together and our unraveling? What does my character in his story think, feel, and do?

Every human, including him, has to live with uncertainty, vulnerability, and injustice. As Art Bochner reminds, there often is "no getting to the bottom, no transcendental point of view, no final truth to be rendered."[5] We move forward with pieces missing. We do not get *over*, which implies resolution, but get *on*—alone and in solidarity.

Of seven friends associated with my work, one survived an alcoholic family system. Two lived through divorces of their parents, both of them while children; at age 40, one bore witness to his mother's second divorce, this one from the only man he ever called "Dad." Five have buried one or both parents. One mom and one dad suffered cardiac arrest and flashed quickly from this life; slowly and cruelly, cancer, ALS, and Alzheimer's took the others. All seven have endured the wrenching end of a partnership. I cannot reveal how many are HIV positive. With the hopeful exception of HIV, these losses will not be overcome; they will be integrated, as those men and I remain integrated in friendship.

I decide that I can do this. I can tell . . . Doug about the subversive and liberatory potential of friendship across difference, offer something helpful to inspire members of dominant groups to become better allies to those marginalized by sexual orientation and/or other social locations. My core feels solid, resolute . . . but my hand shakes when dialing Doug's number.

One ring.

My chest caves.

Two.

Given my own swirling uncertainties, will I be able to frame this in a useful way?

Three rings. Click.

"This is Doug . . ."

"D-doug?"

". . . please leave a message."

I pull my iPhone away from my ear. The "End Call" button beckons. My left index finger swoops.

No. I clear my throat. "Doug, this is Lisa returning your call. I don't know if your story is complete, but I can speak with you. You have my number."

Doug never calls back.[6]

Notes

1   Earlier versions of "Deadline" were presented at the 2009 National Communication Association meetings and published in *Qualitative Inquiry* (Tillmann 2010; used with permission, Sage Publications: http://qix.sagepub.com/content/16/7/596. abstract). A webpage for this chapter may be found at: http://www.insolidarity book.com/deadline.html.

2   According to Carolyn Ellis (2007, 3), "Relational ethics requires researchers to act from our hearts and minds, acknowledge our interpersonal bonds to others, and take responsibility for actions and their consequences."

3   See Kiesinger (2002).

4   See the Appendix and Tillmann-Healy (1998, 2001, 2003).

5   See Bochner (1997, 429).

6   I gave my ex-husband the opportunity to review and respond to this piece. He declined.

References

Bochner, Arthur P. "It's about Time: Narrative and the Divided Self." *Qualitative Inquiry* 3, no. 4 (1997): 418–438.

Ellis, Carolyn. "Telling Secrets, Revealing Lives: Relational Ethics in Research with Intimate Others." *Qualitative Inquiry* 13, no. 1 (2007): 3–29.

Kiesinger, Christine E. "My Father's Shoes: The Therapeutic Value of Narrative Reframing." In *Ethnographically Speaking: Autoethnography, Literature, and Aesthetics*, edited by Arthur P. Bochner and Carolyn Ellis, 95–114. Walnut Creek, CA: AltaMira Press, 2002.

Tillmann, Lisa M. "Deadline: Ethics and the Ethnographic Divorce." *Qualitative Inquiry* 16, no. 7 (2010): 596–598.

Tillmann-Healy, Lisa M. *Life Projects: A Narrative Ethnography of Gay-Straight Friendship*. Ph.D. diss., University of South Florida, 1998.

——. *Between Gay and Straight: Understanding Friendship across Sexual Orientation*. Walnut Creek, CA: AltaMira Press, 2001.

——. "Friendship as Method." *Qualitative Inquiry* 9 (2003): 729–749.

8
BUILD A BRIDGE OUT OF HER[1]

In *Monty Python and the Holy Grail*,
when Sir Bedevere, suspecting a witch
in his midst, asks, "Why do witches burn?"
Peasant Three infers, "Because they're made of wood?"
"So how do you tell," lobs Bedevere, "whether she's made of wood?"
Clever Peasant One conjectures,
"Build a bridge out of her."

Build a bridge out of her.
As I survey the shellacked November landscape,[2] I say let us all
build a bridge out of her.

What sort of bridge?

Sus

pen   s   ion?
Suspended between war ---------- and the promise of peace.

A Golden Gate
from "Mission Accomplished"[3]
to the audacity of hope.[4]

Guantanamo
remains open, but so do I.
I   Still   Hope.

A Golden Gate
suspending 83,000 tons of east coast steel.[5]
SOLID, substantial -------------- yet flexible, agile,
undulating with the wind, swaying nearly 28 feet,[6]
before again finding
her center.

Yes, we can.

Yes, build a bridge out of her.
But not a Bridge to No w h e r e.
No, not a bridge to the 50 residents of Gravina Island, Alaska
who just want to be left the fuck alone. *That's why they live there.*
No, not a 398-million-dollar bridge,[7] enough to build
26 schools, serving more than 16,000 students[8]
each year.

Build a bridge out of her.
Oh, but not the Minneapolis I-35.
No, not the truss arches that
crum
ble
d
to their knees
during rush hour,
August the first, 2007.
No, not the bridge that
tum
ble
d
100 vehicles
and 18 construction workers
toward the rushing river
below.
Thirteen people rushing
with or to their families
would rush
no
more.[9]

Build a bridge out of her.
But no, not the I-35. Not any of our country's
150,000 structurally deficient or functionally obsolete bridges.[10]
Our "representatives" pay for warplanes before commuter trains,
for AIG before levees.
And so our bridges
falling
down,
fall
ing
do
wn,
f
a
l
l
i
n
g
d
o
w
n.

Build a bridge out of her.
Maybe the Hudson River Bridge.
She carried working men and their families through
the Great Depression.

Seventy years later,
on that September Tuesday, this Hudson Bridge,
re-christened the George Washington Bridge,
held working men and women as they wept
for their burning city, their cremated comrades.
Yes, maybe the
George Washington Bridge.

Oh, but no.
No, not the George Washington Bridge.
No, because on the 22nd of September, 2010,
the bridge out of *her* would have said to Tyler Clementi,[11]
"No way. No way no Rutgers Scarlet Knights cheering,
no Phi Delta Theta fraternizing, no violin impresario playing,
no not-yet-out gay boy fretting
leaps from MY arms!"

The bridge out of *her*
would have said: "My sweet Tyler,
I just kicked the ass of your dumbass roommate
and lobbied Congress for you and your future soul mate.
No way you leap
from these trusses, boy."

Build a bridge out of her.
Oh, but not that bridge in Baghdad.
Nearly 1,000 pilgrims drowned, trampled, suffocated
on that bridge, on that August day
in 2005.[12]

Nearly 1,000 pilgrims.
Over 300 more than perished in the South Tower.[13]
The same number of flag-veiled coffins arrived in Dover
in the first *eight years* of the Afghan theater.[14]
Nearly 1,000 pilgrims on one bridge
in one city
on one August day.

Build a bridge out of her.
Perhaps a bridge over troubled water.[15]
That's sounding right. I will lay me down.
Yes, I will lay me down.

But the bridge out of her cannot stay down.
No, I must put this bridge called my back[16]
between facts ------------------------------- and Fox.
Between citizens -------------------------- and Citizens United.[17]
Between reality ------------------------------- and the Tea Party.
Between people ------------------------------- and poverty.
Between sisters -------------------------- and slavery.
Between brothers ------------------ and bombs,
fathers and tombs.
Mother Earth and the plunderers,
poetry and soul murderers.

So yes,   **up!**
build a bridge out of her.   **rise**
But see her. Do you see her now through the fog?   **will**
This is a *draw*bridge, baby, and when she draws, **she**

Notes

1   Earlier versions of "Build a Bridge Out of Her" were presented at the 2010 National Communication Association meetings and published in *Cultural Studies↔Critical Methodologies* (Tillmann 2011; used with permission, Sage Publications: http://csc.sagepub.com/content/11/5/516.abstract). A webpage for this chapter may be found at: http://www.insolidaritybook.com/build-bridge.html.

2   After Republicans gained control of the U.S. House of Representatives in November 2010, President Obama referred to the election results as a "shellacking."

3   President Bush spoke in front of an infamous banner reading "Mission Accomplished" in 2003. Though he announced the end of major combat operations in Iraq, the U.S. occupation would continue until the end of 2011.

4   *The Audacity of Hope* is the title of President Obama's second book.

5   See "Golden Gate Bridge, California" (n.d.).

6   See Creager (June 7, 2010).

7   The proposed "Bridge to Nowhere," eventually scrapped, became a symbol of wasteful spending during the George W. Bush administration; see Schlanger (August 8, 2013).

8   According to the National Clearinghouse for Educational Facilities, the average construction cost in 2010 of an elementary school serving 600 students was $14.8 million; see "Data & Statistics" (June 5, 2014).

9   See "Highway Accident Report: Collapse of I-35W Highway Bridge" (n.d.).

10 See "Structurally Deficient and Functionally Obsolete Bridges by Year" (n.d.).

11 Tyler Clementi's college roommate surreptitiously took video of an intimate encounter between Tyler and another young man. After his roommate broadcast the encounter on the Internet, Tyler leapt to his death from the George Washington Bridge.

12 See Farrell (November 11, 2008).

13 See Lipton (July 22, 2004).

14 See "Operation Enduring Freedom" (n.d.).

15 A nod, of course, to folk singers Paul Simon and Art Garfunkel.

16 A nod to the feminist manifesto *This Bridge Called My Back*, edited by Cherrie Moraga and Gloria Anzaldua (1983).

17 In 2010, the U.S. Supreme Court in *Citizens United v. Federal Election Commission* struck down all limits on corporate funding of political broadcasts.

References

Creager, Ellen. "Take a Walk across Golden Gate Bridge, San Francisco's Icon." *seattletimes.com*, June 7, 2010. Accessed June 5, 2014. http://seattletimes.com/html/travel/2012014206_trgoldengate06.html.

"Data & Statistics." *National Clearinghouse for Educational Facilities*, June 5, 2014. Accessed June 5, 2014. http://www.ncef.org/ds/statistics.cfm#.

Farrell, Stephen. "Baghdad Bridge Reopens, Restitching a Divided Area." *nytimes.com*, November 11, 2008. Accessed June 5, 2014. http://www.infrastructurereportcard.org/a/#e/sd-fo-bridges-year.

"Golden Gate Bridge, California." *American Society of Civil Engineers*. Accessed June 5, 2014.   http://www.asce.org/People-and-Projects/Projects/Monuments-of-the-Millennium/Golden-Gate-Bridge,-California/.

"Highway Accident Report: Collapse of I-35W Highway Bridge." *National Transportation Safety Board*. Accessed June 5, 2014. http://www.ntsb.gov/investigations/summary/HAR0803.htm.

Lipton, Eric. "Study Maps the Location of Deaths in the Twin Towers." *nytimes.com*, July 22, 2004. Accessed June 5, 2014. http://www.nytimes.com/2004/07/22/nyregion/study-maps-the-location-of-deaths-in-the-twin-towers.html.

Moraga, Cherrie, and Gloria Anzaldua, eds. *This Bridge Called My Back: Writings by Radical Women of Color*. New York: Kitchen Table Press, 1983.

"Operation Enduring Freedom." *icasualties.org*. Accessed June 5, 2014. http://icasualties.org/oef/.

Schlanger, Danielle. "Bridge to Nowhere Becomes Ferry to Nowhere as 'Uncle Ted Is No Longer with Us.'" *huffingtonpost.com*, August 8, 2013. Accessed June 5, 2014. http://www.huffingtonpost.com/2013/08/08/bridge-to-nowhere_n_3727865.html.

"Structurally Deficient and Functionally Obsolete Bridges by Year." *infrastructure reportcard.org*. Accessed June 5, 2014. http://www.infrastructurereportcard.org/a/#e/sd-fo-bridges-year.

Tillmann, Lisa M. "Build a Bridge Out of Her." *Cultural Studies↔Critical Methodologies* 11, no. 5 (2011): 516–518.

9

WEDDING ALBUM

AN ANTI-HETEROSEXIST PERFORMANCE TEXT[1]

For Kathryn Norsworthy and Deena Flamm

June the twelfth, 1967,
the Supreme Court renders a unanimous decision.[2]
"Hear ye,"
say they, we find the state of Virginia guilty.
We indict discrimination and segregation in this co-conspiracy
and hereby set free
our Loving citizens:
husband Richard Loving, White,
wife Mildred, African- and Native-American.
Justices White and Black—no fabrication—
join Clark, Fortas, Douglas, Stewart,
Brennan, Harlan, and Warren
to strike down prohibitions to miscegenation
as violations of fourteenth amendment protections.
"Hear ye."

Figure 9.1 Beth and John Tillmann.

1969, June the twenty-first,
my parents wed in a small-town church.
The longest day,
think they, as summer solstice stretches
further than budgets for reception or dress.
A bride of nineteen, four months pregnant;
a groom of twenty, soon to be drafted.
The longest day.

Figure 9.2

To mark my wedding, New Year's Eve, 1995,
bullets of water fire from the sky.
"Signs of luck,"
say they, as wind whips, thunder thwacks, and lightning strikes.
White-lighted, braided-trunk ficus laid waste,
star-patterned luminaries shoot up in flames.
Signs of luck.

Figure 9.3 Jennifer Pickman.

Educations, graduations,
professional-level income.
Adventure, laughter, conversation,
a shared network of friends.
Without children to tend,
we are able to mend
a divorcing couple's dream home
half-renovated, then abandoned.

Good years,
think we,
our parents young and healthy.
A tenure-track job, savings, security.
Not perfectly enchanted.
We lose Jennifer, our maid of honor,
and my dear Aunt Patsy to cancer.
Elders fall to stroke, cardiac arrest, pneumonia.
Still, good years.

The twenty-first of September, 1996:
the sixteenth International Day of Peace.
The irony,
think we, as, of all presidents, Clinton
signs DOMA, Defense of Marriage legislation,
fortifying the institution
against subversion of suburban
families headed by two mothers or fathers
and insurrection of tax-paying same-sex couples.
As for perils posed by cum-stained-dress-saving interns
and narcissistic grandiosity,
simply repeat after me, "I did not have sex with that woman,
Miss Lewinsky."
The irony.

Out of proportion to our privilege and circumstance,
we become Responsible, Sedate, and Serious.
Good enough,
think I, such is the maturation compromise,
the relational pentameter's rise, fall, rise, fall, rise.
Academic vampires suck, veins bleed out, passion cools.
Projects seep into every room.
A summer suspended on scaffolding, he at fifteen feet, I at ten,
double coating our exterior to weather the elements,
while inside the climate
lies dry and silent.

We fight rarely and fairly, so I choose to believe.
We have friendship, respect, mutuality.
Good enough.

Neither proposes disengagement, dropped to one knee,
offering a box of ambivalence, a loneliness ring.
Nothing,
says he, while in the cellar of his conscience
he constructs Betrothed and Beyond compartments.
I misread signs of relational miscarriage.
No legislation passes to defend my marriage.
Nothing.

The eleventh of April, 411, 2006,
seated in our marital therapist's office,
husband looks at his feet, at our counselor, then at me.
"I am leaving,"
says he.
He departs that night; I pack for the next life in June.
How to divide thirteen years' signifiers of two?
Wedding gifts, letters, cards, what do you choose?
What to do with gown and veil of ivory satin and beads,
shrink-wrapped, boxed, preserved, and steam-cleaned,
saved for a daughter not to be?
Photos plucked from frames, some discarded as trash.
Continuity and certainty burned to ash.
Leaving.

The law that once undergirded my marriage
blasts the foundation and scatters the wreckage.
In preparation to attend a post-apocalypse wedding,
I bear arms of a date, dapper, dashing, and handsome.
"Stunning,"
say I with a playful tug to his tie.

This old friend, a gay man,
barred from the institution
I just escaped.
We make quite a pair:
a divorcée with a sensibility queer
and a man who will fall for an international partner,
a legal stranger.
In the incense-perfumed, flower-festooned chapel
we go catty, sarcastic, and cynical,
until we see her,
my beloved student, Laura.
A bride full of light, hope, promise, and faith,
optimism, openness, caring, and grace.
Stunning.

Figure 9.4 John Sansoucie.

A profile photo, a short story, a test of personality,
thirty dollars a month to sing in eHarmony.
Virtual prospects, perhaps two hundred, in the flesh, sixteen men
and then, in March 2008,
John.
Winter turns to spring.
"Marry me,"
says he, an invitation to re-enter a structure of inequity,
a fraternity excluding so many of my friends.
"Marry me."

June the twelfth, 2011: an anniversary, number forty-three.
For Virginia, a beautiful defeat;
for Loving, for justice, a sweet victory.
This June the twelfth, after seventeen years together,
a Boston marriage joins
what no pseudo-defender legislator can tear asunder.
Neither tuxedo nor bustle, neither groom nor bride,
partners, lovers, friends stand side-by-side.
"We do,"
say the two,
"take you Deena, take you Kathryn."
As woman joins with woman,
John, my fiancé, and I rise to defend the sanctity of this union
against heterosexism, homophobia, heteronormativity,
prejudice, discrimination, inequality.
We do.

Figure 9.5 John Sansoucie, Lisa Tillmann, Kathryn Norsworthy, and Deena Flamm.

Coda

In 2012, a Pew poll found for the first time that more Americans support than oppose same-sex marriage;[3] Vice President Biden and President Obama gave their endorsements; and a federal appeals court, consisting of justices appointed by Presidents Reagan, H.W. Bush, and Clinton, ruled unconstitutional the denial of federal benefits to married same-sex couples.[4] On June 26, 2013, the U.S. Supreme Court in *United States v. Windsor* struck down the Defense of Marriage Act (DOMA), opening federal benefits to same-sex couples who marry in the District of Columbia (where Richard and Mildred Loving wed) and in the 19 states in which it is legal as of this writing: Massachusetts,[5] Connecticut,[6] Iowa,[7] Vermont,[8] New Hampshire,[9] New York,[10] Washington,[11] Maryland,[12] Maine,[13] Rhode Island,[14] Delaware,[15] Minnesota,[16] California,[17] New Jersey,[18] Hawaii,[19] Illinois,[20] New Mexico,[21] Oregon,[22] and Pennsylvania.[23] Prior to DOMA's demise, even if legally married, a member of a same-sex couple could not collect a deceased spouse's social security or facilitate immigration of a spouse born outside the United States. The gay male friend I brought as a guest to my first post-divorce wedding decided to live in England with his Scottish husband in no small part due to marriage inequality in the United States.

Seventeen countries on four continents have established a federal right for same-sex marriage.[24] The day after its ruling on DOMA, the U.S. Supreme Court avoided consideration of a federal right by refusing to hear a case challenging a state ban on same-sex marriage.

As indicated, my friends Kathryn Norsworthy and Deena Flamm, to whom this piece is dedicated, legally wed in Massachusetts in 2011. However, we reside in Florida, where a constitutional amendment bars the state from recognizing their union. As of this writing, 30 states have laws or amendments prohibiting same-sex marriage.[25] Among them are 14 of the 16 states that had anti-miscegenation laws struck down by the U.S. Supreme Court in 1967.[26]

The primary rhetorical strategies of opponents to same-sex marriage mirror those used by opponents to interracial marriage. One strategy involves the notion of "God's plan." The trial judge in *Loving v. Virginia*, Leon M. Bazile, proclaimed, "Almighty God created the races white, black, yellow, malay and red, and he placed them on separate continents. And but for the interference with his arrangement there would be no cause for such marriages."[27] His honor's "logic" matches the intellectual heft of "God created Adam and Eve, not Adam and Steve."[28] A second strategy involves the alleged protection of children. Opponents of both interracial and same-sex marriage have argued that growing up in a family headed by a mixed-race or same-sex couple damages children, a claim rejected by every major medical,[29] psychological,[30] and child welfare association. The relevant damaging factors are, of course, *racism* and *homophobia*.

In 2007, a year before her death, Mildred Loving issued a statement marking the 40th anniversary of *Loving v. Virginia*. The conclusion reads:[31]

> Surrounded as I am now by wonderful children and grand-children, not a day goes by that I don't think of Richard and our love, our right to marry, and how much it meant to me to have that freedom to marry the person precious to me, even if others thought he was the "wrong kind of person" for me to

marry. I believe all Americans, no matter their race, no matter their sex, no matter their sexual orientation, should have that same freedom to marry. Government has no business imposing some people's religious beliefs over others. Especially if it denies people's civil rights.

I am still not a political person,[32] but I am proud that Richard's and my name is on a court case that can help reinforce the love, the commitment, the fairness, and the family that so many people, black or white, young or old, gay or straight seek in life. I support the freedom to marry for all. That's what Loving, and loving, are all about.

My own relationship to marriage remains more ambivalent than Mrs. Loving's. On one hand, I love my partner and am committed to our bond. I also appreciate the long-term stability of my parents' union and have experienced and witnessed how extending and withholding social support shores up and undermines relationships. I worry about preceding John in death. He would lose health coverage obtained through my employer, and the taxes on my estate, which he would not pay as my spouse, would be substantial (admittedly a "peril" of the privileged). On the other, I question marriage on both personal and political grounds. I endured a complex and painful divorce. Perhaps by delaying marriage, I am postponing the risk of living through another dissolution. In a larger sense, marriage inequality reflects and reinforces other structural inequities, including those associated with class and gender. Doesn't every person, married or not, deserve emotional and economic security? Knowing what I do now, can I be both a heterosexual ally and married? Is participating in heterosexual marriage in its current form any more ethical than joining an all-White social club?

On February 17, 2012, John and I and Kathryn and Deena became the 265th and 266th couples to sign up for Orlando's domestic partner registry. On May 22, 2012, Orange County, Florida (our home county), adopted a parallel registry. As members of the Orlando Anti-Discrimination Ordinance Committee, Kathryn and I campaigned for both registries. While the rights granted are essential, such as the right to visit John in a hospital or hospice, they represent a tiny fraction of the more than 1100 federal rights and protections that come with marriage.[33] I am fortunate to work for a college that provides domestic partner benefits to both same- and different-sex couples, though under federal law, I pay taxes on those benefits (married employees do not).

Since 2001, I have engaged in civil rights activism as a heterosexual woman, both married and divorced, both partnered and single. In some ways, I felt more effective when I had both heterosexual and marital privilege (I also am rather conventionally feminine in gender presentation, White, comfortably middle-class, educated, and able-bodied). While married, I could speak "purely" as an ally, as someone with nothing immediately personal to gain. In advocating for city and county domestic partner registries, I felt more "in the trenches," fighting for rights I might need to exercise, and as an unmarried woman cohabitating with her partner, I was subject to the same rhetoric of "living in sin" as were my LGBTQ+ friends and fellow citizens.

Full marriage equality will come. In the meantime and thereafter, I hope that LGBTQ+ communities and their allies will pursue a parallel equality agenda, one that seeks to uphold each person's basic human rights—the right to safe, nutritious food; to a clean, sustainable environment; to secure housing; to meaningful work and a living wage; to health care; to freedom from discrimination and violence; and to loving relationships—regardless of marital (or any other) status.

Notes

1 Earlier versions of "Wedding Album" were presented at the 2013 International Congress of Qualitative Inquiry and published in the *Handbook of Autoethnography* (Tillmann 2013; used with permission, Left Coast Press, Inc.). My parents' wedding photograph is courtesy of John and Beth Tillmann. A webpage for this chapter may be found at: http://www.insolidaritybook.com/wedding.html.

2 Mildred Delores Jeter and Richard Perry Loving married in the District of Columbia on June 2, 1958. Police arrested the couple upon return to their home in Virginia, where marriage between White and Black persons was a felony carrying up to a five-year prison term. The Lovings pled guilty and received a one-year jail sentence, suspended if they left the state. The 1967 Supreme Court ruling in *Loving v. Virginia* invalidated anti-miscegenation statutes in 16 states.

3 See "Religion and Attitudes toward Same-Sex Marriage" (February 7, 2012).

4 See Seelye and Bronner (May 31, 2012).

5 Enacted in 2004 via the Supreme Judicial Court of Massachusetts' ruling in *Goodridge v. Department of Public Health* ("Massachusetts" n.d.).

6 Enacted in 2008 via the Connecticut Supreme Court ruling in *Kerrigan and Mock v. The CT Department of Public Health*; in 2009, the legislature and governor reaffirmed the ruling ("Connecticut" n.d.).

7 Enacted in 2009 via the Iowa Supreme Court ruling in *Varnum v. Brien* ("Iowa" n.d.).

8 Enacted legislatively in 2009 with the Vermont House and Senate overriding a veto by Governor Jim Douglas (Gram April 7, 2009).

9 Enacted legislatively in 2010; survived an attempt to repeal in 2012 ("New Hampshire" n.d.).

10 Enacted legislatively in 2011 (Kaplan July 23, 2011).

11 Enacted legislatively in 2012; survived a voter referendum the same year ("Washington" n.d.).

12 Enacted legislatively in 2012; survived a voter referendum the same year ("Maryland" n.d.).

13 Enacted, in 2012, by popular vote, another milestone for marriage equality ("Maine" n.d.).

14 Enacted legislatively in 2013 ("Rhode Island" n.d.).

15 Enacted legislatively in 2013 ("Delaware" n.d.).

16 Enacted legislatively in 2013 ("Minnesota" n.d.).

17 In May 2008, the California Supreme Court in *In Re: Marriage Cases* upheld the right for same-sex couples to marry. That November, the state's electorate narrowly passed Proposition 8, a constitutional amendment banning same-sex marriage. In 2010, a district court found Prop 8 unconstitutional, a ruling upheld by the U.S. Ninth Circuit Court of Appeals in 2012. Prop 8 proponents appealed to the U.S. Supreme Court, which ruled in 2013 that the plaintiffs lacked legal standing. This let stand the lower courts' rulings and cleared the way for same-sex marriage in California ("California" n.d.).

18 In 2012, Governor Chris Christie vetoed a same-sex marriage bill passed by the New Jersey legislature. On September 27, 2013, a Mercer County Superior Court Judge ruled in favor of marriage equality in *Garden State Equality et al. v. Dow et al.* On October 21, 2013, the Christie administration dropped its appeal of the ruling ("New Jersey" n.d.).

19 Enacted legislatively on November 13, 2013 ("Hawaii" n.d.).

20 Enacted legislatively on November 20, 2013 ("Illinois" n.d.).

21 The New Mexico Supreme Court ruled unanimously in favor of same-sex marriage on December 19, 2013 ("New Mexico" n.d.).

22 Enacted in 2014 when Federal District Court Judge Michael J. McShane struck down the state's ban on same-sex marriage. Oregon's attorney general Ellen F. Rosenblum refused to appeal the decision, and the U.S. Supreme Court declined to issue a stay; see Liptak (June 4, 2014).

23 Enacted in 2014 when U.S. District Judge John E. Jones III struck down Pennsylvania's ban, which included not only same-sex marriage but also other forms of relationship recognition for same-sex couples. Governor Tom Corbett announced he would not appeal Judge Jones' ruling. See "Pennsylvania" (n.d.).

24 Marriage equality countries are: Argentina, Belgium, Brazil, Canada, Denmark, England, France, Iceland, Luxembourg, Netherlands, New Zealand, Norway, Portugal, South Africa, Spain, Sweden, and Uruguay ("Freedom to Marry Internationally" n.d.).

25 See "State Laws Prohibiting Recognition of Same-Sex Relationships" (May 15, 2013).

26 The 14 overlapping states are: Alabama, Arkansas, Florida, Georgia, Kentucky, Louisiana, Mississippi, Missouri, North Carolina, Oklahoma, South Carolina, Tennessee, Texas, and Virginia. Delaware and West Virginia also had anti-miscegenation statutes struck down in 1967. In 1996, the Delaware legislature passed a ban on same-sex marriage, which stood until 2013, when the body passed a marriage equality statute. West Virginia neither has a constitutional amendment barring same-sex marriage nor legally recognizes same-sex relationships (see "States" n.d.; "US Miscegenation" July 29, 2009).

27 See *Loving v. Virginia* (1967). Bazile died in 1967, the year of the landmark ruling in *Loving v. Virginia*. How disconcerting it would have been for him to study genetic anthropology and to learn that all modern humans share a common female *African* ancestor.

28 An infamous anti-gay slogan.

29 See "Coparent or Second-Parent Adoption by Same-Sex Parents" (n.d.).

30 See "Sexual Orientation, Parents, & Children" (2004).

31 See Loving (June 12, 2007).

32 Indeed neither Richard nor Mildred Loving attended the U.S. Supreme Court hearing. When asked by his attorney what he should convey to the justices on his behalf, Richard Loving said only, "Tell the Court I love my wife"; see the documentary *The Loving Story* (2011).

33 See "Protections and Responsibilities of Marriage" (n.d.).

References

"California." *freedomtomarry.org*. Accessed May 16, 2014. http://www.freedomto marry.org/states/entry/c/california.

"Connecticut." *freedomtomarry.org*. Accessed May 17, 2014. http://www.freedomto marry.org/states/entry/c/connecticut.

"Coparent or Second-Parent Adoption by Same-Sex Parents." *American Academy of Pediatrics*. Accessed May 16, 2014. http://pediatrics.aappublications.org/content/ 109/2/339.full.

"Delaware." *freedomtomarry.org*. Accessed May 17, 2014. http://www.freedomtomarry. org/states/entry/c/delaware.

"Freedom to Marry Internationally." *freedomtomarry.org*. Accessed May 21, 2014. http://www.freedomtomarry.org/landscape/entry/c/international.

Gram, Dave. "Vermont Legalizes Gay Marriage, Overrides Governor's Veto." *Huffington Post*, April 7, 2009. Accessed May 21, 2014. www.huffingtonpost.com/2009/ 04/07/vermont-legalizes-gay-mar_n_184034.html.

"Hawaii." *freedomtomarry.org*. Accessed May 21, 2014. http://www.freedomtomarry.org/states/entry/c/hawaii.

"Illinois." *freedomtomarry.org*. Accessed May 21, 2014. http://www.freedomtomarry.org/states/entry/c/illinois.

"Iowa." *freedomtomarry.org*. Accessed May 21, 2014. http://www.freedomtomarry.org/states/entry/c/iowa.

Kaplan, Thomas. "After Long Wait, Gay Couples Marry in New York." *nytimes.com*, July 23, 2011. Accessed May 21, 2014. www.nytimes.com/2011/07/24/nyregion/across-new-york-hundreds-of-gay-couples-to-marry-on-sunday.html?_r=1.

Liptak, Adam. "Justices Reject Call to Halt Gay Marriages in Oregon." *nytimes.com*, June 4, 2014. Accessed June 5, 2014. http://www.nytimes.com/2014/06/05/us/politics/supreme-court-rebuffs-call-to-end-same-sex-marriages-in-oregon.html.

Loving v. Virginia, 388 U.S. 1 (1967).

Loving, Mildred. "Loving for All." *freedomtomarry.org*, June 12, 2007. Accessed July 10, 2013. www.freedomtomarry.org/page/-/files/pdfs/mildred_loving-statement.pdf.

The Loving Story. Directed by Nancy Buirski. 2011. United States: Augusta Films.

"Maine." *freedomtomarry.org*. Accessed May 21, 2014. http://www.freedomtomarry.org/states/entry/c/maine.

"Maryland." *freedomtomarry.org*. Accessed May 21, 2014. http://www.freedomtomarry.org/states/entry/c/maryland.

"Massachusetts." *freedomtomarry.org*. Accessed May 30, 2014. http://www.freedomtomarry.org/states/entry/c/massachusetts.

"Minnesota." *freedomtomarry.org*. Accessed May 21, 2014. http://www.freedomtomarry.org/states/entry/c/minnesota.

"New Hampshire." *freedomtomarry.org*. Accessed May 21, 2014. http://www.freedomtomarry.org/states/entry/c/new-hampshire.

"New Jersey." *freedomtomarry.org*. Accessed May 21, 2014. http://www.freedomtomarry.org/states/entry/c/new-jersey.

"New Mexico." *freedomtomarry.org*. Accessed May 21, 2014. http://www.freedomtomarry.org/states/entry/c/new-mexico.

"Pennsylvania." *freedomtomarry.org*. Accessed June 5, 2014. http://www.freedomtomarry.org/states/entry/c/pennsylvania.

"Protections and Responsibilities of Marriage." *freedomtomarry.org*. Accessed May 21, 2014. http://www.freedomtomarry.org/pages/protections-and-responsibilities-of-marriage.

"Religion and Attitudes toward Same-Sex Marriage." *Pew Forum on Religion & Public Life*, February 7, 2012. Accessed July 12, 2013. http://www.pewforum.org/Gay-Marriage-and-Homosexuality/Religion-and-Attitudes-Toward-Same-Sex-Marriage.aspx.

"Rhode Island." *freedomtomarry.org*. Accessed May 21, 2014. http://www.freedomtomarry.org/states/entry/c/rhode-island.

Seelye, Katharine Q., and Ethan Bronner. "Appeals Court Turns Back Marriage Act as Unfair to Gays." *The New York Times*, May 31, 2012. Accessed May 25, 2014. www.nytimes.com/2012/06/01/us/appeals-court-rules-against-federal-marriage-act.html?_r=1&hp&pagewanted=print.

"Sexual Orientation, Parents, & Children." *American Psychological Association*. 2004. Accessed May 16, 2014. www.apa.org/about/policy/parenting.aspx.

"State Laws Prohibiting Recognition of Same-Sex Relationships." *thetaskforce.org*, May 15, 2013. Accessed June 4, 2014. http://www.thetaskforce.org/downloads/reports/issue_maps/samesex_relationships_5_15_13.pdf.

"States." *freedomtomarry.org*. Accessed May 25, 2014. http://www.freedomtomarry.org/states/.

Tillmann, Lisa M. "Wedding Album: An Anti-heterosexist Performance Text." In *Handbook of Autoethnography*, edited by Stacy Holman Jones, Tony Adams, and Carolyn Ellis, 478–485. Walnut Creek, CA: Left Coast Press, 2013.

"US Miscegenation" [graph illustration]. *Wikipedia*, July 29, 2009. Accessed May 27, 2014. www.en.wikipedia.org/wiki/File:US_miscegenation.svg.

"Washington." *freedomtomarry.org*. Accessed May 27, 2014. http://www.freedomtomarry.org/states/entry/c/washington.

10

IN SOLIDARITY

COLLABORATIONS IN LGBTQ+[1]
ACTIVISM[2]

LISA M. TILLMANN AND
KATHRYN L. NORSWORTHY

Figure 10.1 Lisa Tillmann and Kathryn Norsworthy.

What follows is a fictional account. Our "characters" bear our real names; the other eight are composites of students we have taught and from whom we have learned; activists with whom we have worked; and staff, faculty, and administrators we have trained in venues such as Safe Zone. We portray our ally (Lisa)–lesbian (Kathryn) relationship this way for two reasons: one, we had not secured permission from real students, colleagues, or community members to represent their lives and experiences, and two, we seek a way to show our partnership, both personal and professional since 2000, in action. To each of us, the other is a powerful, singular, precious, irreplaceable force in her life. We make every effort here to do that justice.

Saturday, January 11, 2014, 8:45 a.m. Lisa, a 42-year-old White professor, puts down her green and grey backpack. She squares the shoulders of her long-sleeved hot pink top—set off by silver and raw ruby pendant and earrings—and adjusts the waistband of a nearly floor-length travel-knit skirt, black and fluttering. The hot pink complements her chocolate and grey-flecked hair, shoulder-length and spiral-curled.

Lisa uses her key to open Reeves Lodge. Of all training and classroom spaces on campus, this is her and Kathryn's favorite. From the outside, Reeves looks like a tiny Mediterranean villa with peach stucco walls and Spanish tile roof. Inside, the floors, walls, and vaulted ceiling—all of pine—suggest a cabin in the woods. Reeves has both comforts of home, including a restroom and small kitchen, and conveniences of an embedded computer and dual LCD projectors.

"Should we let in some light?" asks Kathryn. Lisa smiles at her colleague, a 60-year-old White professor. As the two begin pulling up shades covering windows on the east, south, and west walls, Lisa notices how movement, color, and sound whirl about Kathryn: brown and silver hair reaching toward her waist; flowing block print top purchased on a trip they took to India last year with their partners and Lisa's parents; jingling bell-trimmed skirt of evergreen silk; swaying beaded earrings. As sunlight floods the room, it reflects off Kathryn's gold, diamond, and mother of pearl wedding band.

They relocate the room's eight tables and 16 chairs, all on rollers, placing four tables along the east wall, one on either side of the whiteboard at the front (south) wall, and two along the west wall. The chairs' seat cushions flip up, allowing them to stack neatly. Kathryn and Lisa make four rows of four chairs, tucking two rows under each south window.

Crossing to the wide, floor-to-ceiling east window, they appreciatively note the well-tended yard with mature palm tree, picnic table, and barbecue grill. Tennis courts occupy the space behind the south windows; a mixed doubles match underway, the whaps of balls intersperse with players' laughter.

"Thank you for bringing supplies," Lisa says, setting Kathryn's canvas tote onto the computer station's desk along the west wall. "I put instructions for the Web of Oppression on a PowerPoint slide that can stay up throughout that exercise."

"Terrific," Kathryn responds. "Say, how are you doing?"

Lisa sighs. "Mmm ... my anxiety has spiked. Probably the book deadline and the three preps—including two new classes—that start next week. I'm not sleeping well." Kathryn's brown eyes fill with concern. Lisa then says, "Plus, I miss you to pieces." She reaches out for Kathryn, and the two embrace.

"Miss you too," Kathryn says into Lisa's ear. "Fall semester swallowed us both." They pull back to look at each other again. Kathryn continues, "I love teaching Engaged Buddhism, but I have to do it as an overload. As usual, I've got Practicum students collaborating every week with farmworkers in Apopka. You and I have been coordinating the proposal for a masters program in Peace and Social Justice . . ."

Lisa knows her friend's list of commitments goes on and on. She observes, "Sounds like that would provide meaning but leave little room for decompression and joy."

"A familiar theme for us," says Kathryn. "Here we stand on a Saturday morning, about to embark on a four-hour training."

"When we could be sipping mimosas on your back porch," Lisa replies.

Just then, Masao, a 40-year-old Japanese-American faculty colleague, enters. Seeing Kathryn and Lisa, he says, "Obviously this is the right room."

"Welcome, welcome, welcome!" greets Kathryn.

Admiring Masao's fitted t-shirt and jeans, both black, Lisa adds, "And aren't you too cool for school?"

Zach, a White 34-year-old colleague in Residential Life, enters next. He wears Levi's and a polo sporting school colors: navy with "Rollins" stitched in gold. "Hello, comrades," says Zach, hugging Kathryn, then Lisa. A tall and fit late-20s man accompanies Zach. Lisa and Kathryn note the man's shaved head and brown eyes, but neither recognizes him. "Meet Fernando, an old friend from church."

"Wonderful," says Lisa, offering her hand, which Fernando encloses between his.

Responding to Lisa's typically cold hands, Fernando says, "Warm heart." He steps back and straightens his neatly pressed steel-grey shirt tucked into black Kenneth Cole pants.

Lisa spots Naomi and Helen, two community activists she and Kathryn have known for more than five years. "Oh, yay!" Lisa rushes over to hug them while Kathryn continues talking to Fernando.

Two more colleagues enter: Jackie, a 25-year-old intern at the counseling center and Violet, 52, from Student Services.

Finally, a mid-40s man with brown eyes and sandy hair arrives. Lisa approaches him. "Have we met? I'm Lisa Tillmann."

"Blake," he says. "I've seen you around. You've testified at several public hearings."

"Do you work in media?" Lisa asks.

"Good memory," Blake replies. "I did for many years."

Kathryn glides over, introduces herself to Blake, and says to Lisa, "That's everyone."

Together Lisa and Kathryn walk toward the south wall, the front of the classroom. Kathryn opens her arms wide, as if ready to embrace the group. "Good morning. Could we please form a circle?" The group quickly falls in. "Welcome to Mindful Activism: LGBTQ+."

Lisa breaks in, "Probably the LGBT—lesbian, gay, bisexual, transgender—is familiar. We mean the Q+ to include queer, questioning, gender queer, plus asexual, pansexual, etcetera."

"Yes, thank you," says Kathryn, warmth radiating from her. "I see friends here, some old, some new. I am Kathryn Norsworthy, professor of Graduate Studies in Counseling here at Rollins."

Lisa smiles. "And I'm Lisa Tillmann, professor of Critical Media and Cultural Studies. We feel honored to join forces with you in exploring how to develop and hone our skills as activists engaged in the struggle for civil rights. Kathryn and I share a particular interest in how members of and allies to the LGBTQ+ community can collaborate effectively in this activism."

"Let me tell you a bit more about my colleague," Kathryn says. "Dr. Tillmann, Lisa, accepted a position at Rollins in 1999. She had written her dissertation on her husband's and her integration into a network of gay male friends and was rewriting that as a book that would be published in 2001 as *Between Gay and Straight*."

Lisa chimes in, "Kathryn, who came to Rollins in '92, was on sabbatical my first year. We met in the fall of 2000 at a screening of a documentary, *Our Voices*."

Kathryn explains, "Donna Lee, then-director of Multicultural Affairs, had interviewed minority students about their experiences in the classroom and on campus."

"During the debrief," Lisa says, "a woman with a rustling skirt and lion's mane . . ." Lisa winks at Kathryn. ". . . talked of how the students' testimonies of marginalization and exclusion moved and disturbed her. She gave voice to my responses to the film."

Kathryn tells the group, "I don't recall what either of us said, except that when Lisa spoke, she conveyed passion and conviction. I knew I needed to connect with her. What we expressed must have impacted others present because within a week, the Dean of Students called each of us, asking if we would co-chair the College's inaugural committee on diversity."

Lisa adds, "That committee provided the initial context for working together on social justice initiatives, at Rollins and in the community, and for becoming friends."

"In our many years of personal and activist collaboration," says Kathryn, "we have organized and co-facilitated trainings, helped implement policy changes at the College . . ." She nods toward Naomi and Helen. ". . . and participated in successful efforts in Orlando and Orange County to secure domestic partner registries and non-discrimination protections on the bases of sexual orientation and gender identity."

Lisa reports, "Meanwhile, we helped infuse our departments' curricula with the values of multiculturalism and social justice. Kathryn also has become a campus leader on community engagement pedagogy as well as a renowned scholar on decolonizing international psychology. In the U.S. and in Thailand, she advocates for women; for national, cultural, and religious minorities; and for the LGBTQ+ community."

"And Lisa has expanded her activism into social justice documentary filmmaking.[3] Two of her films have opened at the Global Peace Film Festival.

"Now let's hear from each of you," Kathryn directs. "Please tell the group where you stand in your journey on LGBTQ+ issues, what brought you to the training today, and to what initiative you wish to apply practices of mindful activism."

Running fingers through floppy red hair, Zach clears his throat. "My name is Zach. I work in Residential Life at the college. I'm married; my wife and I have a six-year-old daughter and a four-year-old son. My family attends a Lutheran church, and we recently elected our first gay bishop. This has divided our congregation. Many people, including me, wholeheartedly support this change. Others threaten to break from the ECLA."

Fernando explains, "Evangelical Lutheran Church in America."

"Right," says Zach. "At this workshop, I want to focus on fostering tolerance among people of faith, on helping them see that homosexuals are equal in the eyes of God."

Naomi bristles at the words "tolerance" and "homosexuals" but says nothing.

Café con leche skin sets off Fernando's brilliant smile. "Fernando. I'm 29. I grew up in the same church as Zach. I'm home on winter break until tomorrow, when I return to Gainesville. At UF, I study journalism full time, master's level. I did not attend Rollins for my BA, and I never worked here, so I'm not a member of the Rollins community. I am, however, part of the LGBTQ+ community.

"Anyway, Zach thought I should come because I've talked to him about exclusion. I'm biracial. My dad's Cuban and my mom's Irish, so in some circles I'm not Latino enough; in others, not White enough. And I'm bisexual. I encounter gay men who assume I'm 'really gay' but holding onto my heterosexual privilege, and I confront straight people who can't imagine why, if I'm attracted to women, I don't take the path of least resistance."

Kathryn asks, "And on what initiative will you center your work today?"

"When the Lake County school board blocked formation of a GSA, gay-straight alliance, I covered the story for the *Independent Florida Alligator*. So something pertaining to a GSA."

Naomi's dancing blue eyes complement her short salt-and-pepper hair. "I'm Naomi. Like Fernando, I neither attend nor am employed by Rollins, but for years, I have been in the trenches—or at least near them—with Kathryn and Lisa.

"As you can see," Naomi continues, running her hands over a loose-fitting man's shirt tucked into carpenter jeans, "my gender presentation is rather masculine—has been since I can remember, maybe age four. I haven't had surgery, and I don't take hormones, but in public, people sometimes read me as male. Restrooms have been a particular problem. Some women have flown into a panic, called security . . ." Her voice trails off.

Naomi steadies herself. "I manage the cafeteria at Orlando Memorial. I have witnessed how the healthcare system fails our community, especially lesbians and trans—transgender—folks, *my* folks. So that's my initiative: improving healthcare services."

Lisa smiles at Helen, noting her autumn appearance: short auburn hair, amber eyes, and button-down shirt covered with red and orange leaves. "Like Naomi and Fernando," says Helen, "I'm not part of the Rollins community, but I am part of the gay community. My name's Helen. I'm a probate attorney. I was raised Catholic, which presented problems when I came out to my parents ten years ago; I'm 38 now. I identify as somewhere between agnostic and atheist. I don't talk about that *at all* with my family, and frankly, I still speak very little with them about my sexuality.

"Given what I've seen in the aftermath of a gay person's death—the homophobic family swoops in, leaving the surviving partner in the lurch[4]—I hope to help establish a statewide domestic partner registry."

Blake grins widely, revealing the braces he'll have for five more months. "Hi, I'm Blake. I had a career in corporate media but never found it fulfilling. When my dad died last year and left me some money, I struck out on my own.

"What else? I came out late, after college. I don't have a partner, though I long for that. Being middle-aged and an independent—i.e., low-income—media-maker are not qualities atop many gay men's partner wish list. So much of our community's effort focuses on marriage equality. While I'm elated that public sentiment has improved, I often wonder, what about those of us for whom marriage is *not* in the picture? What about our need for social support, for economic security? I want to explore that in my initiative: my first documentary."

"I'm Jackie," says our blue-eyed colleague, smartly dressed in a tan button-down shirt and chocolate Capri pants. She twirls a sun-kissed blond curl around her index finger. "I intern at the Rollins counseling center. I attended this workshop because my 24-year-old brother just came out to our family. I want to learn more about how best to support him. My public initiative will pertain to gay youth, maybe homelessness or suicide prevention."

"I work at the college as well," says Masao, adjusting his hipster glasses, "teaching courses in methods and Queer Sociology. I serve on the Professional Standards Committee, and we've been charged with assessing the current Course and Instructor Evaluation, CIE, process. I recently read a study showing that Black faculty got lower evaluations than White faculty.[5] In another study, a lecturer presented to eight sections of the same course on the same day. He standardized the material, except in four sections, he three times referred to his partner Jason; in the other four, he three times referred to his partner Jennifer. Students rated teaching quality and their own learning far lower in the 'Jason' sections.[6] As far as I know, Rollins never has measured the relationship between minority status and CIE results. That's something for which I want to push."

Violet says to Masao, "As someone of Latin-, African-, and Native-American heritage, I'm very interested in what you find."

She turns to the group, "My name's Violet. I spent ten years in the army." She looks down at her khaki t-shirt tucked into camouflage pants. "Guess I dressed the part today. I work in Student Services, am married, and have three daughters. I think my 17-year-old might be gay. I've tried to engage my husband in conversation about it; he's burying his head. I considered speaking to our pastor, but my church is quite conservative."

"And your initiative?" prompts Kathryn.

"Before coming today, I researched the number of states without discrimination protections on the basis of sexual orientation—29, Florida among them. I hope to plug into state-level activism on that issue."

"Thank you, everyone," says Lisa. "Now, please grab a chair. Stay close to the front so you easily can see the whiteboard." The group moves as instructed.

Kathryn tells them, "As we know, effective activism involves understanding a problem and its root causes. To facilitate such understanding, we begin with an exercise developed by my Thai collaborators and me: Tip of the Island." She walks to the whiteboard. With a blue marker, Kathryn makes a wavy line to signify the sea, then a black marker to draw a landmass, most of it submerged.

Lisa says, "The tip represents visible manifestations of heterosexism, homophobia, biphobia, and transphobia. What forms does LGBTQ+ oppression take in everyday life?"

The group remains silent a moment before Blake puts forward, "Stereotypes."

Kathryn writes the word beside the island's tip. "Can you give examples?"

Blake replies, "Gay men as promiscuous, shallow, flaky. Jack on *Will and Grace*." He glances around the group. "I hope I'm not offending anyone. I know a lot of people think he's hilarious. But that's not me at all."

Helen adds to the list of stereotypes. "Lesbians as titillation for straight men."

"Or as nonexistent," Naomi offers.

Fernando says, "Also true of bi and trans folk—maybe more so."

Lisa paraphrases, "So stereotypes *and* silences."

"Great," Kathryn says. "What other manifestations come to mind?"

"Not sure how to categorize this," says Jackie. "In one of my counseling courses, I had a classmate: lesbian, maybe 25. She shared a story of reflexively reaching for her partner's hand. The two women looked up and saw a group of fraternity-shirted guys walking their way. Remembering they were on campus, they panicked and dropped hands."

"We could call that affection inequality," Violet suggests.

"How about relational inequality?" Helen amends. "Then it would encompass marriage inequality." Kathryn nods, writing "relational inequality" on the board.

Blake says, "That term also would capture the energy we expend managing our identities with significant others: whether to come out, to whom, when, in what way."

Masao observes, "Prohibitions on foster parenting and adoption fit here as well."

Adding these examples to the list, Kathryn says, "You may know that Florida banned adoption by GLB individuals and couples until 2010. Vicki Nantz, whom Lisa and I have known and worked with for years, made a film about it called *In Anita's Wake*."[7] Blake makes a mental note.

Masao says, "Also next to relational inequality we could put rejection—that which LGBTQ+ people face from family and friends that heterosexual and cisgender folks do not."

"Please explain cisgender," Kathryn requests. "That term may be unfamiliar to some."

"It refers to one whose gender identity and presentation generally conform to what's expected: biological males will be masculine and biological females will be feminine."

Helen studies the board. "Sodomy laws also cohere with relational inequality."

"That's right," says Lisa. "Fourteen states—including Florida—had them on the books until 2003, and dozens of countries still have them. In 2013, the Supreme Court of India *re*criminalized same-sex relations."

Fernando adds, "Some countries still *execute* people for same-sex relations."

"A manifestation I mentioned earlier is discrimination," Violet says. "A lot of people don't know that in most states, you still can be fired for being gay. Until I began questioning my daughter's orientation, I didn't know."

Kathryn replies, "Some of us work at an institution and live in a county with non-discrimination protections, but that wasn't always the case. Even today, once we cross from Orange to Seminole County, we lose those protections."

"Bullying belongs on our list," suggests Zach.

"And hate crimes," says Jackie.

The group's contributions now fill the whiteboard area surrounding the island's tip. Kathryn observes, "We can observe these manifestations of oppression." She then moves her hand over the island's submerged area. "Now, let's name the social systems that support these manifestations."

"When I put forward stereotypes," Blake tells the group, "I had the mass media in mind." Kathryn writes "media system" in the underwater region.

Naomi says, "We talked a lot about relational inequality. Hard to ignore the church's role." Kathryn adds "religious system."

Reading the material next to "relational inequality," Violet offers, "the family system."

Zach looks at "bullying" and says, "your peers." Kathryn jots "peer social system."

The group then begins calling out in rapid succession: "Education." "Health care." "Employment." "Legal/political."

Kathryn records quickly, repeating what she heard. "What was that last one?"

Helen tells her, "Legal/political system."

"Got it," says Kathryn, making a loop on the final "m." "Great work, everyone."

Lisa directs, "In our next exercise, each of you will be assigned one system that fosters LGBTQ+ oppression. Please take a five-minute break while we set up." Fernando crosses to and enters the restroom at the northwest corner. Violet and Helen line up outside. Masao walks to the kitchen and begins opening cabinets.

"Another restroom?" requests Naomi.

"Outside the Faculty Club," says Kathryn, "the building just to our east. And a one-minute walk past that is Dianne's Café."

Lisa catches Kathryn's eye and points toward Jackie. Getting Lisa's drift, Kathryn nods. Before Jackie can file out with Naomi, Helen, Blake, and Zach, Lisa lightly touches her arm. "Jackie, you feeling strong and solid today?"

"I, uh, guess so."

"Instead of representing a system," Lisa explains, "we'd like you to stand in for the LGBTQ+ community. The exercise can be intense, and we prefer to have an ally play this role."

"Oh, sure!" replies Jackie. "It will be good for me to step into my brother's shoes."

"Thank you so much," Lisa says. "See you in five."

Fernando exits the restroom and follows Jackie out the door. Masao, carrying a cup of water from the kitchen tap, is not far behind.

While Kathryn strides to the desk, Lisa moves the chairs from the room's center, placing one at each table. From her tote, Kathryn pulls seven stiff white cards, 11 inches by four inches. Each has a hole punched in the two top corners and two feet of yarn fed through and tied, the card serving as a pendant for the yarn necklace. Using Tip of the Island results, she takes a black Sharpie and writes the name of one system on each card: Media, Religious, Family, Education, Health Care, Employment, and Legal/Political. Lisa crosses to the desk area and powers on the LCD projectors. On a slide, she has:

I represent the ___ system.

One way I contribute to LGBTQ+ oppression is ___.

My message to you as an LGBTQ+ person is ___.

Lisa turns to Kathryn. "How do you think it's going?"

"The group had no trouble with examples for Tip of the Island," Kathryn reflects.

Lisa nods. "They also seemed quick to identify systems supporting oppression."

"We recruited an invested and sophisticated group," says Kathryn. "Their introductions and initiatives show that each has a personal and political stake in being here."

Participants begin returning from break, some sipping at coffees. Masao munches the last bite of a protein bar retrieved from his nearby office.

"Welcome back," greets Kathryn, gathering the group into a circle.

Lisa says, "In Tip of the Island, we talked about systems that support heterosexism, homophobia, biphobia, and/or transphobia at a structural level, beyond the level of any individual. Each of you will be assigned a system. You will generate two statements about how your system fosters queer oppression."

"I was born in 1953," interjects Naomi. "In my day, people hurled 'queer' as an epithet, one of the worst things you could call someone."

Lisa now realizes that, although "queer" has been mentioned, the group has not yet discussed its meanings.

Blake tells the group, "I still hear 'queer' that way, and I was born in '67."

"Please employ your terminology of choice," says Kathryn. "Use 'LGBTQ+' if that feels more congruent."

"How about 'anti-gay oppression'?" queries Blake. "A lot of folks utilize 'gay' as the catch-all term. It sounds less loaded than 'queer.'"

Fernando says, "I'm not sure 'anti-*gay* oppression' applies to me as a bisexual man. Does it apply to Naomi or Helen as lesbians, to Naomi as transgender?"

"I *hate* the term 'lesbian,'" says Helen. "Always have. Such an ugly word." Naomi clenches her jaw as Helen continues, "I have no problem with 'gay.' I always think of myself as a member of the gay community."

Naomi takes a deep breath. "I use 'lesbian' very deliberately and self-consciously. I feel adamant about explicitly representing women in the community and reclaiming 'lesbian,' just as some people do with 'queer.'"

Kathryn reports, "Last semester, Lisa and I visited a class to provide a Safe Zone training. I presented myself to the group as a lesbian; Lisa referred to herself as a 'queer-identified heterosexual.'"

Lisa explains, "It all hinges on context. That course centered on LGBTQ+ histories and social movements. In some situations, I will advocate for LGBTQ+ equality but consciously not disclose my heterosexuality. I will allow others to wonder if I may be lesbian. In other contexts, I will identify as heterosexual and try to mobilize that privilege in support of others' rights and welfare."

"In this training," says Kathryn, "we employ the term 'queer' to be inclusive and to expose gender and sexual orientation as social constructions, as language categories created by particular people at particular times for particular purposes. A queer perspective challenges heteronormativity. Masao, can you please explain that?"

"It equates heterosexuality with 'normalcy' and associates all other sexualities with deviance. If you contest heteronormativity, you can self-define as queer, regardless of your sexual orientation or gender expression —thus Lisa as a 'queer-identified heterosexual.'"

"Important discussion," affirms Lisa. "In the next exercise, Jackie will stand in for the LGBTQ+ community. In addition to writing statements about how your system contributes to oppression, you'll write second-person statements directed at her: 'My message to you, Jackie, as an LGBTQ+ person is ___.'"

Zach closes one eye and purses his lips. "Hmm . . . can you give us an example?"

"Absolutely," says Kathryn. "I'll pick a system we won't be covering. 'I represent the criminal justice system. One way I support LGBTQ+ oppression is through dismissive and insensitive responses to hate crimes.'"

Lisa improvises the second part. "Jackie, my message to you as an LGBTQ+ person is: 'Perhaps if you'd behaved *normally*, this wouldn't have happened to you.'"

"Let's offer a second example for this system," suggests Kathryn. "Another way I foster oppression is through sexist and homophobic language in training and on the job."

Lisa adds, "My message to you, Jackie, is: 'I protect and serve—but only heterosexual and cisgender citizens. You're on your own. You're not worth protecting or serving.'"

"All right," says Kathryn, "Lisa will distribute pencils and cards, assigning each of you a different system. Write your statements on the backs of your cards."

Kathryn approaches Jackie, handing her a notepad and pencil. "While the rest of the group prepares, we'd like you to compose first-person

statements about everyday fears and concerns of an LGBTQ+ person."
Jackie nods.

Lisa announces, "System representatives: feel free to work with a
partner on your statements and messages."

The group disperses, each taking a seat. For perhaps three minutes,
no one speaks as they jot down ideas, erase, cross out, reword. Lisa
consults with Jackie while the system representatives run their drafts by
a peer or two, trying to get the wording just right.

Hearing a lull, Kathryn says, "Sounds like we're ready. Please keep
your chairs where they are, leaving the center of the room clear. Jackie,
you will stand in the middle; system representatives, please encircle
Jackie." The group moves into formation.

Lisa explains, "We asked an ally, Jackie, to represent the LGBTQ+
community. She now will read statements she generated about life as a
member of that group."

Jackie clears her throat. "Whenever I plan a trip with my partner, we
extensively research the climate for LGBTQ+ persons. In many locations
around the world, in the U.S., and in Florida, we just don't feel safe."

Kathryn nods encouragement to Jackie, who continues: "I grew up
really close to my sister, who just gave birth. I want to tell her about
my girlfriend, but my family holds very traditional values. If I come out,
will they allow contact with my nephew?" The group listens intently.

Jackie then reads, "Ryan Skipper, a gay man exactly my age, 25, was
murdered in nearby Polk County. The perpetrators stabbed Ryan
multiple times and left him to die. One assailant said he acted in
retaliation for 'unwanted sexual advances.' Sometimes when I walk alone
at night, I watch as men pass by on the street. I wonder, Can they see
who I am? Will they lash out at me?" Jackie glances up from her paper,
indicating she has finished.

"Thank you, Jackie," says Kathryn, taking a ball of string from her
tote. "We will start with Blake. Please offer your first statement, then
deliver your message directly to Jackie." She hands Blake the ball. "Then
wind the string around your wrist and lob the ball to someone across
the circle—anyone but those right next to you."

Blake, positioned at 12:00 at the front of the room, says, "I represent
the media system. I support oppression through portrayals of swishing

sissies and man-hating dykes. Jackie, my message to you is that I have the power to show everyone, including you, who you are."

Lisa nods. Blake loops the string around his left wrist and tosses the ball toward 5:00. Zach, the closest, catches it and says, "I, the religious system, uphold oppression by demonizing homosexuality from the pulpit. Jackie, my message to you: if you fail to change your wicked ways, God condemns you to hell for eternity." A few beads of sweat appear on Jackie's brow. Zach wraps the string and throws overhand to 10:00. It bounces off Masao's hands, falls to the floor, and rolls about eight feet toward the east wall.

"Sorry," says Masao, looking flustered.

"No problem," Kathryn encourages. "Take your time."

Masao winds excess string around the ball before announcing, "Employment system. One way I support oppression is by refusing to interview or hire a queer person." He glowers at Jackie. "I reviewed your resume: interest in counseling gay youth; service to the campus LGBTQ+ group. I said to myself, 'Not a good fit' and moved on to the next application."

Masao sees Jackie's upper front teeth gnaw at her lower lip. He then looks to 2:00 and tosses the ball to Violet, enclosing Jackie in a triangle of string.

"Legal/political system," says Violet. "I support LGBTQ+ oppression by voting down or blocking consideration of fair housing legislation. Why should I care, Jackie, if you can't find a place to live? I don't want your kind in my neighborhood anyway."

Glancing toward Naomi at 8:00, Violet raises the ball, signaling an overhand throw. Jackie realizes that she's in the way, takes a half step to the right, and crouches down. Kathryn and Lisa lock gazes and nod as Violet sends the ball over Jackie's head.

"Health care system," says Naomi. "I foster oppression by refusing partners and children access to loved ones. My message, Jackie, is that we have a 'family only' policy," then, performing disdain, "and whatever your group is, it's not a family."

Naomi meets Helen's gaze and tosses the ball to 3:00. "Speaking of family," says Helen, "I represent that system. Oppression manifests in my context through gendered socialization. Jackie, my message is: act like a girl. Don't be too strong. Don't be too loud. Don't take up too much space." Noticing that Fernando at 6:00 is the only member of the circle without a wrist wrapped in string, Helen makes the short throw.

"Education system," he says. "I support oppression by ignoring queer contributions to history and culture. Jackie, my message to you is . . ." His voice breaks. "N-no one came before you. You are alone. Indeed, you don't exist."

The group absorbs this before Fernando looks directly across the group and makes a perfect throw to Blake. "Media system," he reminds. "A second way I enact oppression is by distorted coverage of hate crimes. My message, Jackie, is that you were asking for it. What did you expect, wearing men's clothes and leaving that dyke bar?" Jackie's face flushes.

Blake offers a short toss to Helen at 3:00. "Family system," she says. "Another way I foster oppression is through heteronormative socialization. Jackie, my message is that we reserve sexuality for married procreating adults. Shame on you for any behavior or even desire that falls outside our parameters."

Helen directs her focus across the circle to 10:00. Masao holds up his hands, ready to catch. When the ball lands, he says, "Employment system. A second way I support oppression is through a closed and hostile climate. My message, Jackie, is keep it to yourself. No one wants to hear about your partner or see on your desk a picture of your *wedding*, or whatever it was. We will accept your professional contributions and benefit from your expertise and skills, but we refuse to know *you*." Masao nods toward Fernando and throws him the ball.

"Education," he says. "I foster oppression by dismissing reports of bullying as 'kids will be kids.' Jackie, your wellbeing and safety do not concern me."

Fernando tosses underhand toward Violet at 2:00, but the ball bounces off the web and to the floor. Jackie, struggling to navigate string that boxes her in on all sides, picks it up and hands the ball to Violet. "Legal/political," Violet reminds. "A second way I institutionalized oppression until 2011 was barring from military service anyone openly gay, lesbian, or bisexual. Your deviance, Jackie, threatened group morale, cohesion, and safety."

Realizing several participants have read both statements, Violet scans the group. Naomi raises her free hand, and Violet tosses the ball. "Health care. Oppression manifests in my context through non-inclusive forms. Check one box, Jackie: 'single,' 'married,' 'divorced,' 'widowed.' Don't see yourself? We don't see you either."

"Okay," says Naomi, "is that everybody?"

"Just me left," replies Zach at 5:00. Naomi sends the string high over the web. Catching it, Zach says, "Religious system. A second way I enact oppression is by refusing to ordain gay leaders. Jackie, how could you guide others spiritually? You can't even guide yourself."

Jackie now directly faces Lisa. Shoulders slumped, Jackie seems overwhelmed. The group absorbs the cumulative impact of the messages they have delivered.

Kathryn breaks the silence. "Jackie, please tell the group how you feel."

"Wow . . ." she says, gathering her thoughts. "Um . . . it's hard to express. At first, I experienced it as an intellectual exercise: how do the systems support oppression? But when Masao talked of rejecting my job application, I thought about my brother—an untenured high school teacher in a rural town. He really *could* lose his job.

"Then, as it went on and I kept getting more and more hemmed in, I started to feel disheartened, beaten down. Everybody's against me. I'm alone in here."

Lisa asks, "System representatives: how did this exercise impact you?"

"I had a related experience to Jackie's," says Blake. "I first approached it like a screenplay: I can write these lines and recite them convincingly. But when I looked directly at Jackie, I saw tears in her eyes. She wasn't acting; this was having a real impact."

"I noticed that too," says Masao. "Then I felt my chest cave. Look at what my system—employment—does; look at what *I* am doing as its representative."

Zach speaks next. "I don't know if you gave me the religious system on purpose."

"We did," says Kathryn, smiling.

"Faith has been a huge part of my life. As I mentioned, I was raised Lutheran."

"I was raised Pentecostal," says Naomi.

Zach's mouth falls open. "So was my mother."

"Believe me," Naomi tells the group, "if it were possible to 'pray away the gay,' I would have done it. For years, I went to bed every night imploring God, 'Take away these feelings.'

"Anyway, I interrupted you, Zach. Please continue."

"The Pentecostal side of my family viewed homosexuality as an abomination. In the Lutheran church we attended, the rhetoric was softer: 'love the sinner; hate the sin.' That seemed fair to me, loving even. But to brand the expression of love toward another human as sinful is the antithesis of loving."

"It's oppressive," adds Blake. "It's *hateful*."

Naomi says, "The examples from my system—health care—came directly from my experience working in the industry. People become doctors and nurses to help others. I cannot fathom how a so-called 'professional' could look a partner or child in the face and say, 'I can't let you in; you're not family.' Even if others are not family in someone's bullshit definition, who cares? If a friend, a coworker, or a compassionate acquaintance is there for me, let her in! Would it be better if I suffered— if I *died*—alone?"

"Recently," Helen tells the group, "a gay man had a heart attack at an area hospital. He kept asking—begging—for his partner. When staff wouldn't let his partner in, the patient pulled off the monitors and yanked out his IV. The man stumbled into the ER waiting room and found his partner, who drove him to another hospital. He could have died." Blake wipes away a tear as Helen says, "People *die* from homophobia."

Blake speaks haltingly. "I . . . I felt grateful that Jackie stood in for me—for us—because I navigate these systems every day. At the same time, I thought of ways I actually do foster oppression. I've come a long way in my development as a gay man, but day to day, how effective an ally am I for lesbians, for bi or trans folk? How many times have I stood by silently while my gay male friends disparage 'dykes' and drag queens?"

Kathryn says, "To me, some of the saddest outcomes of oppression are the ways it can divide members of the community from our allies and even from each other."

"How did we see a manifestation of that here?" Lisa asks. "How did Jackie facilitate the web of oppression?"

It takes the group a few moments to process. "When she realized that her body blocked my throw," recalls Violet, "she stepped aside."

Jackie says, "Another time, I did more than that. The ball bounced off the web, and I picked it up and handed it to Violet!"

Kathryn observes, "So this exercise illustrates that oppression occurs at the structural level, and that LGBTQ+ people at times contribute to that. Sometimes we see oppression and step aside; other times we actively facilitate it. What else can we learn?"

"Look at the web," Helen says. "These oppressions work together."

"Oppressions confine us," adds Blake.

"Yes," says Masao, "emotionally, relationally, educationally, professionally, legally."

"Although I am significantly 'webbed in,'" notes Jackie, "I'm not totally immobilized." She waves her arms and takes a half-step forward. "I do have some agency."

Violet says, "The lessons here pertain to but also transcend LGBTQ+ oppression. We could apply this exercise to religion, race, sex."

Kathryn nods. "Exactly right. A couple years ago, we engaged Lisa's senior seminar in a Web of Oppression on socioeconomic class."

"The more we practice LGBTQ+ activism," Lisa says, "the more invested we can become in redressing other inequities. Kathryn is a longtime advocate for farmworker rights."

Kathryn adds, "And Lisa has authored public writing critical of the Iraq war[8] and will teach a class this fall called Incarceration and Inequality."

"Now," says Lisa, "how could our social systems operate differently, more justly?"

Zach replies, "At minimum, we would have to be more inclusive, to ensure representation of a range of persons."

"Those persons would need to be heard," says Fernando, "taken seriously, respected."

Naomi offers, "People within our systems would have to band together, within and across groups, to work for change."

"It's like that quote attributed to Margaret Mead," says Masao. "'Never doubt that a small group of thoughtful, committed citizens can change the world. Indeed it is the only thing that ever has.'"

Kathryn asks, "To become LGBTQ+ affirmative, what new messages would your systems need to send?"

Of the media system, Blake says to Jackie, "I will represent you fairly and accurately."

"We welcome you in our houses of worship," Zach says. "We will consecrate your relationship."

Helen looks at Jackie. "We always will be your family. We love you just as you are."

Of health care, Naomi says, "And we honor *your* definition of family."

Masao tells Jackie, "We value both your professional skills and your humanity."

"We will teach the history of your community," says Fernando. "Your sexuality will be affirmed in health education, and *you* will be affirmed by colleagues."

Kathryn smiles. "Before concluding, what might we do with the string?"

"Cut it," suggests Fernando.

"Burn it," says Violet.

The group unwraps their wrists and throws the web to the floor.

Naomi observes, "Jackie remains alone in there."

"What would you like to do about that?" Lisa asks.

"Join us," invites Helen, stepping to her right. Zach moves the same distance to his left to make room.

Kathryn catches Jackie's gaze and asks, "How do you feel now?"

"Exhausted!" she replies. The group laughs. "But better. I am especially moved by the invitation into the circle. This web binds us all, but each of us can play a role in unraveling it!"

"Wonderful," says Lisa, walking to the desk and reaching into the tote for legal pads.

Kathryn reports, "For our final exercise today, we will focus on the initiatives you brought to the training." She crosses through the group to the whiteboard.

Beginning in the northeast corner by the door, Lisa circles the room, placing a pad at each table. Kathryn erases Tip of the Island results, grabs the blue dry erase marker, and explains, "The Web of Oppression helps us get at the structural level—how inequalities infuse each social system and intersect with inequalities of other systems. We could do a web exercise for each institution and for each system within that institution. For example, we could illuminate how LGBTQ+ oppression circulates within Rollins College and the systems that comprise it. That kind of analysis helps us figure out how to spark change.

"So, for this exercise, we request that you briefly analyze the systems connected to the inequality you wish to help remedy. Then brainstorm strategies you might employ. Here are your questions," Kathryn says, writing them as she speaks. "What is the issue, problem, inequity? How does it manifest? What more must I learn? From where or whom can I acquire the relevant information and skills? What would it take to redress the inequity? What role am I best suited to play? Whom can I enlist to collaborate and how?"

"So have a seat," directs Lisa, "and for ten minutes, reflect on these questions as they apply to your initiative."

As the group disperses, Kathryn and Lisa meet in the room's center. They clasp hands and give each other a hug. Pulling back, Lisa studies Kathryn's eyes, noting their redness and the dark circles beneath. Referring to Kathryn's mom, Lisa asks, "How is Mother Norsworthy?" On Lisa's first trip to Kathryn's hometown of Perry, Georgia, she spontaneously addressed Mrs. Norsworthy this way. Tickled by it, Kathryn's mom began replying in kind with "Daughter Lisa."

Kathryn exhales. "Her diabetes seems under control, but if they don't get her blood pressure medication right, I know she'll be back in the hospital."

Lisa shakes her head. "She must be so scared and frustrated."

"Yes and very confined. Mom loses her breath so easily now, even in everyday activities."

"That's a lot to manage from over 300 miles away."

"It is," says Kathryn with a sigh. "I need to get there within a week or two—sooner if she's hospitalized.

"What about you? Your folks all right?"

"Better than that," Lisa responds. "They decided to buy that house in Gainesville, so they'll be snowbirds come November. When my folks visit in April, they want you and Deena to come to dinner."

"We would love that. I still marvel that we shared India with them. Hard to believe that was a year ago!"

Lisa checks the clock, noting that 11 minutes have passed. To the group she says, "You now will collaborate with a partner. Zach and Naomi: could you find a spot? Also Masao and Fernando, Jackie and Helen, Violet and Blake. Talk through your initiatives, solicit input from your partner, and Kathryn and I will come around to consult."

Before they separate, Kathryn asks Lisa, "Can you come to my house after?"

Lisa smiles. "I was counting on it!"

Kathryn grabs a chair from the nearest stack, rolling it less than a foot to the southeast corner, where Zach and Naomi compare notes. When Kathryn sits down, Naomi reminds, "My initiative involved improving healthcare services, especially for lesbians and trans women. At the root of this problem are doctors and other staff who show contempt for LGBTQ+ patients, making them feel uncomfortable and thus less likely to seek care. In terms of strategies, where to begin? I'm not a professor. I didn't even finish college. I work in food service. I'm a butch dyke. As you know, Kathryn, I've been involved in public initiatives, but I contribute behind the scenes: hosting activists at my house, cooking a meal for them."

"As one who has partaken in those meals," Kathryn says fondly, "let me affirm their personal and social importance!" Naomi blushes. Kathryn then asks, "From what direction would you most like to improve health care: from within existing heterosexist systems or by helping build new ones?"

"Hmm . . . since I work in a hospital, I was thinking internally, maybe organizing a training. What might creating a new system look like?"

Zach ventures, "Do you know other gay healthcare professionals?"

"Let's see . . . I have a lesbian gynecologist; I know a gay male surgeon and a few nurses, several support staff: aides, janitors, grounds-keepers."

Kathryn asks, "Would each of them be connected to additional LGBTQ+ folks in the health field?"

"I would assume so," says Naomi. "What if I helped form some kind of network, a support group . . . no, more like an advocacy and referral group? We could call it . . . uh . . . Queer Care." Zach and Kathryn laugh. "Maybe not; I have made clear how I feel about that word!"

"What would be the group's mission?" queries Kathryn.

"Maybe to identify LGBTQ+ affirmative providers in the area."

"Sounds like a great goal," says Kathryn.

Zach asks, "Using your contacts—people you know and people they know—could you assemble a steering committee?"

"Probably," Naomi responds. "I've worked locally in health care for over 30 years."

Kathryn suggests, "You also could check with the Center. Dozens of LGBTQ+ groups meet there regularly. Maybe something related already is underway."

"I've been there a couple of times," Naomi says. "You were there, Kathryn, speaking at the Town Hall on the Orange County domestic partner registry."

"That's right," Kathryn tells her. "This pair is on a roll!" She turns to face Zach. "Now, I recall your introduction; you want to change the climate at your church."

"Exactly. As I mentioned, some parishioners support the full integration of gay people as members and leaders; others actively oppose. Our church lacks a clear position on inclusion, and that allows homophobia to circulate within our system.

"Some concrete ideas I wrote down: letter of support for gay bishop, one-on-one lobbying of those threatening to split off, study session on homosexuals and the Bible."

Softly, Naomi says, "Zach, that's the second time today I heard you use the term 'homosexuals.' Helen said she hates the term 'lesbian,' which I don't understand, frankly; to me, that smacks of internalized homophobia. 'Homosexual' has the same impact on me. It sounds like a disease."

Kathryn adds, "Indeed, the American Psychological Association classified homosexuality as a disorder until 1973. Prior to that, one could be committed to a mental hospital and given electroshock therapy on no other basis than having a same-sex orientation. Many of us avoid the term 'homosexual' because it calls up that history and because a same-sex orientation involves not only sex but also attachment, love, and community."

Zach's freckled face flushes. "I'm sorry. You'd think at only 34, I'd be more hip."

"It's not about being hip," says Naomi. "It's about learning our history and tuning in to people's preferences. Cut yourself some slack. You attended this training—more than we can say for most people, including LGBTQ+ people. By the way, I hear members of my community use that term, sometimes in jest, the way a gay man might call another a 'fag,' and sometimes totally unselfconsciously—like it's a neutral descriptive term.

"Anyway, let's get back to your initiative."

"To which of your ideas do you feel most drawn?" asks Kathryn.

Zach replies, "Initially, the lobbying. I have two close friends and several acquaintances thinking of founding their own congregation. But then I wondered what might happen if my lobbying worked, if they stayed. What will the climate be like for . . ." Deliberately he says, "LGBTQ+ members, or even for allies? How much do we *want* to keep trying to hold back their conservative tide?"

Kathryn offers, "In this work, these kinds of questions often arise. Lisa and I have faced that here at Rollins. Both of us feel drawn to teaching at institutions more diverse racially and socioeconomically, less exclusive, more affordable."

"So why devote your careers to a school whose tuition, room, and board run over $50,000 a year?" asks Zach.

Kathryn responds, "My program, located in the Holt evening degree school, costs far less than that. But it's a fair question. A few reasons: both Lisa and I have carved out spaces in the curriculum infused with social justice values. Elsewhere, we could be lone voices in the wilderness of large heterogeneous departments. Mainstream programs would expect more mainstream research and publications. I doubt my social change fieldwork in Thailand or Lisa's social justice documentary work would receive the consistent institutional funding and support that they do here. Also, at a smaller school like Rollins, one person—or one lesbian-ally pair—can make a real difference. I participated in lobbying for domestic partner benefits for both same- and different-sex couples, which we secured in 2001. That coverage has taken pressure off both Lisa's and my partners. Her partner John found corporate America stifling. Rollins' health benefits helped facilitate his administering a small business and consulting full time. My partner Deena, a mental health counselor who retired at 50, has significant health problems. She could not risk going without insurance until of Medicare age. At the same time, I have seen how homophobia and transphobia undermine her health. If she had to stay in a traditional clinical setting to maintain health coverage . . ."

Naomi finishes, "It would shave years off her life." She reaches for and squeezes Kathryn's hand.

Kathryn nods, grateful that Naomi has allowed her—even in her facilitator role—to be vulnerable and to receive support. For years, Kathryn and Lisa have talked about how teachers, mentors, and activists can be objectified by others, who operate as if caring and compassion flow in only one direction: from teacher to students, from mentor to protégées, from activist to community members.

"Listening to you talk," says Zach, "I sense that, although I will be sad to see my friends and acquaintances leave, it may be best for everyone. I want to put my energy into making the remaining group safe and affirming."

"And how might you best do that?" queries Kathryn.

"The same idea we generated with Naomi: a steering committee. I could ask Fernando to help me convene it. We'd need a balance of LGBTQ+ folks and allies. We could follow a process like this, assist each other in identifying and executing initiatives."

Kathryn asks, "Would your initiatives be more internally or externally focused?"

Zach turns this over. "Meaning within each person or between people?"

"Yes to both," says Kathryn. "Though I was thinking of internal or external to your church. On every public initiative on which Lisa and/or I have worked, people of faith have been instrumental—on both sides.

The religious right often tries to define our civil rights as affronts to God. It's been crucial to have more progressive people of faith offer messages of God's openness, care, and love."

"In what contexts do they convey those messages?" asks Zach.

"At public hearings," says Kathryn, "and in meetings with elected officials. Lisa and I recently consulted with a budding group of activists in Lake County. Fernando mentioned the middle school that blocked formation of a GSA. When the ACLU stepped in, the school board threatened to eliminate all student clubs. Lisa and I could have tried to meet with board members, but we are outsiders in every sense. Neither of us lives in Lake County. All board members are Republicans, more than one elected with Tea Party and religious right support. Lisa and I are progressive Democrats; she is agnostic, I am a practicing Buddhist. We told the activists, 'Expand the circle. Find the moderate Republicans and faith leaders. Identify someone in each district, and get that person to meet with her representative.'"

Zach nods. "I absolutely could see myself helping build a team like that."

"You two are well on your way," Kathryn observes. "Keep talking while I move on."

During Kathryn's consultation with Naomi and Zach, Lisa engages Fernando and Masao, who sit at a table beneath a southwest window. "As I indicated," says Fernando, "I covered the Lake County GSA controversy for the UF paper. The public hearings took my breath away. They revealed many root causes of the problem, ranging from the community's heterosexist and homophobic attitudes and beliefs to the lack of non-discrimination protections in Lake County schools. Some people viewed a GSA as usurping parental rights, showing how the larger community supports the school's failure to protect queer kids." Fernando's voice rises in pitch and intensity. "What about the rights of kids to have a safe space, to connect with advocates, to be free of bullying, to know how to practice safe sex, to be caught before falling into a suicidal abyss?" He inhales deeply. "I remember the Rollins contingent testifying at hearings: Kathryn, Lisa, and two male faculty members . . . I forget their names."

"Sam and Erik," Lisa says. "Sam is a junior colleague in Kathryn's department; Erik is a young visiting professor. Kathryn and I have been helping cultivate the next generation."

Fernando reports, "I also saw that awful web posting, 'Parental Rights Shredded by Wolves,' by Patricia Sullivan, a Tea Party leader in Florida." He explains to Masao, "At one school board meeting, Lisa's testimony immediately followed Sam's and Erik's. She introduced herself by saying, 'Lisa Tillmann, also from Rollins. We travel in packs.' People laughed; it broke some of the tension."

Lisa nods. "I briefly posted a link to Sullivan's blog on my Facebook as an example of the heat—and distortion—you likely will take when doing this kind of work. Worried that driving traffic to the site could invite additional blowback, I deleted it from my timeline an hour later.

"A few years ago, the *Sandspur*, the Rollins newspaper, published an op-ed on 'anchor babies' and a cartoon of a bug-like alien that has commandeered the easy chair, TV, and snacks of a young White man, who looks on in disgust. Kathryn requested and received permission from her department to send a campus-wide email denouncing the rhetoric as racist and harmful. I then asked for and got my department's support to do the same, in part because I firmly agreed with Counseling's stance and in part because I didn't want them—or Kathryn—to stand alone."

Masao adds, "Their emails—more than the op-ed and cartoon themselves—sparked a firestorm. A town hall drew a standing-room-only crowd. Some students, staff, and faculty rebuked their departments' 'misuse' of the campus email system. The Fox network spotlighted members of the *Sandspur* staff, as if heroes for free speech."

Lisa says, "Then a series of right wingnuts began an online character assassination of Kathryn specifically, accusing her of trying to 'intimidate' the op-ed writer and calling her a 'bully' and a leader of the 'Thought Gestapo.' For a time, when you googled 'Kathryn Norsworthy,' those posts would appear first. Of all the backlash we have encountered since our collaboration began in 2000, this took the greatest emotional toll on her."

"How do you prepare yourself to be branded a 'wolf' or a 'bully'?" Fernando asks.

Lisa replies, "I doubt anyone gets used to having one's words taken out of context or being the target of mean-spirited rhetoric. I cannot compare my case to Kathryn's. Sullivan posted her drivel, 50 people commented, and the controversy died down. In some ways, I actually don't mind being likened to a wolf. You come after someone vulnerable, a gay kid or an undocumented worker, I want to be there at that person's side, growling and ready to pounce. Though Kathryn has that side as well, she is, at heart, a peacemaker. She embodies love and harmony. I can't think of anything more unfair than calling Kathryn a 'bully.'"

"Fernando," redirects Lisa, "where are we in analyzing and addressing your issue?"

"At first, I considered helping Lake County form their GSA. Masao asked how far I live from there, and I said, 'At least 70 miles.' I think we both realized that with my full-time studies, that might be unsustainable. Then I used my iPad to search for a GSA closer to home, finding one at Gainesville High—less than five miles from my apartment. I sent an email to the 'contact us' address, requesting to meet with the advisor."

Lisa smiles. "Great! What do you hope to bring to the GSA?"

"Since I'm a journalist," says Fernando, "I thought of offering writing workshops. In middle school, journaling saved my life. Maybe I can support the kids in becoming more introspective and better able to utilize writing to process their experiences and struggles."

Masao suggests, "If Gainesville High has a newspaper, maybe you can mentor them to write personal and/or investigative pieces that could help change the climate."

Fernando beams. "I *love* that!"

"Perfect!" says Lisa. She turns to Masao. "All right, dear colleague, let's talk about the instructor evaluation initiative."

"As you know, some research has shown that minority status correlates with lower student ratings. When I read junior colleagues' course evaluations, I see evidence of these disparities, but that can be dismissed as anecdotal. If we don't establish a pattern, how will we convince the institution to factor relevant statuses into the evaluation process?"

"Will you collect and analyze data yourself?" Lisa queries.

"Fernando asked about ethical issues like informed consent and confidentiality. I may need a third party to redact names and department affiliations, not to mention clearance from the dean and provost."

"The provost oversees the Office of Institutional Research," Lisa recalls. "What might motivate the provost to allocate resources for this purpose?"

"As you know," Masao says, "I serve on the Professional Standards Committee, PSC. Our chair sits on the Arts and Sciences Executive Committee, EC, as do the dean, provost, and president. Maybe I could start with a resolution from PSC to EC. If it then passes EC, the resolution goes to the faculty."

Lisa nods. "Let's say the resolution passes PSC, EC, and the faculty, and the provost agrees to devote resources from Institutional Research. What do we do with the results?"

"They would need to be interpreted," Masao replies.

"By whom?" Lisa asks.

"I have a fairly extensive background in quantitative methods," says Masao, "and I bet I could enlist a methodologist in the psychology department."

Lisa queries, "Is this a topic on which you'd like to publish?"

"Yes, though I have a book manuscript due May 15. Until then, my research time is fairly locked."

Lisa adds, "You'd need IRB approval to use the data outside of Rollins." Masao nods, looking a bit dispirited.

Fernando asks, "Is there someone else who could oversee the analysis, a consultant maybe?"

Lisa tells Masao, "Though Kathryn and I feel competent to design and conduct trainings, we also find it important to bring in external people. Over the years, we have attended and/or helped arrange workshops led by Lee Mun Wah, Maurianne Adams, George Lakey, and others. They possess expertise we don't, and sometimes folks who don't live in the Rollins house better facilitate discussions of hot-button issues."

"If minority status indeed correlates with lower ratings, that could be a hot button," Masao reflects.

"Indeed," says Lisa. "What will that mean for department review committees, the college-level Faculty Evaluation Committee, the dean, the provost, the president, the board—all of whom participate in tenure and promotion decisions?"

Masao replies, "People would need to be trained on how to read student evaluations through this lens." Lisa and Fernando nod.

"Well done, you two," Lisa praises. "Keep talking and refining while I move on."

Leaving Zach and Naomi to their work, Kathryn rolls a chair to the table near the lodge's entrance occupied by Jackie and Helen. "Helen should go first," suggests Jackie. "Her initiative is more clearly formulated than mine."

"Statewide domestic partner registry?" Kathryn recalls.

Helen finger-combs her short red hair. "Yes. The problem is inconsistent coverage, a patchwork of city and county registries. From what I understand, most legislators oppose a statewide registry or are undecided. While the number of Florida citizens supporting equality continues to grow, our community still faces loud and well-funded opponents, for example, the Florida Family Council, which has the ear of Governor Rick Scott.

"In terms of concrete steps, I attended the public hearings for the Orlando and Orange County registries but didn't feel ready to testify."

"I can appreciate that," says Kathryn. "It's not my preferred way of contributing."

Helen reports, "I did sign the Equality Florida petitions, and I emailed city and county commissioners."

"Terrific!" Kathryn replies. "Lisa and I did that too. Those communications add up."

Jackie says to Kathryn, "What you said about testifying surprises me. You seem so comfortable in front of a group."

Kathryn smiles. "I've had to cultivate that. I'm fairly introverted and much more at ease collaborating with a small group, like the Orlando Anti-Discrimination Ordinance Committee, OADO, or visiting one person, such as an elected official."

"Not sure I could do the latter," Jackie reflects, shaking her head. "I'd be so nervous!"

"It helps not to be alone," says Kathryn. "I always have gone with at least one other person, most often Lisa. Since 2002, we have met with our own city and county commissioners and, when deemed helpful by OADO, with other officials as well."

"What's it like to talk with them?" Jackie asks.

"Not as intimidating as you might think. You discover that they are human beings with expertise in some areas and blind spots in others. Many are attorneys, so Helen, you'd have common ground where Lisa and I don't. Officials may understand a lot more about some aspects of the law than do we, but frankly, even the lawyers don't tend to know more than Lisa and me about civil rights law."

Kathryn says to Helen, "How might you help secure a statewide registry?"

"I'm not sure," Helen responds, "though I know of a fellow attorney, Mary Meeks. She has been at the forefront of this."

"Lisa and I know her well. Mary is part of OADO. No one was more important than she in the push for the local registries. Since then, Mary and her wife Vicki Nantz, the filmmaker, have traveled across the state, helping other municipalities pass registries."

Helen's amber eyes widen. "I'd love to take Mary to lunch!"

"Do that," encourages Kathryn. "Mary has her finger on the pulse of the statewide initiative. She would have a dozen ideas of how you could contribute: whom to write, whom to visit, where and when to testify— if you felt ready."

A surge of excitement courses through Helen. "Fantastic!"

Kathryn smiles at Jackie. "Something involving youth, right?"

"Yes, but my thinking is all over the place. I know that LGBTQ+ youth are at particular risk for bullying, family rejection, homelessness, and suicidality. I don't know which system to analyze because my issue cuts across so many."

"It does," says Kathryn. "To where does your heart gravitate: on campus, like college-age youth, or off-campus, like LGBTQ+ middle- and high-schoolers?"

Jackie tucks a blond curl behind her right ear. "Open to all of the above."

Kathryn asks, "Have you been through Safe Zone training?"

"No," Jackie says apologetically.

"Oh, don't worry," Kathryn tells her. "There should be one this fall. In 2007, Lisa and I participated in a Safe Zone training of trainers. Since then, our group has facilitated levels one and two trainings for students, staff, faculty, and administrators."

"I definitely will attend the next one," Jackie says. "What about off-campus options?"

Kathryn nods. "I could put you in touch with Michael Slaymaker, the founder of OADO and president of the Orlando Youth Alliance, a peer-based support and education service. Michael also serves Zebra Coalition, who assist young people facing isolation from their families, bullying, abuse, and homelessness."

"Zebra sounds amazing," says Jackie. "I cannot imagine what it would've been like if my parents had abused my brother, if he'd ended up addicted to drugs or homeless."

"Involvement with either of these organizations would help you understand more deeply the issues they address as well as expose you to effective models of how to serve queer youth.

"Send me an email," Kathryn requests, "and I'll reply with Michael's contact information."

"I'll do it right now," Jackie says, pulling a bright purple phone from her handbag.

During Kathryn's consult with Helen and Jackie, Lisa engages Violet and Blake, seated near the computer desk. After sliding a chair from the nearest stack, Lisa sits. She gathers the sides of her skirt, piling fabric in her lap so it does not catch under the chair's wheels. "As I worked with Fernando and Masao," Lisa remarks, "I could hear you two talking excitedly."

Blake responds, "If Violet's daughter is gay, she's lucky to have this incredible woman as a mom! Well . . . gay or not, she's damn lucky!"

Violet's cheeks flush. "What about you, Blake? Kind, gentle, conscientious: a mother's dream!"

"My mom . . ." Blake reflects, "has come a long way. She loves me, for sure. The gay part . . . uh . . . probably not what she would have chosen for me."

Violet asks, "Would you have chosen it for yourself?"

"I did not choose," Blake says with uncharacteristic firmness.

"I understand," Violet replies. "I don't see my daughter as making a choice either."

Familiar with and often frustrated by the limitations of "born this way" exchanges, Lisa offers, "However you became who you are, Blake, I hope you now would elect to be gay. I feel drawn to all dimensions of you, including that one. If you were not gay, you might not be at this workshop. I might never have met you."

"The loss would be mine," Blake says.

"*Ours*," Lisa amends. "Now, Blake, shall we talk about your budding career in film?"

He smiles. "When we did Tip of the Island, we discussed relational inequality and how that manifests in the family, religious, and legal/political systems. I mentioned in my introduction wanting to advocate for the *non*-partnered. I'd like to influence people across social systems to consider our humanity, our rights.

"Kathryn said she knew Vicki Nantz, whom I googled from my tablet and found vickinantzfilms.com. Vicki has built an impressive body of work, including two films on marriage equality, one on Florida's adoption ban, and one on the murder of Ryan Skipper."

"Does she earn her living from this work?" asks Violet.

Lisa explains, "Her wife is the activist and attorney Mary Meeks. Vicki donates far more time and resources than she brings in. Mary's law practice is their primary source of income. Of course, Mary donates incalculable time and energy as well. She was a major force behind local partner registries and the Orange County HRO, Human Rights Ordinance. Mary has testified before the Florida legislature and met with state representatives. She would be a great resource for you, Violet, in how to do state-level activism. You want to work on non-discrimination protections, yes?"

"Exactly," says Violet. "The problem in Florida is uneven protections from organization to organization, city to city, county to county. I spoke to Helen during the break. We agreed that obstacles to statewide change include legislators' ignorance and oppressive attitudes."

Blake suggests, "Violet, why don't we take Vicki and Mary out for coffee? I'd love to know both of them. I could get advice from Vicki about producing socially conscious documentaries, and you could ask Mary to mentor you on state-level activism."

"I would be thrilled to provide an introduction," says Lisa.

"And don't forget, Blake," Violet says, "Lisa has written and produced films."

"Oh, I haven't forgotten!"

Violet continues, "One centers on the ways we relate to our bodies and to food and how those practices reflect larger inequalities."

"*Off the Menu*,"[9] Lisa says.

Violet tells Blake, "Another is about LGBT civil rights … *Remembering.*"

"Yes, *Remembering a Cool September*, and the one I'm finishing now is *Weight Problem: Cultural Narratives of Fat and 'Obesity.'*"[10]

"So I should treat you to coffee as well," Blake says.

"How about we treat each other?" Lisa proposes.

"Since you're a professor," he observes, "you obviously don't make films full time. Your films don't pay the bills."

"True. My films contribute to the scholarship I'm expected to produce. They've been supported by several small- and medium-size grants at Rollins. I sell DVDs through an LLC, as does Vicki Nantz, but the revenue generated has never come close to covering the costs of production—let alone my mortgage."

Blake looks down at Lisa's left hand. On it sits her 1920s platinum engagement ring of diamonds with sapphire accents. "You're married," he notes.

"Engaged," says Lisa, not understanding the relevance.

"And Vicki and Mary are partners," Blake continues.

"They married in Massachusetts a few years ago," Lisa tells him.

"I am alone," Blake says, "and I no longer have a full-time job to cover living expenses."

Lisa responds, "You mentioned that your dad passed away, leaving you some money. May I ask how long you could live on that?"

"Hmm … two years, maybe three."

Violet asks, "And could you fund a film out of that?"

Blake looks at Lisa. "How much did your films cost?"

"Maybe $30,000 total. A couple years back, Scott Hamilton Kennedy, producer of the Oscar-nominated documentary *The Garden* offered a filmmaking workshop. Doing this work full time, he said, means devoting 20 percent of your professional life to grant writing and fundraising."

Blake says, "I don't know the first thing about that."

"I didn't either," Lisa replies. "Rollins now has an office that sends out a monthly notice about available grants. If I see any that pertain to your project, I'll forward the links."

"And I'll watch for grant-writing workshops," says Violet. "The Rollins Philanthropy Center offers them."

Lisa then recalls, "Another filmmaker who visited Rollins said he had learned to live a simple, scaled-down life, less than $15,000 a year."

"I could do that for a few years," Blake reflects. "I don't know about indefinitely."

"Any other advice for me?" queries Violet.

"Just know your representatives," says Lisa, "at all levels: city, county, state, federal. All have offices in your district. Visit them. If your daughter does come out, see if she'll go with you. Humanize yourselves and these issues."

Violet nods. "Much of this runs on relational capital."

"Exactly right," Lisa says. "I can't think of a single public initiative that 'just happened,' where officials woke up one morning, understood the oppression, and voted for change. Human beings showed up, told their stories, went back a second time, a third time."

Lisa continues, "In 2002, Orlando amended Chapter 57 of its city code, adding non-discrimination protections based on sexual orientation."

"I remember seeing those hearings on Orange TV," says Blake. "The rhetoric shook me to my core."

Lisa exhales audibly. "Kathryn, her partner Deena, and I suffered through the hearings together—hours of testimony, *dozens* of opponents. 'You will see God's wrath,' they said. 'God sent AIDS as his judgment.' 'Gay men are rapists and pedophiles.' It was vile.

"After the Council approved the new protections by a four-to-three vote, our group, OADO, turned our attention to Orange County.

It took four years to get even the Fair Housing Code updated and another four years for a full-scale Human Rights Ordinance, this one inclusive of gender identity."

"So *eight years* to move from city to county," Violet marvels, "from sexual orientation only to sexual orientation and gender identity. That's tenacity."

Lisa says, "Kathryn is one of the most tenacious people I know."

"I bet she says the same of you," Blake responds.

Lisa smiles, then looks across the room at Kathryn, who rises from her chair. When Lisa does the same, the two make eye contact and nod. Kathryn reaches into the tote for her tingshas. She and Lisa converge at the front of the room. Kathryn gently rings the bells three times. By the third, the group silences.

Kathryn says, "Please stand and form a circle." The group moves slowly but purposefully. "What amazing conversations, from your insightful systemic analyses to the multitude of creative ideas about where to go from here. To absorb what we've just experienced, let's all close our eyes and take a few signal breaths: deep inhalations through the nose, holding for a second or two, then a slow release through the mouth." The group breathes in unison five times, and Kathryn sounds the bells again.

Lisa requests, "What was it like to have these conversations?"

Group members call out "Invigorating." "Energizing." "A bit daunting."

"To distill our discoveries," suggests Lisa, "let's devote a few minutes to reflecting on the question, 'What is one pearl of wisdom, a key guideline for activism, that emerged from my conversation with my partner?'"

Jackie offers, "Each of us has a responsibility to develop knowledge and skills."

Blake nods. "We must understand deeply the systems we seek to change. Where do we possess resources and power? What resources and power do others hold?"

Violet adds to Blake's list: "Who makes the relevant decisions? Where do they stand on these issues? What motivates them? What relational strategies work best with them?"

"Interpersonal competence is paramount," says Masao.

"We cannot do this alone," Helen observes. "We must act in solidarity with others. Seek out mentors."

Masao nods. "When possible, enlist people in key positions of influence. For me, that could be the dean or provost."

Fernando says, "And to build confidence, start with something concrete and doable."

"From there," adds Zach, "be thoughtful, intentional. I need to immerse myself in LGBTQ+ contexts. As Jackie suggested, there is a lot I need to learn."

"And do the work *with* me," says Naomi, "not for me. I don't require rescuing from above. I need allies at my side."

Kathryn records the group's list of guidelines on the board. When the energy begins to wane, Lisa invites, "Let's close by offering something that captures the sentiment each of us is leaving with today. Anyone may start."

Just to Kathryn's left, Naomi speaks first. "I feel hopeful. I didn't expect that half the attendees today would be allies, and their level of commitment has really moved me."

Masao says, "I am enlivened. I've been studying queer theory since grad school and teaching it for five years. But this is the first time I've engaged in this kind of experiential learning. It helped me link theory to practice, to go from consciousness-raising to action."

At 11:00, Blake tells the group, "I really relate to that. In corporate media, I covered stories about ordinary citizens 'being the change,' as Gandhi said. Now I can *write* those stories; *I* can be one of those citizens."

On his left, Lisa shares, "I feel inspired by this dialogue. Hearing your stories, taking in your wisdom, and consulting on your initiatives have given me ideas for class activities, public and academic writing, and my own activism. Thank you for that."

Violet speaks next. "'Supported' captures my sentiment. I know I'll continue thinking about this workshop and about everyone here—especially you, Blake." He blushes as Violet continues, "I have formulated next steps on the non-discrimination initiative. I am ready to enlist my daughter and husband in this journey. If they're not ready to march beside me, I'll forge ahead and prod them gently along."

Helen wipes both palms on her jeans. "Naomi used the word that came to my mind: 'hopeful,' but I also am absorbing the seriousness of it all. There's so much to do!" Several people nod. "But at least each of us now has a vision or plan, resources, a person to contact."

Jackie says, "My sentiment is gratitude. Thank you all so much for everything you taught me. I can't wait to call my brother!" The group laughs. "When the school year ends, he plans to return to Orlando for the summer. If our combined skills can meet some need identified by the Zebra Coalition, maybe he and I can collaborate on an initiative."

The group looks to Zach. "'Dedicated' expresses my sensibility." He locks gazes with Naomi. "I feel a responsibility to live up to the trust you're placing in me as an ally. As I navigate this rupture in my church, I will ask myself, WWND—What Would Naomi Do?"

"How about instead you pick up the phone and call me?" quips Naomi.

"Would you mind?" asks Zach.

"Not only would I not mind," says Naomi, "I would appreciate the opportunity to weigh in—and to get to know you better."

Fernando exhales. "I feel . . . not quite ready to part. Kathryn and Lisa emailed us prior to the workshop, so I know how to contact everybody. Once I hear from the GSA, there may be ideas I want to run by particular individuals, like Jackie and Masao, or by the whole group. Plus I'd love to continue learning about your initiatives: successes, setbacks, redirections." Everyone smiles and nods, relieved that though the workshop is ending, the group's relationships and collaboration will live on.

Finally, it's to Kathryn. "I feel so blessed for these hours together. I have strengthened ties to members of the LGBTQ+ community," she says, looking to Blake, Naomi, Helen, and Fernando. Then, addressing Jackie, Zach, Masao, Violet, and Lisa: "And I have deepened my already profound regard for our allies. Let us all work together in service of peace, equality, and justice—for *everyone*, in and outside the LGBTQ+ community."

Participants bid farewell to each other and their facilitators. Filing out of Reeves Lodge, they leave Lisa and Kathryn in the quiet of a room smelling of pine and flooded with midday light. Amid an embrace Lisa asks softly, "Is it too early for wine on your back porch?"

"Never," says Kathryn.

Figure 10.2 Kathryn Norsworthy and Lisa Tillmann.

Notes

1 LGBTQ+ refers to lesbian, gay, bisexual, transgender, and queer, plus identities such as intersex and asexual.
2 Deena Flamm shot the photographs in this chapter, whose webpage may be found at: http://www.insolidaritybook.com/in-solidarity.html.
3 See Tillmann (2014), Tillmann, Hall, and Dietz (2014), and Tillmann and Dietz (2014).
4 See Nantz (2013).
5 See Smith (2009).
6 See Russ, Simonds, and Hunt (2002).
7 See Nantz (2010).
8 See Tillmann (October 8, 2008).
9 See Tillmann et al. (2014).
10 See Tillmann (2014) and Tillmann and Dietz (2014).

References

Nantz, Vicki. *In Anita's Wake* [motion picture]. United States: Vicki Nantz Films, 2010.
——. *Billy & Alan* [motion picture]. United States: Vicki Nantz Films, 2013.
Russ, Travis, Cheri Simonds, and Stephen Hunt. "Coming Out in the Classroom . . . an Occupational Hazard? The Influence of Sexual Orientation on Teacher

Credibility and Perceived Student Learning." *Communication Education* 51, no. 3 (2002): 311–324.

Smith, Bettye P. "Student Ratings for Teaching Effectiveness for Faculty Groups Based on Race and Gender." *Education* 129, no. 4 (2009): 615–624.

Tillmann, Lisa M. "Without a Balance of Stories, Elite Media Report Same Old War." *Orlando Sentinel*, A19, October 8, 2008.

——— . *Weight Problem: Cultural Narratives of Fat and "Obesity"* [motion picture]. United States: Cinema Serves Justice, 2014. http://cinemaservesjustice.com/weight-problem.html.

Tillmann, Lisa M., and David Dietz. *Remembering a Cool September* [motion picture]. United States: Cinema Serves Justice, 2014. http://cinemaservesjustice.com/Remembering.html.

Tillmann, Lisa M., Rex Hall, and David Dietz. *Off the Menu: Challenging the Politics and Economics of Body and Food* [motion picture]. United States: Cinema Serves Justice, 2014. http://cinemaservesjustice.com/off-the-menu.html.

EPILOGUE

I sip coffee, reflecting on what moves toward closure and what remains unfinished. If *Between Gay and Straight* bookends this leg of the journey, *In Solidarity* required 13 years to live, compose, and publish. So much happened:

9/11.
U.S. invasion
and occupation.
Recession.
Mass incarceration.
Hope.
Healthcare legislation passing.
Boots-on-ground militarism waning.
LGBT equality ascending.
Change?
NSA watching,
listening,
meta-data analyzing.
Drones' Hellfire raining.
A sick planet perilously warming.

Rereading this manuscript, I note that *In Solidarity* has a more serious tone and political thrust than did *Between Gay and Straight*—a product of the years in which I wrote; of the shift in my professional life from a mainstream department of Communication to a program I spearheaded in Critical Media and Cultural Studies; and of the trajectory of my personal life: divorce, disillusion, dating, dissolution, and depression, with which I have struggled much of my life but most acutely in 2006 and 2013.

As fingers tap keys, I ponder that transformative period from 1994 to 1998, when my graduate education at the University of South Florida intertwined with the lives, relationships, and stories of a network of gay male friends. Emotion rises in my chest as I think of David Holland, the man who invited me into that network. I saw David most recently in June 2014, when he drove to Orlando to provide dinner and cheer.

Thinking of my old friend sparks memories of my ex-husband, Doug Healy, who introduced me to David and connected me to the Suncoast Softball League. I stare at a white screen a long time before words come. Though I haven't seen Doug since 2012, I feel profound gratitude for the many ways he facilitated this project. I send a blessing of loving kindness: Doug, may you be safe; may you be happy; may you be healthy; may you live with ease.

I sit back, hands encircling a steaming mug. I call voices and faces of other old friends to mind: Tim Mahn, Rob Ryan, Pat Martinez, Jeff Grasso, Al, Stew, Joe, Bob, and Kem of the Cove team; Mike Fried, a political soul mate, and his partner and my friend since 1997, Rick Merrifield, who shot key photographs for *Between Gay and Straight*, including the one on its cover.

As I lean back in my white leather swivel chair, warm thoughts arise of Matt Moretti ("Don't Ask, Don't Tell") and his siblings Elisabeth, Paul, and Ashley. In November 2013, Matt invited me to the home he still shares with Josh to reunite with a patio full of Moretti siblings, spouses, and children, including Elisabeth and her partner Ruth and Paul and his wife Faye. The boisterous group clearly relished being together—and made me long for a larger family!

Next to enter my mind: the Wise men, Ray and Steven ("Father's Blessing"), among the most committed and facilitative participants with whom I ever have worked. In 2010, Ray earned a combined MBA and Masters in Healthcare Administration. Employed as a project manager for a large managed care consortium, he now resides in Colorado.

I head downstairs for a fresh cup of Sumatra. While steaming water hisses and spits from my Kuerig, a smile crosses my lips. I think of Gordon Bernstein ("Passings"), his father Tex, his late mother Marilyn, his godfather Bob, and Bob's wife Eve. Gordon gave us a scare in 2012. Crushing headaches and a meningioma diagnosis required radiation and entail continued monitoring and stress management. My friend still lives with Todd, his partner since 2000, in the same house in Ft. Lauderdale. Tex winters nearby and has a lady companion. Gordon said recently of his dad, "He's as happy as I've ever seen him."

Ascending the stairs, I pause to regard another family: Donovan Marshall, his parents John and Barb, and his former partner, Jackson Jones. In some ways, "Revisiting Don/ovan" ends quite unhappily, with relational dissolution: Donovan and Jackson, Doug and me, and later, John and Barb as well. Sometimes endings open new possibilities. In 2009, Donovan moved to Madison to be with his current partner, to whom he got engaged on June 7, 2014. Hopefully by the time you read this, there will be marriage equality in Wisconsin—if not the entire United States. Other times, however, endings close doors. In November 2013, Donovan told me that he and his dad had not spoken for some time. I send peace and light to them, hoping they find their way back together.

Back at my desk, I feel overwhelmed with gratitude toward my parents John and Beth Tillmann and my academic parents, Art Bochner and Carolyn Ellis. Art and Carolyn mentored me through my dissertation and its publication as *Between Gay and Straight*. Both also reviewed the entire *Going Home* section of this book as well as several other pieces and consulted on my proposal for *In Solidarity*. Other "without whom" mentors include Robert Ruberto, retired from Lincoln High School, and professors Lynn Turner and Helen Sterk.

My mind runs through a slide show of other key colleagues and friends: Kathryn Norsworthy, Norman Denzin, Mitch Allen, Keith Berry, Carol Rambo, Stacy Holman Jones, Tony Adams, Chris Poulos, Bill Rawlins, Ron Pelias, Derek Bolen, Christine Kiesinger, Carrie

Schulz, Saleem Yusuff, and Rajesh Kannan, all of whom have facilitated production, presentation, and/or publication of my work. With elbows propped upon the desk, I rest my chin on folded hands.

Next to cross my mental screen are those especially influential in my development as a campus activist and progressive academic: Donna Lee and Mahjabeen Rafiudden, former directors of Multicultural Affairs at Rollins College; Denise Cummings, my Critical Media and Cultural Studies collaborator; and my Faculty United (FU) comrades: Kathryn Norsworthy, Larry VanSickle, Ed Royce, and Eric Schutz.

I bring my left foot to rest on the chair as I contemplate fellow members of the Orlando Anti-Discrimination Ordinance (OADO) committee: founder and master organizer Michael Slaymaker, force of nature Mary Meeks, Joe Saunders (now a state representative), Pat Padilla (also of PFLAG), Joyce Hamilton Henry (also of the ACLU), Mallory Garner-Wells and Michael Farmer (also of Equality Florida), poet and caretaker Drew Weinbrenner, filmmaker Vicki Nantz, Tom Woodard, Randy Stephens, Patrick Howell, and of course, Kathryn Norsworthy, the best friend, collaborator, co-author, and human being one could encounter. Thank you, Kathryn, for your presence and humanity and for loving Deena, my other sounding board in life and love and my key mentor in music and mischief.

My mind then beholds Dave Dietz, my friend since 1995 and film collaborator since 2005. No one has been more influential in developing my artistry, and no one better affirms that laughter saves projects, relationships, and lives.

As I type, something familiar pricks in my chest. More than usual today, I grieve the 2012 deaths of ethnographer-tricksters Bud Goodall and Nick Trujillo. I hope they would have been moved by *In Solidarity* and would have found it worthy of use in their classes.

My gratitude toward Bud and Nick mixes with that which I feel toward my academic home since 1999. Rollins College has supported this project via a McKean and several Critchfield research grants. I then consider the incalculable debt I owe to Phillip Vannini, Margaret Moore, Samantha Barbaro, Gail Newton, Abigail Stanley, and Gail Welsh at Routledge/Taylor & Francis as well as the reviewers of my proposal and manuscript, Tony Adams, Northeastern Illinois University; Keith Berry,

University of South Florida; William K. Rawlins, Ohio University; Bernadette Calafell, University of Denver; and Amy Kilgard, San Francisco State University. Thank you for believing in the merit of this work and for helping it find an audience.

And finally, I begin formulating thoughts of my two main men, Linus, the basset hound asleep at my feet, his body stretched from his doggie chaise to the tribal rug of magenta, violet, and pink, and John, my love since 2008. I close with a story whose conclusion has yet to be written.

June 26, 2013. Kathryn Norsworthy, Deena Flamm, Margaret McLaren, and I hear Jeff Toobin, CNN Senior Legal Analyst, say, "DOMA is gone."

We hop around Kathryn and Deena's back bedroom whooping and cheering. Deena reaches for Kathryn, telling her, "I love you."

"Love you too, baby girl."

"We love you BOTH!" Margaret and I chorus. Kathryn and Deena open their arms and bring us in for a group hug.

Into my ear, Deena says, "Love you too."

"So, so much," adds Kathryn.

I look at my three friends' joyful faces and say, "I think I'll get married."

Their shouts overlap: "Whoa!" "Woo hoo!" "Hoopla!"

At last, Margaret queries, "Um . . . does John know?"

"He will soon," I say. "A long time John has waited—for me to heal, for a less unequal terrain. If you need me, I'll be at home, awaiting his return."

At 6:15 p.m., our electronic gate beeps and swings open as John's half-ton Tundra lumbers over the pavers. Linus bounds clumsily down the staircase, yelping. John and I cross paths in the doorway between the dining room and kitchen. "Congratulations," he says, arms encircling my waist. "I know today meant a lot to you and our friends."

I clear my throat. "Hon . . . I'm thinking . . . maybe it's time to get married."

"I've been thinking that for five years," he quips. I return his smile. John then asks, "Is this because of DOMA?"

"This is because I love you," I reply. "And because of DOMA." I stare into his camouflage green eyes and stroke the mountain-man scruffle on his chin. "What do you say? Will you marry me, John Sansoucie?"

"Any day, any place."

"Well, we can't do it in Florida," I muse.

He grins. "Now how did I know you would say that?"

Later that night, I phone my friend Al, a member of the original Cove softball team. He now lives in San Francisco with his partner Marc. In May 2013, at their home just outside the Castro, they hosted John, John's parents, and me for dinner. When Al picks up, I barely can hear him over the revelry. Today Californians celebrate both the demise of DOMA and the Supreme Court's Prop 8 decision, which stopped short of establishing a federal right to same-sex marriage but cleared the path for marriage equality in California. "Hey, my dear!" Al says, sounding high on justice and maybe a bit of champagne.

"I'm calling to say congratulations," I loudly reply, "and to let you know I'm getting married!"

"What's that, honey?" asks Al amid a cacophony of car horns and cheering.

"Married! I'm getting married!"

Beat. Then, "Oh, yay! When? Where?"

"Not sure," I say. "Maybe on this historic date. But definitely in a marriage equality state."

Al lets out a full-throated laugh. "That is so *you*! Say, you could marry at our house."

My eyes open wide. "We just might do that!"

So that's the plan: Al and Marc's house, June 2014. John and I decided against the 26th, but only because it fell on a Thursday. Except Al and Marc, everyone in attendance will be traveling, most of us cross-country. We settled instead on Saturday, June 21. It will be my parents' 45th wedding anniversary.

* * *

The above would have made an "into the sunset" ending to *In Solidarity*. Indeed it *was* the ending until April 25, 2014, when tread marks appeared suddenly on the road to John's and my wedding. We remain domestic partners, committed to each other and to discovering where our path now leads.

Thus the personal mirrors the political. We try to look deeply and see clearly exactly where we are. We celebrate achievements, face setbacks, and grieve losses. At the same time, we keep envisioning a place of greater equity, peace, hope, joy, and love and doing what we can to co-create it.

In solidarity,
Lisa M. Tillmann

APPENDIX
FRIENDSHIP AS METHOD[1]

During the research and composition of my Ph.D. dissertation[2] and first book, *Between Gay and Straight*,[3] friendship emerged not only as a subject of my research but also as its primary *method*. In my dissertation, I coined the term "friendship as method." Expanding on ideas developed there, this appendix discusses my project and other interpretive and critical studies that exemplify elements of friendship as method.

I begin by defining friendship, positing friendship as a kind of fieldwork, and establishing the methodological foundations of friendship as method. Next, I propose that this mode of qualitative inquiry involves researching with the practices, at the pace, in the natural contexts, and with an ethic of friendship. Finally, I describe this approach's strengths and considerations for both researcher and participants.

Friendship Defined

In *Friendship Matters*, William K. Rawlins defines a close friend as "somebody to talk to, to depend on and rely on for help, support, and caring, and to have fun and enjoy doing things with."[4] Like romantic and family relationships, friendship is an interpersonal bond characterized by the ongoing communicative management of dialectical tensions, such as those between affection and instrumentality, expressiveness and protectiveness, and judgment and acceptance.[5]

Unlike romance and kinship, friendship in Western cultures lacks canonical status. In the United States, we tend to accord friendship second-class status. For example, we might say, "We're *just* friends," to mean, "We're neither family nor lovers." On confronting the chasm between unsanctioned and sanctioned ties, Andrew Holleran reflects:

> I was always discomfited whenever I accompanied friends to hospitals, or emergency rooms, at having to answer the question of the doctor, "Who are you?" with the words, "A friend." It sounded so flimsy—so infinitely weaker than, "His brother," "His cousin," "His brother-in-law." It sounded like a euphemism; a word that did not, could not, convey what our bond really was.[6]

Holleran's experience supports Rawlins' claim that friendship occupies a marginal position within the matrix of interpersonal relations and has "no clear normative status."[7] Kathy Werking affirms this, deeming friendship "the most fragile social bond."[8]

We can attribute some of friendship's unstable footing in Western societies to the absence of obligatory dimensions. We are not born into friendships, as most are into families. Like marriage, friendship is a voluntary relationship;[9] but unlike marriage, friendship lacks religious and legal grounding, rendering the creation, maintenance, and dissolution of friendship an essentially private, negotiable endeavor.[10]

Friends come and stay together primarily through common interests, a sense of alliance, and emotional affiliation.[11] Friendship, according to Rawlins, "*implies affective ties.*"[12] In friends, we seek trust, honesty, respect, commitment, safety, support, generosity, loyalty, mutuality, constancy, understanding, and acceptance.[13]

In addition to emotional resources, friendships provide identity resources. Humans form, reinforce, and alter conceptions of self and other in the context of ongoing relationships. This explains why Gary Alan Fine calls friendship "a crucible for the shaping of selves."[14]

Friendships tend to confirm more than contest conceptions of self because we often befriend those similar to ourselves, those more "self" than "other." As Rawlins points out, this begins in early childhood, when young persons typically have more access to playmates of the same age, sex, and physical characteristics.[15] Similarly, adolescent friends tend to be of the same race, school grade, and social standing. Throughout life, friendships have a pronounced likelihood of developing within (rather than across) lines such as culture, education, marital and career status, and socioeconomic class. Because of this, posits Rawlins, friendships more likely "reinforce and reproduce macrolevel and palpable social differences than . . . challenge or transcend them."[16]

When friendships do cross social groups, the bonds take on political dimensions. Opportunities exist for dual consciousness-raising and for members of dominant groups (e.g., men, Euro-Americans, Christians, and heterosexuals) to serve as allies for friends in marginalized groups. As a result, those who are "just friends" can become *just* friends, interpersonal and political allies who seek personal growth, meaningful relationships, and social justice.[17]

Friendship as Fieldwork

When I began proposing friendship as a method of inquiry, I received some quizzical looks. Even some who view friendship as an important topic and who recognize that friendships sometimes arise in the context of research expressed skepticism about a methodological link between friendship and fieldwork.

In many ways, though, friendship and fieldwork are similar endeavors. Both involve being in the world with others. To friendship and fieldwork communities, we must gain entrée. We negotiate roles (e.g., student, confidant, advocate), shifting from one to another as the relational context warrants. Our communication might progress, in Martin Buber's terms, from "seeming" to "being," from I-It (impersonal and instrumental), to I-You (more personal yet role-bound), to moments of I-Thou, where we are truly present, meeting one another in our full humanity.[18]

We navigate membership, participating, observing, and observing our participation.[19] We learn insider argot and new codes for behavior. As we deepen our ties, we face challenges, conflicts, and losses. We cope with relational dialectics, negotiating how private and how candid we will be, how separate and how together, how stable and how in-flux. One day, finite projects—and lives—end, and we may "leave the field."

Foundations

Friendship as method builds on several established approaches to qualitative research. It is based on the principles of interpretivism, which according to Thomas Schwandt, stem from the German intellectual traditions of hermeneutics (interpretation) and *verstehen* (understanding), from phenomenology, and from the critiques of positivism.[20]

Interpretivists take reality to be both pluralistic and constructed in language and interaction. Instead of facts, we search for intersubjective meanings, what Clifford Geertz, following Max Weber, calls the "webs of significance";[21] instead of control, we seek understanding. For interpretivists, "objectivity becomes a synonym for estrangement and neutrality a euphemism for indifference."[22] According to Norman Denzin, we research and write not to capture the totality of social life but to interpret reflectively slices and glimpses of localized interaction in order to understand more fully both others and ourselves.[23]

Feminist researchers laid additional groundwork for friendship as method. Standpoint feminism focuses on intersecting systems of institutional and cultural oppression.[24] According to Kristen Intemann, "standpoints do not automatically arise from occupying a particular social location. They are achieved only when there is sufficient scrutiny and critical awareness of how power structures shape or limit knowledge in a particular context."[25] A standpoint, writes Sandra Harding, "is an achievement" and "a collective one, not an individual one."[26]

Feminists have been instrumental in debunking the myth that inquiry can or should be free of politics and values[27] and in promoting communitarian ethics. According to Patricia Hill Collins, we must move from colonization to an "epistemology of empowerment."[28] Pathways toward this way of knowing include an ethic of caring that invites expressiveness, emotion, and empathy;[29] "dialogical knowledge production";[30] and collaborative social change work.[31] Feminist projects reflect and advance commitments to consciousness-raising, empowerment, equity, and justice.[32] According to Intemann, such inquiry aims "to examine power relations, institutions, policies, and technologies that perpetuate oppression from the perspective of the oppressed, so that they may be changed, undermined, or abolished."[33]

Queer researchers pursue a similarly political agenda. We queer a text or project when we problematize the binary constructions and the conflation of sex, gender, and sexual orientation; challenge heteronormativity; and interrogate and seek to dismantle heterosexual privilege.[34]

Michelle Fine's notion of "working the hyphens"[35] also influenced friendship as method. Like other interpretive and critical approaches, Fine's rejects scientific neutrality, universal truths, and dispassionate inquiry and works toward social justice, relational truths, and passionate inquiry. Through authentic engagement, the lines between researcher and researched blur, permitting each to explore layers of self, other, and relationship. Instead of "speaking for" or even "giving voice," researchers *get to know* others in meaningful and sustained ways.

Fine's philosophy shares much common ground with participatory action research (PAR). According to Reason, this type of inquiry emerged from liberationist movements.[36] Action researchers view truth as a product and instrument of power. PAR honors lived experience and aims to produce knowledge and action directly useful to those with whom we collaborate. Under this model, we evaluate research by what Patti Lather and Peter Reason term "catalytic validity," the degree to which it empowers our research communities.[37] As we centralize dialogue, the subject–object relationship of positivism becomes a subject–subject one, in which academic knowledge combines with everyday experience to reach new and profound understandings.[38]

Closest methodologically to friendship as method are interactive interviewing[39] and collaborative witnessing.[40] These demand more sharing of personal and social experiences on the part of the researcher than does PAR. But, like participatory action research, interactive interviewing and collaborative witnessing are interpretive practices, require intense collaboration, and privilege lived, emotional experience.

Friendship as Method

Calling for inquiry that is open, multi-voiced, and emotionally rich, friendship as method involves the practices, the pace, the contexts, and the ethics of friendship. Researching with the *practices* of friendship, first, means that although we employ traditional forms of data gathering (e.g., participant observation, systematic note-taking, and informal and formal interviewing), our primary procedures are those we use to build and sustain friendship: conversation, everyday involvement, compassion, generosity, and vulnerability.

Keith Cherry's ethnographic account of a community of people living with AIDS exemplifies practices of friendship.[41] To chronicle participants' experiences and relationships, Cherry conducted fieldwork, shot photographs, and recorded interaction, but he also played ping pong and watched soap operas with residents, drove them to doctor appointments, visited them in the hospital, and helped arrange birthday parties and funerals. These activities added emotional and relational layers to Cherry's intellectual pursuits. Responding to the changing needs of community members, his friend and researcher roles shifted from center to periphery and back again. Sometimes Cherry had the emotional space to reflect on the meanings residents assigned to everyday practices, such as gossiping and watching television; other times, fear and grief consumed him. The depth of his connections to this community rendered him a vulnerable observer,[42] a compassionate witness, and a true ally.

Second, friendship as method demands that we research at the natural *pace* of friendship. The tempo is that of anthropology, whose practitioners typically stay a year or more in fieldwork communities, and of psychotherapy, a process that, in the words of Liz Bondi, "needs to enable 'nothing to happen' or 'time to be wasted' and similar 'inefficiencies.'"[43] Over the course of 18 months, Cherry spent 25 to 40 hours per week at the Tahitian Islander, an apartment complex for people living with AIDS.[44] Carol R. Rinke and Lynnette Mawhinney each conducted research in urban schools over the course of two academic years.[45] Christine Kiesinger, who composed life histories of four women with eating disorders, devoted three years of academic and personal involvement to the lives of her participants.[46] Between formal interviews, Kiesinger shared meals, transcripts, and confidences with respondents. Barbara Myerhoff based *Number Our Days* on four years of participant observation and life history interviewing within an elderly Jewish community.[47] *Between Gay and Straight* required three years of participant observation and interviewing and three additional years of writing, sharing drafts with community members, and rewriting. My follow-up project, *Going Home*, has kept me connected to my friends/collaborators' lives and families of origin since 2003. Michael Angrosino volunteered at a group home for three years before even beginning his study of persons with mental retardation, which lasted another nine years.[48] Since 1999, Kathryn Norsworthy and Ouyporn Khuankaew have facilitated "training of social action trainers" across Thailand and along the border with Burma.[49] Each project mentioned here involved (or still involves) a serious time commitment, but in every case, both profound relationships and provocative accounts resulted.

With friendship as method, a project's issues emerge organically, in the ebb and flow of everyday life: leisurely walks, household projects, activist campaigns, separations, losses, recoveries. The unfolding path of the relationships becomes the path of the project.

The length of time needed may vary depending on whether the researcher and participants begin the study as strangers, acquaintances, friends, or close friends. This approach requires multiple angles of vision. Strangers tend to have keener observational eyes yet must cultivate more intersubjective views, which develop gradually over time. Close friends already may share deeper, more intricate perspectives of one another but must continually step back from experiences and relationships and examine them analytically and critically.

Figure A.1 Members of the Cove softball team

Third, friendship as method situates our research in the natural *contexts* of friendship. *Between Gay and Straight* takes readers into multiple sites: gay bars and clubs, softball fields, restaurants, and coffee houses. For the *Going Home* project, I traveled across the United States to places defined by participants as important, such as childhood homes, schools, and houses of worship. The sites themselves hold less significance than what they mean to our collaborators and who we become within them. In Kristen C. Blinne's words, "Employing 'friendship as method' captures my desire to remain connected to my field site as an active, compassionate, and embodied participant."[50]

Perhaps the most important aspect of this methodology is that we research with an *ethic* of friendship, a stance of hope, caring, justice, even love.[51] Friendship as method is neither a program nor a guise strategically aimed at gaining further access. It is a level of investment in participants' lives that puts fieldwork relationships on par with the project.

We sacrifice a day of writing to help someone move. We set aside our reading pile when someone drops by or calls "just to talk." When asked, we keep secrets, even if they would add compelling twists to our research report or narrative. We consider our participants an audience and struggle to write both honestly and empathically *for them*.[52] We lay ourselves on the line, going virtually anywhere, doing almost anything, pushing to the furthest reaches of our being. We never ask more of participants than we are willing to give. Friendship as method demands radical reciprocity, a move from studying "them" to studying *us*.[53]

For researchers, this means that we use our speaking and writing skills and our positions as scholars and critics in ways that transform and uplift our research, local, and global communities.[54] Since 2001, my friend and colleague Kathryn Norsworthy and I have been members of the Orlando Anti-Discrimination Ordinance Committee (OADO), a nonpartisan social advocacy group of LGBT persons and allies. In Orlando and Orange County, OADO played an instrumental role in securing domestic partner registries and non-discrimination protections based on sexual orientation and gender identity. Kathryn and I have spearheaded resolutions and petition drives on our campus; met with city and county officials; composed newspaper editorials;[55] spoken at public rallies; and testified before the Orlando Human Relations Board, the Orlando City Council, the Orange County Board of Commissioners, and the school boards of Orange and Lake counties.

Myerhoff contributed to a film that won an Academy Award for best short documentary, bringing renewed visibility and resources to the Aliyah Center. Angrosino developed such close relationships with staff and clients at Opportunity House that they elected him to its board of trustees. Since 1990, Stephen John Hartnett has been teaching not only about but also *within* the U.S. prison system as well as protesting the death penalty and the prison industrial complex.[56] In these and many other ways, researchers can become allies with and for their research communities. Making this move, we do not deny or efface privilege associated with education or any other dominant group identity; instead, we try to use that privilege for liberatory ends.

This ethic of friendship also extends to our relationships with readers. We research pressing social problems that undermine freedom, democracy, equity, and peace. We strive to ensure that our representations expose and contest oppression associated with race, nationality, gender, class, sexual orientation, religion, age, and ability. With compelling, transgressive accounts, we seek to engage readers, and on multiple levels: intellectually, aesthetically, emotionally, ethically, and politically.[57] Together, researchers, participants, and readers learn to practice a more active and responsible citizenship.

Strengths of Friendship as Method

For everyone involved, friendship as method can provide a unique perspective on social life. In the ethnographic dialogue,[58] we bring together personal and academic discourses, comparing, contrasting, and critiquing them.

For the Researcher

This move offers much to qualitative researchers. Perhaps the most meaningful benefit is the relationships themselves. Total immersion of both our academic and personal selves can foster multifaceted bonds. Of his relationships with the men of Opportunity House, Angrosino writes, "I didn't want to be thought of as just the guy who showed up every so often with the tape recorder. I wanted to remain someone who had connections to their lives in general."[59]

Such relationships can provide what Kenneth Burke calls "equipment for living."[60] By befriending Jewish elders at the Aliyah Center, Myerhoff rediscovered her roots. Through interactive, reciprocal bonds with Abbie, Liz, Eileen, and Anna, Kiesinger added layers of meaning to her own account of bulimia.

Friendship as method can bring us to a level of understanding and depth of experience we may be unable to reach using only traditional methods. In my work, by studying LGBTQ+[61] literatures, I learn about my friends/participants historically and politically; by observing their interactions, I get to know them interpersonally and culturally; by giving them my compassion and devotion, I experience them emotionally and spiritually.

Between Gay and Straight and *In Solidarity* involved multiple cycles of conversing, sharing activities, reading LGBTQ+ literatures, exchanging material, writing about the group, distributing the writing, and talking about it. Throughout these cycles, my researcher and friendship roles wove together, each expanding and deepening the other. My participants became (and remain) family. The impact of our relationships ripples through every dimension of my life.

One area profoundly affected has been my connections with women, both lesbian- and heterosexually identified. Observing my participants' same-sex bonds, I have been prompted to seek new levels of affiliation in my own. I am better able to tap into the loving—even erotic—possibilities of female friendship, and I believe this renders me a more feminist ally to other women.

These layered connections also allow me to see the many faces of oppression.[62] As a result, I work continually to infuse my research, my pedagogy, and my institutional and community service with the values of anti-oppressive education.[63] In all of these ways, this academic project has become my *life project*.

For Participants

Respondents can benefit from participation in such projects as well. Through the experience of empathic connection with the friend/

researcher, participants can feel heard, known, and understood.[64] Those with whom we collaborate have unique opportunities to (co-)construct meaningful accounts and to offer those to others as gifts. Previously hospitalized for anorexia, a participant named Liz said to Kiesinger, "I have been to hell and back and if I can prevent anyone from going where I've been, I will tell my story."[65] Respondents also can take pride in the contributions they make to the researcher's life. About her relationship with a participant who has struggled with bulimia, Kiesinger writes: [66]

> Abbie took a liking to me almost instantly. She seemed very interested in my life, my story, and my bulimia. In our interactions, she played a "motherly" role and seemed eager to take me under her wing. She expressed this most strongly in the intense maternal embrace she gave me after each meeting. She would hold me close to her for a long time, patting the back of my head. I knew that she felt valued, useful, and strong when consoling me. Given that she felt unworthy, useless, and weak for most of her life, I was thrilled to let her shower me with all the advice, nurturance, and counsel she could.

By engaging the friend/researcher in a long-term, multi-faceted relationship, participants can learn as many new ways of thinking, feeling, and relating as the researcher can. Rob Ryan, a friend since 1996 and participant in *Between Gay and Straight*, reported on some specific lessons learned:[67]

> I remember talking to you about what it meant to be gay and some of my hang-ups about it. You were the first person— whether you knew it or not—who clarified for me that being gay related to my sexual orientation and not necessarily to being masculine or feminine. I didn't see myself as feminine, but my upbringing was that if you were gay, you were feminine, and that was a bad thing.
> A year later, I asked if you saw me as "the woman" in my relationship with Tim. Your answer was: "If you're asking

whether I see you as the one who tends to be more sensitive and nurturing, then yes, I see you as the woman." You turned being "the woman" from a weakness—as I unknowingly had made it out to be—to a strength. Suddenly, it dawned on me: I should value *all* my good qualities, masculine and feminine.

At the oral defense for my Ph.D. dissertation, Gordon Bernstein, my friend since 1995 and a participant both in the original project and in *Going Home*, said this:[68]

I grew up playing baseball, played it in college for a couple years. Was very much socialized with middle-class, beer-drinking, heterosexual ideals. Socialized that way all my life. Our group has thought and talked about things since meeting Lisa that we didn't before. Our conversations were very unemotional. I don't know how often we expressed ourselves—what we thought, how we felt, how we came to terms with things. Lisa facilitated those kinds of conversations, and I don't think anyone else here could have facilitated them. I know that I couldn't have been as open, pushed the envelope that often, and really shared my views, because I was socialized not to feel pain. "Deal with it, suck it up, and move on." But Lisa made it comfortable for us, and that made it possible for her to establish the kind of friendships we have with her.

Though it brings unusual dimensions to our relationships, my dual role of friend/researcher provides additional reasons and ways to connect. Because I study them/us, my friends/participants can count on my intellectual interest in their emotional and relational lives. Rob indicated that had I been "just a friend," he may not have perceived a standing invitation to share personal experiences. At the same time, because I care about them so much and embody that ethic of caring, they can trust that I will honor their confidences; do everything in my power to support them and to act in their best interest; and engage in teaching, research, and service pursuits that promote liberation and justice for them and for everyone.

Figure A.2 Lisa Tillmann and Gordon Bernstein.

When we approach research as an endeavor of friendship, the emergent texts can have additional benefits for participants, including self-understanding and acceptance. Asked what he learned from the dissertation, Rob told me, "I wish I had read this before I came out. This has helped me become more comfortable with myself." On a similar note, Pat Martinez, another participant in the original study, said:[69]

> I think that I have benefited more from Lisa writing her dissertation than *she* has, or will, even by getting a Ph.D. Becoming involved with Lisa and the work she was doing . . . enabled me to deal with my coming out. It helped me combine my old athletic, fraternity-brother self and my emerging gay self. I saw that I could be a *gay* athlete, a *gay* man with gay *and straight* friends . . . The only "drawback" for me is that I wish the project would have started earlier. We met just as I was coming out at 35. I wonder how different my twenties would have been had I crossed paths with someone like [Lisa], had I been asked to look within myself and discuss my inner struggles—as I have in my late thirties.

Figure A.3 Patrick Martinez.

What we write even can strengthen connections among members of one's research community. Rob said of the dissertation, "I wasn't involved with [my partner] Tim when many of the early events were occurring. So I felt like I got to know the group and the group's history better." David Holland, a friend since 1994 and participant in the original project, made a similar observation:[70]

> I never imagined that the dissertation would have such an impact on all of us as friends. My friendships with these guys were pretty solid before, but the project has brought us even closer. Reading the dissertation, we all learned about each other. Since

then, we've talked about the events Lisa wrote about, and those discussions have re-forged the bonds between us. This was a very, very unique experience that we all shared.

These works then can be taken outside the fieldwork community and used as sources of education. Tim Mahn, a friend since 1994 and participant in the original study, said of *Between Gay and Straight*, "There are so many people I meet, or I'm friends with, or acquaintances, or family members, or people from my past that I'd like to send a copy. I think they could be enlightened. It's going to be a great tool."

Finally, our writings from friendship as method can promote social change. In Tim's words, "As a reader, I kept thinking, 'I want to do something; I *have* to do something.' [The project] gave me energy. I feel like I'm now a bit of an activist." On a similar note, Rob told me, "You've shown us that we have a lot of responsibility, and that being out is courageous. If we can be that, I know we can help others."

Considerations of Friendship as Method

For both researcher and participants, friendship as method raises the ethical stakes. The demands are high and the implications can be daunting.

For the Researcher

Every researcher must consider practical issues. Deadlines for publication, grant applications, tenure, and promotion structure and constrain our work lives. Not all researchers can afford to spend at least a year in the field and another year or more writing, revisiting, and rewriting.

Questions graduate students have asked include, "How do I get a project like this through my thesis/dissertation committee?" and, "Will anyone hire this kind of researcher?" Students interested in such work must find programs that support it. Some of the projects I have discussed (my own, Cherry's, and Kiesinger's) came out of the Ph.D. program in Communication at the University of South Florida. The Communication departments at the University of Illinois at Urbana-Champaign and the University of Southern Illinois at Carbondale also encourage critical, ethnographic, and action research. With respect to the job-seeking process, it probably is safer professionally to conduct more traditional studies. But one's passion for unconventional research and for close relationships in the field need not preclude academic employment. In my first year on the job market (1998–9), I was invited to four campus interviews and received two offers.

On the other hand, practicing friendship as method does make it challenging to specify, in advance, research questions and objectives for external evaluators such as dissertation committees and institutional review boards. Our work also may be difficult to contextualize for more traditional colleagues and funding agencies. To help provide such a context, I included a detailed statement of my methodological philosophy, articulating many ideas contained in this appendix, in a professional assessment report for evaluations at mid-tenure, tenure, and promotion to full professor. The statement sparked discussions with the multi-disciplinary evaluation committees, but I was not asked to defend my approach. Each researcher has to gauge the political and methodological climate of her or his department and institution in order to frame what s/he does in terms that peers and evaluators will find understandable and persuasive.

Careful consideration must be given to emotional demands as well. With friendship as method, researchers must examine, scrutinize, and critique ourselves in ways not required by traditional qualitative inquiry. Kiesinger's relationship with Abbie, whose account of bulimia centers on a long history of sexual exploitation, evoked a vague yet haunting sense that Kiesinger also had been sexually abused as a child. Close relationships with my friends/collaborators make it impossible to shirk from my heterosexism and heterosexual privilege. Though such radical reflexivity can take us to the darkest corners of our socialization and experience, it also can enlighten our thinking, our accounts, and our being.

Relationally, doing fieldwork this way carries all the risks that friendship does. Because we must reveal and invest so much of ourselves, researchers are more vulnerable than we ever have had to be, which means we can be profoundly disappointed, frustrated, or hurt. For three years, Kiesinger witnessed four women battle anorexia and/or bulimia.

Three of them followed no clear path toward recovery, and their struggles at times exacerbated Kiesinger's own struggles with body and food. By exploring the borderlands between Jewish and Christian identities, Leigh Berger learned to live with uncertainty and began to work through the conflicted feelings she had for her estranged, mentally ill father.[71] Just as she felt ready to reconnect with him, he suddenly died. During my fieldwork, members of my research community tested positive for HIV, rendering me a fellow traveler down emotional, medical, and political pathways. Myerhoff and Cherry grieved the deaths of virtually every participant in their studies.

Another consideration involves our sometimes-conflicting obligations. On one hand, we must respect and honor our relationships with participants; on the other, we owe readers as comprehensive and complex an account as possible. After collecting narratives of conversion to Messianic Judaism, Berger wanted to interview participants' significant others about their reactions to the person who had changed faiths. In the end, she rejected the idea, concluding that this "would be too disruptive to the delicate truce many family members share when one member has converted."[72] Though such interviews would have brought a new and provocative dimension to her project, Berger privileged her ethic of friendship over her ethnographic interest.

As mentioned, due to our deep and sustained involvement, we may be told secrets that would add significant layers to our accounts. Even with non-privileged information, the dual role of friend/researcher makes it difficult to decide what to divulge, especially regarding information that potentially discredits our participants.

Berger reports being disconcerted by the conservative attitudes toward abortion and same-sex relations that her participants expressed. On several occasions, the sexism exhibited by my gay male friends/ participants troubled me. In face-to-face encounters in the field, both Berger and I tended to suppress much of our disapproval.[73] Had our participants been strangers or simply "subjects," we may have maintained a more critical distance and felt more empowered to challenge their views directly.[74] Later, we included these issues in our written accounts, hoping our portrayals would spark reflection and action, both in and outside our fieldwork communities. At some level, though, even this felt like a betrayal to our friends/participants, already members of stigmatized and marginalized groups.

Under friendship as method, researchers must pay constant close attention to ethical issues, including informed consent, confidentiality, and beneficence. At times, we navigate their pathways in unconventional ways. Angrosino's research, for example, centered on adults with mental retardation, many of whom also have a history of mental illness and/or criminal behavior. Because his participants may have difficulty assessing the consequences of consent, Angrosino wrote ethnographic fiction and created composite characters.

My approach to confidentiality changed as the relationships changed. In my first class paper on the network of friends, I followed social science conventions by using pseudonyms and altering other identifying details. Later, as the project became more collaborative, I asked my friends/ participants to choose between having a pseudonym, including their real first name only, or using their real first and last names.[75] I explained that pseudonyms were the standard and safest approach. For the dissertation, one primary participant, Adam (not out at work or to his family), requested a pseudonym and asked that I write only generally about his occupation and hometown. Others (David, Gordon, Rob, and Pat) had me use real first and last names. Because *Between Gay and Straight* would be a more public and accessible document, I contacted the group again. This time, "Adam" gave permission to use his real first name (Al), while another participant, embarking on a new career, asked that I alter his last name. All men consented to having photographs of them in the book, and Tim and Rob agreed to appear on the cover with my husband and me.

When Tim and Rob decided to use their real names, each said to me, "I want to do this for you." While this reflects their level of investment in our relationships and in the project, I urged them not to base consent on their feelings for me or on what they imagined I wanted. We talked at length about the personal and professional risks they would be taking. My friends could be fired for no other reason than being gay—something still true as of this writing. When *Between Gay and Straight* came out in 2001, Tim and Rob could not even legally have sex in Florida and 13 other states. From conversations I had with them, I came to believe that, while my friends' connections with me could not be completely disentangled from their decisions, each perceived himself to be acting in his own best interest, as well as the interests of other— especially younger—gay men, who need role models for coming out. Had I not believed that, I would have tried to convince them to change their names.

In re-securing informed consent for *In Solidarity*, I opened myself to the possibilities that participants would request significant revisions or even withdraw. I reached out in the fall of 2013 and spent more than a month not knowing whether *any* of the *Going Home* chapters could appear in this book. One chapter entailed significant negotiation and substantive changes. When researchers share decision-making, we give up a lot of control.

In terms of beneficence, I clearly have profited more professionally than have my non-academic collaborators. The original project and its publications proved central to my earning a Ph.D., getting an academic job, and receiving tenure, and my follow-up work was instrumental in my promotion to full professor. My most recent scholarship, however, has involved co-authorship with my friend and colleague, Kathryn Norsworthy,[76] who identifies as lesbian, and co-production with a friend since 1995, David Dietz,[77] who identifies as gay. Also, in the interest of distributing the benefits of my LGBTQ+ work, I have donated royalties from *Between Gay and Straight* to activist groups (e.g., the ACLU, the Human Rights Campaign, Equality Florida, GLSEN, and PFLAG) and continually offer myself as a resource to community groups, the media, educators, and students.

When researchers become allies to groups the dominant culture has constructed as deviant (e.g., gay men, Messianic Jews, women struggling with bulimia, people with AIDS) and assign the resultant texts in their classes, not all students respond positively. Confronting this kind of work may challenge deeply held values and assumptions. I have had to answer complaints (e.g., this work as "gay propaganda") on course evaluations and directly to my department chair and senior administrators. One student had to be removed from my class before the semester even began. Seeing *Between Gay and Straight* on the reading list, this student called my chair and provost, demanded an alternative to my class (a require-ment for the major), and made veiled threats. I am fortunate to be at an institution whose administration supports and defends my work. Nonetheless, these student complaints have been both time- and energy-sapping.

When our projects center on oppression, our emotional and physical safety can be jeopardized as well. My friends/participants and I have been verbally accosted by homophobic slurs. Those politically and/or religiously opposed to my work have sent me virulent anti-gay literature and targeted me in online smears. Enduring still another level of risk, Khuankaew and Norsworthy conduct workshops on violence, trauma, and HIV-awareness on the Thai–Burma border, where it has been illegal for them to organize. With each training session, Norsworthy, a psychologist from the United States, has risked deportation and blacklist status, and her Thai collaborator, Khuankaew, has faced incarceration.

Friendship as method, while incredibly rewarding, comes with a set of obligations that do not pave a smooth, easily traveled path. When we engage others' humanity, struggles, and oppression, we cannot simply turn off the recorder, turn our backs, and exit the field. Anyone who takes on this sort of project must be emotionally strong and willing to face pressure, resistance, backlash, and perhaps even violence.

For Participants

When we approach research as an endeavor of friendship and we approach participants as friends, we also heighten some considerations for them. Because of the power imbalance between researcher and participants, field relationships can be exploitive. Friendship as method seeks to undermine and disrupt this. However, if researchers do not maintain an ethic of friendship in their fieldwork practices and accounts, our participants, readers, and/or listeners can sustain emotional damage.[78]

In "Emotional and Ethical Quagmires in Returning to the Field,"[79] Carolyn Ellis writes poignantly about the anger and pain members of her fieldwork community suffered when a third party informed them that she had published *Fisher Folk*,[80] a book containing unflattering portrayals of their "backwoods" lifestyle. An extended family had taken in Carolyn as a friend, giving her years of virtually unfettered access, but as a then-realist ethnographer, she rarely allowed herself to be similarly open. Ellis also admits to taping conversations surreptitiously, to securing consent so early in the 12-year project that many forgot about her researcher role or assumed it had ended, and to sharing none of her published work. The honesty of "Emotional and Ethical Quagmires" helps readers become, as Ellis herself has become, a more dialogical and relationally ethical researcher.[81]

Friendship as method all but demands that writings be taken back to the community for examination, critique, and further dialogue. I have given my central participants interview transcripts, drafts of class papers, the dissertation, proposed changes for *Between Gay and Straight*, drafts of several articles, and the manuscript for *In Solidarity*. Several attended my dissertation defense having read the document, and many participated in the discussion. I also conducted follow-up interviews to attain additional reactions and reflections. At each stage, I incorporated their feedback and suggestions and renegotiated informed consent. Their participation at so many stages required repeated intrusions on their time and energy. Had they been working class or in poor health, they may not have had these resources to devote.[82]

While this process helped the projects become more egalitarian, it also rendered my friends/participants vulnerable. As with *Between Gay and Straight*, *In Solidarity* exposes once-private aspects of my collaborators to family, friends, and co-workers. In reading interview transcripts for *Going Home*, three primary informants had to confront heterosexist and/or homophobic comments made by a relative. Seeing such comments, one relative felt so uncomfortable and ashamed that this person insisted that several lines be removed. In the case of "Revisiting Don/ovan," requesting that participants reread the chapter in 2014 also meant asking them to re-immerse themselves in three partnerships—Donovan Marshall and Jackson Jones, John and Barb Marshall, and Doug Healy and me—all of which dissolved painfully.

In some cases, our participants risk not only emotional but also physical harm. To attend Khuankaew and Norsworthy's workshops, for example, Burmese women have defied laws against organizing and risked arrest, abuse, and imprisonment. For me, few thoughts are more sobering than the possibility that one of my friends could become the victim of a hate crime as a result of visibility in my work.

Friendship as method requires that ethics remain at the forefront of our research and our research relationships. Confidentiality and informed consent become ongoing negotiations. Researchers and participants reflexively consider and discuss power dynamics at every turn and constantly strive to balance the need to advance the interpretive and critical agendas of their projects and the need to protect one another from harm.

Conclusion

Most any study involving human "subjects" can incorporate some aspect of friendship as method. Even in the most empirical, double-blind research, we can treat participants with an ethic of friendship. We can solicit fears and concerns, listen closely and respond compassionately, and use such exchanges to refine the study and direct its implications.

Friendship as method well suits the study of close relationships, including friendship. In contrast to one-time, retrospective surveys, a primary means of studying relationships, friendship as method involves sustained immersion in participants' lives, offering a processual and longitudinal perspective. But most any topic could be investigated with the practices, at the pace, in the contexts, and/or with an ethic of friendship. Topics like living with disability,[83] navigating racist discourse in the classroom,[84] the experience of incarceration,[85] or surviving genocide,[86] probably lend themselves best to friendship as method, because the more emotional and multi-faceted the topic, the more appropriate it becomes for researchers and participants to share emotional and multi-faceted ties.

For a mutual, close, and/or lasting friendship to develop between every researcher and all participants is unrealistic. Regardless, we can approach respondents from a stance of friendship, meaning we treat them with respect, honor their stories, and try to use their stories for humane and just purposes.

In a strange aligning of the universe, the oral defense for my dissertation took place the same day and time as Matthew Shepard's memorial service. Jim King, a member of my committee, posed this question: "But what if *they* are not humane and just? Would you study Matthew Shepard's killers this way?"

I responded with this:[87]

> That would be extremely difficult. When something like this murder happens, "we"—the non-perpetrators—often are so shocked and disheartened that we distance ourselves from "them"—the perpetrators. We tell ourselves that they must be crazy or evil. Such explanations come quickly and easily. The hardest question to ask is this: what kinds of personal, familial, and cultural conditions have to exist for this act to make sense somehow, to seem almost *rational*? We don't ask this because it implicates us in the problem; it forces us to identify with the killers, to bring them close and see them as part of us. Russell Henderson and Aaron McKinney were unable to experience their interconnection with Matthew Shepard; that's exactly what made him so disposable. But if we dispose of them in the same way, we come no closer to creating the kind of world where such actions become less possible. It would be profoundly un-comfortable and disturbing to study Henderson and McKinney with the practices and/or with an ethic of friendship, but that may be what's most needed.[88]

Certainly, the full scope of friendship as method does not fit every qualitative project. Time, career, and interest constraints limit our ability to study social life at the natural pace of friendship. Likewise, our purposes may not best be served in the natural contexts of friendship. When doing oral history, for example, we must contrive an interview setting where high-quality recording can occur. Practices of friendship, moreover, such as compassion, might feel inappropriate when doing research on groups we consider dangerous or unethical.[89]

Between Gay and Straight and *In Solidarity* are unique because some of my participants already were friends or acquaintances when I began the projects, and friendship was also a subject of my research. But qualitative researchers need not adopt the whole vision to benefit from friendship as method. Moving toward friendship as method may be as simple as turning off the recorder and cooking dinner with participants; investing more of ourselves in their emotional, relational, and political welfare; inviting respondents further into our lives than we ever dared before; hanging around longer; writing texts that are as enlightening and useful to our research, local, and global communities as to our academic careers; and/or approaching participants as we would potential or actual friends: with a desire for mutual respect, understanding, growth, and liberation.

Figure A.4 Lisa Tillmann and Tim Mahn.

Notes

1   Material from this appendix has been adapted from my Ph.D. dissertation, *Life Projects* (Tillmann-Healy 1998), my book *Between Gay and Straight* (Tillmann-Healy 2001; used with permission, AltaMira Press), and an article published in *Qualitative Inquiry* (Tillmann-Healy 2003; used with permission, Sage Publications: http://qix.sagepub.com/content/9/5/729.abstract). Portions of this chapter were presented at the 2003 meetings of the National Communication Association. Dave Dietz and Doug Healy shot the photographs in this chapter.

   Other researchers have employed friendship as method in studies utilizing autoethnography (see, e.g., Blinne 2011), co-constructed autoethnography (see, e.g., Ellis and Rawicki 2013; Hill and Holyoak, 2011), participant observation (see, e.g., Bonnin 2010; Rinke and Mawhinney 2014), in-depth interviews (see, e.g., Owton and Allen-Collinson 2013; Rinke and Mawhinney 2014), life history (see, e.g., Roets, Reinaart, and Van Hove 2008), and even archival research (Mattingly and Boyd 2013).

2 See Tillmann-Healy (1998).

3 See Tillmann-Healy (2001). As indicated in the Introduction, my dissertation and first book grew out of an ethnographic and interview study of the network of gay male friends that became family to me and to Doug Healy, my husband until 2006.

4 See Rawlins (1992, 271).

5 See Rawlins (1992, 2009).

6 See Holleran (1996, 34–35).

7 See Rawlins (1992, 9).

8 See Werking (1997, 18).

9 See Rawlins (1992, 2009) and Weiss (1998).

10 See Rawlins (1992, 2009).

11 See Weiss (1998).

12 See Rawlins (1992, 12).

13 See Rubin (1985, 7).

14 See Fine (1981, 265).

15 See Rawlins (1992, 44).

16 See Rawlins (1992, 274).

17 For an application of friendship as method in the context of a relationship between a man with a physical disability and his "frien-tendant," a "nondisabled ally," see Kelly (2013).

18 See Buber (1988).

19 See Tedlock (1991).

20 See Schwandt (1994).

21 See Geertz (1973, 5).

22 See Jackson (1989, 4).

23 See Denzin (1997).

24 See, for examples: Collins (1991, 1998, 2012); Harding (1991, 2009); and Intemann (2010).

25 See Intemann (2010, 785).

26 See Harding (2009, 195).

27 See Harding (1991).

28 See Collins (1998, 229).

29 See Collins (1991).

30 See Collins (2012, 15).

31 See, for examples, Khuankaew and Norsworthy (2000), Norsworthy with Khuankaew (2005), Norsworthy and Khuankaew (2012), and Chapter 10.

32 See, for examples: Cook and Fonow (1986), Lather (1991), McLaren (2011), Norsworthy with Khuankaew (2005), Norsworthy and Khuankaew (2012), Reinharz (1992), and Roberts (1990).

33 See Intemann (2010, 786).

34 Texts that contributed to the development of my own LGBTQ+ affirmative perspective include: Bornstein (1995), Bronski (2011), Butler (1999), Eaklor (2008), Foucault (1988, 1990a, 1990b), Gamson (2000), Jagose (1996), Katz (1996), Miller (2006), Sedgwick (1990), and Warner (1999). *In Solidarity* attempts to show queer-informed scholarship, activism, and pedagogy. For other examples of queer-informed autoethnography, see Adams (2011), Adams and Holman Jones (2011), and Holman Jones and Adams (2014).

35 See Fine (1994).

36 See Reason (1994).

37 See Lather (1991) and Reason (1994).

38 See Reason (1994).

39 See Ellis, Kiesinger, and Tillmann-Healy (1997) and Tillmann-Healy and Kiesinger (2001).

40 See Ellis and Rawicki (2013).

41 See Cherry (1996).

42 See Behar (1996).

43 See Bondi (2013).

44 See Cherry (1996).

45 See Rinke and Mawhinney (2014).

46 See Kiesinger (1995, 1998a, 1998b).

47 See Myerhoff (1978).

48 See Angrosino (1998).

49 See Khuankaew and Norsworthy (2000), Norsworthy (2002), Norsworthy with Khuankaew (2005), and Norsworthy and Khuankaew (2012).

50 See Blinne (2011, 253).

51 Christine Kelly (2013, 788) discusses "relational and representational conundrums" that arise in striving to practice an ethic of friendship, and Carol Rinke and Lynnette Mawhinney (2014, 11) highlight the sometimes-delicate balance between the researcher's personal and relational ethics.

52 See Ellis (1995).

53 In Sandra Harding's (2009, 193) words, "It is one thing to gesture toward 'including the excluded' in our thinking and social projects. It is quite another to engage seriously not only with their ways of understanding themselves and their social relations, but also with their ways of understanding us and our social relations."

54 See Christians (2000).

55 See Norsworthy (May 29, 2013) and Tillmann-Healy (October 12, 2001; April 13, 2002; October 24, 2002).

56 See Hartnett (2003, 2010) and Hartnett, Novek, and Wood (2013).

57 See Bochner (1994).

58 See Tedlock (1991).

59 See Angrosino (1998, 38).

60 See Burke (1973).

61 Refers to lesbian, gay, bisexual, transgender, queer, plus identities such as intersex and asexual.
62 See Young (2000).
63 See Freire (1999).
64 See Hutchinson, Wilson, and Wilson (1994).
65 See Kiesinger (1995, 54).
66 See Kiesinger (1995, 52).
67 See Tillmann-Healy (2001, 217).
68 See Tillmann-Healy (2001, 217–218).
69 See Tillmann-Healy (2001, 218).
70 See Tillmann-Healy (2001, 218).
71 See Berger (2000, 2001).
72 See Berger (2000, 180).
73 Lynnette Mawhinney (in Rinke and Mawhinney 2014, 10–11) also writes about conflicts between personal and relational ethics. As Mawhinney builds rapport with Shanae, a participant and fellow African-American, Shanae becomes more open about her views on urban education, which include cultural and racial stereotypes. "Not once did I challenge Shanae's views in the year I worked with her," admits Mawhinney. Working as co-researchers, co-authors, and friends, Theon Hill (evangelical Christian, heterosexual, and African-American) and Isaac Holyoak (agnostic, gay, and White) do confront their differences directly (Hill and Holyoak 2011).
74 At the same time, more conventional researchers may have defined their function as observation as opposed to social justice intervention.
75 This approach to informed consent and confidentiality may mitigate the hierarchical separation between researcher and participants. However, so long as the researcher determines the options, the differential is not eliminated. Perhaps only co-authorship and co-production have that potential; for examples, see Chapter 10; Ellis and Rawicki (2013); Roets et al. (2008); and Tillmann and Dietz (2014).
76 See Chapter 10.
77 See Tillmann and Dietz (2014).
78 See Chapter 6.
79 See Ellis (1995).
80 See Ellis (1986).
81 See Ellis and Rawicki (2013) for an example of how her approach to research has evolved.
82 See de Leeuw, Cameron, and Greenwood (2012) for a discussion of how participatory projects can burden research communities, especially those already marginalized.
83 See Kelly (2013) and Owton and Allen-Collinson (2013).
84 See Sassi and Thomas (2012).
85 See Hartnett (2003).
86 See Ellis and Rawicki (2013).

87   See Tillmann-Healy (2001, 212–213).

88   Members of the Tectonic Theater Project did exactly that, interviewing Henderson and McKinney for *The Laramie Project: Ten Years Later* (see Kaufman, Fondakowski, Pierotti, Paris, and Belber 2012). Rebecca Barrett-Fox (2011) pursues a parallel endeavor in her ethnographic study of the Westboro Baptist Church.

89   See Dawes (July 1, 2013).

References

Adams, Tony E. *Narrating the Closet: An Autoethnography of Same-Sex Attraction.* Walnut Creek, CA: Left Coast Press, 2011.

Adams, Tony E., and Stacy Holman Jones. "Telling Stories: Reflexivity, Queer Theory, and Autoethnography." *Cultural Studies↔Critical Methodologies* 11, no. 2 (2011): 108–116.

Angrosino, Michael V. *Opportunity House: Ethnographic Stories of Mental Retardation.* Walnut Creek, CA: AltaMira Press, 1998.

Barrett-Fox, Rebecca. "Anger and Compassion on the Picket Line: Ethnography and Emotion in the Study of Westboro Baptist Church." *Journal of Hate Studies* 9, no. 11 (2011): 11–32.

Behar, Ruth. *The Vulnerable Observer: Anthropology That Breaks Your Heart.* Boston, MA: Beacon Press, 1996.

Berger, Leigh. *Messianic Judaism: Searching the Spirit.* PhD diss., University of South Florida, 2000.

———. "Inside Out: Narrative Autoethnography as a Path toward Rapport." *Qualitative Inquiry* 7 (2001): 504–518.

Blinne, Kristen C. "'I Rained': On Loving and (Un)becoming." *Journal of Loss and Trauma* 16 (2011): 243–257.

Bochner, Arthur P. "Perspectives on Inquiry II: *Theories and Stories.*" In *Handbook of Interpersonal Communication* (2nd ed.), edited by Mark L. Knapp and Gerald R. Miller, 21–41. Thousand Oaks, CA: Sage, 1994.

Bondi, Liz. "Research and Therapy: Generating Meaning and Feeling Gaps." *Qualitative Inquiry* 19, no. 1 (2013): 9–19.

Bonnin, Christine. "Navigating Fieldwork Politics, Practicalities and Ethics in the Upland Borderlands of Northern Vietnam." *Asia Pacific Viewpoint* 51, no. 2 (2010): 179–192.

Bornstein, Kate. *Gender Outlaw: On Men, Women, and the Rest of Us.* New York: Vintage Books, 1995.

Bronski, Michael. *A Queer History of the United States.* Boston, MA: Beacon Press, 2011.

Buber, Martin. *The Knowledge of Man: Selected Essays.* Atlantic Highlands, NJ: Humanities Press International, Inc., 1988.

Burke, Kenneth. *The Philosophy of Literary Form: Studies in Symbolic Action.* Berkeley, CA: University of California Press, 1973.

Butler, Judith. *Gender Trouble: Feminism and the Subversion of Identity (10th Anniversary Edition).* New York: Routledge, 1999.

Cherry, Keith. "Ain't No Grave Deep Enough." *Journal of Contemporary Ethnography* 25 (1996): 22–57.

Christians, Clifford G. "Ethics and Politics in Qualitative Research." In *Handbook of Qualitative Research* (2nd ed.), edited by Norman K. Denzin and Yvonna S. Lincoln, 133–155. Thousand Oaks, CA: Sage, 2000.

Collins, Patricia Hill. *Black Feminist Thought: Knowledge, Consciousness, and the Politics of Empowerment.* New York: Routledge, 1991.

——. *Fighting Words: Black Women and the Search for Justice.* Minneapolis, MN: University of Minnesota Press, 1998.

——. "Looking Back, Moving Ahead: Scholarship in Service of Social Justice." *Gender & Society* 26, no. 1 (2012): 14–22.

Cook, Judith A., and Mary Margaret Fonow. "Knowledge and Women's Interests: Issues of Epistemology and Methodology in Feminist Sociological Research." *Sociological Inquiry* 56 (1986): 2–29.

Dawes, James. "Understanding Evil." *Chronicle of Higher Education*, July 1, 2013. Accessed May 17, 2014. http://forums.chronicle.com/article/Understanding-Evil/140025/.

de Leeuw, Sarah, Emilie S. Cameron, and Margo L. Greenwood. "Participatory and Community-Based Research, Indigenous Geographies, and the Spaces of Friendship: A Critical Engagement." *The Canadian Geographer* 56, no. 2 (2012): 180–194.

Denzin, Norman K. *Interpretive Ethnography: Ethnographic Practices for the 21st Century.* Thousand Oaks, CA: Sage, 1997.

Eaklor, Vicki L. *Queer America: A People's GLBT History of the United States.* New York: The New Press, 2008.

Ellis, Carolyn. *Fisher Folk: Two Communities on Chesapeake Bay.* Lexington, KY: University Press of Kentucky, 1986.

——. "Emotional and Ethical Quagmires in Returning to the Field." *Journal of Contemporary Ethnography* 24 (1995): 68–98.

Ellis, Carolyn, Christine E. Kiesinger, and Lisa M. Tillmann-Healy. "Interactive Interviewing: Talking about Emotional Experience." In *Reflexivity & Voice*, edited by Rosanna Hertz, 119–149. Thousand Oaks, CA: Sage, 1997.

Ellis, Carolyn, and Jerry Rawicki. "Collaborative Witnessing of Survival during the Holocaust: An Exemplar of Relational Autoethnography." *Qualitative Inquiry* 19, no. 5 (2013): 366–380.

Fine, Gary Alan. "Friends, Impression Management, and Preadolescent Behavior." In *Social Psychology through Symbolic Interaction*, edited by Gregory P. Stone and Harvey A. Farberman, 257–272. New York: John Wiley & Sons, 1981.

Fine, Michelle. "Working the Hyphens: Reinventing Self and Other in Qualitative Research." In *Handbook of Qualitative Research*, edited by Norman K. Denzin and Yvonna S. Lincoln, 70–82. Thousand Oaks, CA: Sage, 1994.

Foucault, Michel. *The History of Sexuality: The Care of the Self.* New York: Vintage Books, 1988.

——. *The History of Sexuality: An Introduction.* New York: Vintage Books, 1990a.

——. *The History of Sexuality: The Use of Pleasure.* New York: Vintage Books, 1990b.

Freire, Paulo. *Pedagogy of the Oppressed.* New York: Continuum, 1999.

Gamson, Joshua. "Sexualities, Queer Theory, and Qualitative Research." In *Handbook of Qualitative Research* (2nd ed.), edited by Norman K. Denzin and Yvonna S. Lincoln, 347–365. Thousand Oaks, CA: Sage, 2000.

Geertz, Clifford. "Thick Description: Toward an Interpretive Theory of Culture." In *The Interpretation of Cultures*, by Clifford Geertz, 3–30. New York: BasicBooks, 1973.

Harding, Sandra. *Whose Science? Whose Knowledge? Thinking from Women's Lives.* Ithaca, NY: Cornell University Press, 1991.

——. "Standpoint Theories: Productively Controversial." *Hypatia* 24, no. 4 (2009): 192–200.

Hartnett, Stephen John. *Incarceration Nation: Investigative Prison Poems of Hope and Terror.* Walnut Creek, CA: AltaMira Press, 2003.

——, ed. *Challenging the Prison-Industrial Complex: Activism, Arts, and Educational Alternatives.* Champaign, IL: University of Illinois Press, 2010.

Hartnett, Stephen John, Eleanor Novek, and Jennifer K. Wood, eds. *Working for Justice: A Handbook of Prison Education and Activism.* Champaign, IL: University of Illinois Press, 2013.

Hill, Theon E., and Isaac Clarke Holyoak. "Dialoguing Difference in Joint Ethnographic Research: Reflections on Religion, Sexuality, and Race." *Cultural Studies↔Critical Methodologies* 11, no. 2 (2011): 187–194.

Holleran, Andrew. "Friends." In *Friends and Lovers: Gay Men Write about the Families They Create*, edited by John Preston and Michael Lowenthal, 31–37. New York: Plume, 1996.

Holman Jones, Stacy, and Tony E. Adams. "Undoing the Alphabet: A Queer Fugue on Grief and Forgiveness." *Cultural Studies↔Critical Methodologies* 14, no. 2 (2014): 102–110.

Hutchinson, Sally A., Margaret E. Wilson, and Holly Skodol Wilson. "Benefits of Participating in Research Interviews." *Image: The Journal of Nursing Scholarship* 26 (1994): 161–164.

Intemann, Kristen. "25 Years of Feminist Empiricism and Standpoint Theory: Where Are We Now?" *Hypatia* 25, no. 4 (2010): 778–796.

Jackson, Michael. *Paths toward a Clearing: Radical Empiricism and Ethnographic Inquiry.* Bloomington, IN: Indiana University Press, 1989.

Jagose, Annamarie. *Queer Theory: An Introduction.* New York: New York University Press, 1996.

Katz, Jonathan Ned. *The Invention of Heterosexuality.* New York: Plume, 1996.

Kaufman, Moises, Leigh Fondakowski, Greg Pierotti, Andy Paris, and Stephen Belber. *The Laramie Project: Ten Years Later.* New York: Dramatist's Play Service, 2012.

Kelly, Christine. "Building Bridges with Accessible Care: Disability Studies, Feminist Care Scholarship, and Beyond." *Hypatia* 28, no. 4 (2013): 784–800.

Khuankaew, Ouyporn, and Kathryn L. Norsworthy. "Struggles for Peace, Justice, Unity and Freedom: Stories of the Women of Burma." *Seeds of Peace* 16 (2000): 16–18.

Kiesinger, Christine E. *Anorexic and Bulimic Lives: Making Sense of Food and Eating.* PhD diss., University of South Florida, 1995.

——. "From Interview to Story: Writing Abbie's Life." *Qualitative Inquiry* 4 (1998a): 71–95.

——. "Portrait of an Anorexic Life." In *Fiction & Social Research: By Ice or Fire*, edited by Anna Banks and Stephen P. Banks, 115–136. Walnut Creek, CA: AltaMira Press, 1998b.

Lather, Patti. *Getting Smart: Feminist Research and Pedagogy with/in the Postmodern.* New York: Routledge, 1991.

Mattingly, Doreen J., and Ashley Boyd. "Bringing Gay and Lesbian Activism to the White House: Midge Costanza and the National Gay Task Force Meeting." *Journal of Lesbian Studies* 17 (2013): 365–379.

McLaren, Margaret. "Women's Rights and Collective Resistance: The Success Story of Marketplace India." In *Gender & Globalization: Patterns of Women's Resistance*, edited by Erica G. Polakoff and Ligaya Lindio-McGovern, 191–210. Whitby, Ontario: de Sitter Pubications, 2011.

Miller, Neil. *Out of the Past: Gay and Lesbian History from 1869 to the Present.* New York: Alyson Books, 2006.

Myerhoff, Barbara. *Number Our Days.* New York: Touchstone, 1978.

Norsworthy, Kathryn L. "Feminist Interventions for Southeast Asian Women Trauma Survivors: Deconstructing Gender-Based Violence and Developing Structures of Peace." Greensboro, NC: ERIC CASS, 2002.

——. "Scouts' Decision on Gay Boys Bittersweet." *Orlando Sentinel*, May 29, 2013. Accessed May 21, 2014. http://articles.orlandosentinel.com/2013–05–29/news/os-ed-scouts-pro-gay-myword-052913–20130528_1_gay-scouts-boy-scouts-gay-adults.

Norsworthy, Kathryn L., with Ouyporn Khuankaew. "Bringing Social Justice to International Practices of Counseling Psychology." In *Handbook for Social Justice in Counseling Psychology: Leadership, Vision, and Action*, edited by Rebecca L. Toporek, Lawrence Gerstein, Nadya Fouad, Gargi Roysircar-Sodowsky, and Tania Israel, 421–441. Thousand Oaks, CA: Sage, 2005.

Norsworthy, Kathryn L., and Ouyporn Khuankaew. "Feminist Border Crossings: Our Transnational Partnership in Peace and Justice Work." In *Helping Beyond the 50-Minute Hour: Therapists Involved in Meaningful Social Action*, edited by Jeffrey A. Kottler, Matt Englar-Carlson, and Jon Carlson, 222–233. New York: Routledge, 2012.

Owton, Helen, and Jacquelyn Allen-Collinson. "Close But Not Too Close: Friendship as Method(ology) in Ethnographic Research Encounters." *Journal of Contemporary Ethnography* 43, no. 3 (2013): 283–305.

Rawlins, William K. *Friendship Matters: Communication, Dialectics, and the Life Course.* New York: Aldine de Gruyter, 1992.

——. *The Compass of Friendship: Narratives, Identities, and Dialogues*. Thousand Oaks, CA: Sage, 2009.

Reason, Peter. "Three Approaches to Participative Inquiry." In *Handbook of Qualitative Research*, edited by Norman K. Denzin and Yvonna S. Lincoln, 324–339. Thousand Oaks, CA: Sage, 1994.

Reinharz, Shulamit. *Feminist Methods in Social Research*. New York: Oxford University Press, 1992.

Rinke, Carol R., and Lynnette Mawhinney. "Reconsidering Rapport with Urban Teachers: Negotiating Shifting Boundaries and Legitimizing Support." *International Journal of Research & Method in Education* 37, no. 1 (2014): 3–16.

Roberts, Helen, ed. *Doing Feminist Research*. London: Routledge, 1990.

Roets, Griet, Rosa Reinaart, and Geert Van Hove. "Living between Borderlands: Discovering a Sense of Nomadic Subjectivity throughout Rosa's Life Story." *Journal of Gender Studies* 17, no. 2 (2008): 99–115.

Rubin, Lillian B. *Just Friends: The Role of Friendship in Our Lives*. New York: Harper & Row, 1985.

Sassi, Kelly, and Ebony Elizabeth Thomas. "'If You Weren't Researching Me and a Friend . . .': The Mobius of Friendship and Mentorship as Methodological Approaches to Qualitative Research." *Qualitative Inquiry* 18, no. 10 (2012): 830–842.

Schwandt, Thomas A. "Constructivist, Interpretivist Approaches to Human Inquiry." In *Handbook of Qualitative Research*, edited by Norman K. Denzin and Yvonna S. Lincoln, 118–137. Thousand Oaks, CA: Sage, 1994.

Sedgwick, Eve Kosofsky. *Epistemology of the Closet*. Berkeley, CA: University of California Press, 1990.

Tedlock, Barbara. "From Participant Observation to the Observation of Participation: The Emergence of Narrative Ethnography." *Journal of Anthropological Research* 47 (1991): 69–94.

Tillmann, Lisa M., and David Dietz. *Remembering a Cool September* [motion picture]. United States: Cinema Serves Justice, 2014. http://cinemaservesjustice.com/Remembering.html.

Tillmann-Healy, Lisa M. *Life Projects: A Narrative Ethnography of Gay-Straight Friendship*. PhD diss., University of South Florida, 1998.

——. *Between Gay and Straight: Understanding Friendship across Sexual Orientation*. Walnut Creek, CA: AltaMira Press, 2001.

——. "Matthew Shepard: Three Years Later." *Orlando Sentinel*, October 12, 2001.

——. "Equal Rights, Not Special Rights." *Orlando Sentinel*, April 13, 2002.

——. "Coming Out of Homophobia's Closet." *Orlando Sentinel*, October 24, 2002.

——. "Friendship as Method." *Qualitative Inquiry* 9 (2003): 729–749.

Tillmann-Healy, Lisa M., and Christine E. Kiesinger. "Mirrors: Seeing Each Other and Ourselves through Fieldwork." In *The Emotional Nature of Qualitative Research*, edited by Kathleen Gilbert, 81–108. Boca Raton, FL: CRC Press, 2001.

Warner, Michael. *The Trouble with Normal: Sex, Politics, and the Ethics of Queer Life*. New York: The Free Press, 1999.

Weiss, Robert S. "A Taxonomy of Relationships." *Journal of Social and Personal Relationships* 15 (1998): 671–683.

Werking, Kathy. *We're Just Good Friends: Women and Men in Nonromantic Relationships.* New York: Guilford Press, 1997.

Young, Iris Marion. "Five Faces of Oppression." In *Readings for Diversity and Social Justice: An Anthology on Racism, Antisemitism, Sexism, Heterosexism, Ableism, and Classism,* edited by Maurianne Adams, Warren J. Blumenfeld, Rosie Castañeda, Heather W. Hackman, Madeline L. Peters, and Ximena Zúñiga, 35–49. New York: Routledge, 2000.

AUTHOR BIOGRAPHIES

Lisa M. Tillmann, Ph.D., is an activist researcher, social justice documentary filmmaker, and professor of Critical Media and Cultural Studies (CMC), a program she founded at Rollins College. Grounded in values of peace, equity, and justice, CMC examines the world's most pressing issues and challenges and helps students envision ways to work toward change. On campus and in central Florida, Dr. Tillmann has participated in numerous activist initiatives, many centering on civil rights. She authored the book, *Between Gay and Straight: Understanding Friendship across Sexual Orientation*, produced the film *Weight Problem: Cultural Narratives of Fat and "Obesity,"* and co-produced the films *Off the Menu: Challenging the Politics and Economics of Body and Food* and *Remembering a Cool September* (about LGBT civil rights). To learn more about her film work, please visit: CinemaServesJustice.com. She may be contacted at: Ltillmann@rollins.edu.

Kathryn L. Norsworthy, Ph.D., is an activist researcher, counseling psychologist, and professor of Graduate Studies in Counseling at Rollins College. She has engaged in several years of LGBT civil rights activism in her home community in central Florida as well as immigrant and farmworker rights work. In South and Southeast Asia, she collaborates with local colleagues on projects supporting peace building in areas of ethno-political conflict, women's leadership within the Burma refugee communities engaged in the democracy movement, socially just HIV/AIDS counseling, mindful activism, social movement building within the Thai LGBTQ+ activist community, and Global South–North power-sharing partnerships for social change. She may be contacted at: knorsworthy@rollins.edu.

INDEX

Added to a page number 'n' denotes notes.